Nuts Ab

NUTS ABOUT SQUIRRELS

The Rodents That Conquered Popular Culture

Don H. Corrigan

McFarland & Company, Inc., Publishers
Jefferson, North Carolina

ISBN (print) 978-1-4766-7596-1
ISBN (ebook) 978-1-4766-3635-1

LIBRARY OF CONGRESS CATALOGUING DATA ARE AVAILABLE

BRITISH LIBRARY CATALOGUING DATA ARE AVAILABLE

Front cover images © 2019 Shutterstock

Printed in the United States of America

McFarland & Company, Inc., Publishers
Box 611, Jefferson, North Carolina 28640
www.mcfarlandpub.com

This squirrel treatise is dedicated to Captain Meriwether Lewis—explorer, soldier, politician, and public servant, best known as the leader of the Corps of Discovery, which explored the new American territory known as the Louisiana Purchase in 1804. Lewis marveled at the ways of squirrels when he first witnessed a mass migration of the creatures on the waters of the Ohio River. On his travels up the Missouri River with William Clark, his fascination with the barking squirrel inspired him to send one back to President Thomas Jefferson; the squirrel subsequently became a vocal inhabitant of the White House. This author pays homage to Lewis at his statue in St. Charles, Missouri, whenever traveling the Katy Trail along the Missouri River, a favored habitat of the gray squirrel.

Table of Contents

Acknowledgments

There are many companions, colleagues and scholars to be acknowledged here. First, I must reference my late father, who was no friend of squirrels. His antipathy for them attracted my attention at an early age. My father always tried to outsmart squirrels—to no avail. When squirrels took a liking to his chimney stack, he took my toy saxophone and tried to drive them out by playing discordant notes into the flue. Later, he climbed to the roof to place a barbecue grill grate atop the chimney to screen out the squirrels. After retirement, he sat on his backyard porch with a BB gun aimed in the direction of the squirrels that raided his tomato garden. It was a long saga without a happy ending (unless this book constitutes a happy ending).

Other kind kindred souls who merit acknowledgment are my wife, Susanne, and Millennial children, Christa and Brandon. My wife showed immense patience with my hours of researching and talking about squirrels. My daughter, Christa, drew on her vast knowledge of Sandy Cheeks, the squirrel from *SpongeBob SquarePants*, to assist with the chapter on squirrels in animated cartoons. Likewise, my son, Brandon, provided an assist with his video game knowledge of the squirrel in *Conker's Bad Fur Day*, though he remains skeptical that I have any business writing about video games.

As a college student, I enjoyed the many squirrels on the campus of Knox College on the plains of western Illinois. My fraternity brother, Greg Divers, was also in the thrall of squirrels. A very successful quarterback for Knox's Old Siwash, Greg channeled his inner squirrel before many a football contest. He would hop on his waterbed and emulate a squirrel anxiously examining and gnawing on an acorn, which somehow served as preparation for winning football games against the likes of Monmouth, Grinnell and St. Olaf colleges. In graduate school, I enjoyed watching the many squirrels outside of Walter Williams Hall and Neff Hall at the University of Missouri School of Journalism. The oldest school of journalism in America prepared me for a career in community journalism and occasionally writing stories and columns about (what else?) squirrels.

Squirrel articles have been published in my time as editor of the *Webster-Kirkwood Times* newspapers in suburban St. Louis. It's important to thank my newspaper partner, Dwight Bitikofer, and managing editor, Kevin Murphy, and the staff and photographers of the newspapers for their forbearance with my frequent forays into squirrel journalism. I must also acknowledge the late Kirkwood, Missouri, councilman Francis Scheidegger and the Wildlife Rescue Center for their story leads on illegal squirrel trapping and releases in the St. Louis area. In addition, Erin Shank, a wildlife biologist with Missouri's Powder Valley Nature Center, has been a font of knowledge on squirrel behavior and population fluctuations.

On the academic side, my dean and department chair at the Webster University School of Communications, Eric Rothenbuhler and Gary Ford, have my gratitude for approving a year-long faculty development leave to complete this book project on squirrels. My teaching career at this global institution in Webster Groves has spanned four decades, during which my colleagues have assisted me on a number of projects. Faculty members knowledgeable about animation, film and video games—Van McElwee, Chris Sagovac and Josh Yates—contributed to this project. A past department chair, Art Silverblatt, has joined me in efforts to get a star for Marshall McLuhan on the University City Walk of Fame in St. Louis. McLuhan, who is referenced frequently in this book, distinguished himself on the faculty at St. Louis University for several years before becoming an international guru of mass media.

Finally, it would be impossible to thank all the people who have forwarded me audio, video and newspaper clips about squirrels after learning about this project. I would, however, like to single out Mark Sableman, a media attorney with Thompson Coburn, LLC; Bill Ruppert and Dave Slane, professional tree huggers and squirrel lovers; Jim Wright of the Kirkwood–Des Peres Chamber of Commerce; Roland Klose, an editor with the *St. Louis Post-Dispatch*, as well as members of the St. Louis Press Club; and Mike Phoenix, Daniel Yezbick, Dan Martin, Bill Smith, and members of the St. Louis Comic Book Club. Last but not least, I must thank Holly Shanks, a Webster University journalism graduate familiar with my lectures on squirrels and mass media. Holly has been instrumental in the editing and formatting of this book. She has also served as a journalist with the *Webster-Kirkwood Times* and joins me as coeditor of the blog *Environmental Echo*.

Preface:
Mass-Mediated Squirrels

The uncompromising mission of this book is to make the point that, collectively, squirrels are a major presence in our flesh-and-blood lives as well as in the virtual lives that we enjoy through popular culture and as delivered via the channels of mass communications. When it comes to animated creatures on television and in film, everybody knows about the famous mice and the ducks. Mickey and Minnie Mouse are celebrated worldwide (Mickey even has theme parks dedicated to him), and Donald Duck and his nephews, Huey, Dewey, and Louie, can be found in comics, cartoons, television shows and movies. But what about the squirrels? Squirrels have a lot more personality, energy and natural genius than either mice or ducks. Squirrels deserve some special attention.

Thanks to our mass-mediated world, we do know a few celebrity squirrels on a first-name basis. We may be surprised at just how many squirrels are in our circle of acquaintances. In books, some of the better-known squirrels include characters named Cyril, Earl, Nutkin, Tippy-Toe and Mr. Peanuts. On television and in the movies, there are such well-known squirrels as Twiggy, Tommy, Rally, Rupert and more. In popular cartoons and animated movies, squirrels named Rocky, Slappy, Skippy, Sandy, Hammy and Surly scamper across screens and into our living rooms and family rooms. In comic books and video games, squirrels are tagged with odd monikers like Nutsy, Ray the Flying Squirrel, Conker, Squirrel Girl and many more. The irony of all this hoopla is that none of these squirrels will answer to the names they've been given. These squirrels are, for the most part, just figments of fertile imaginations that created them for our entertainment, if not necessarily for our edification.

The maw of mass media is vast, voluminous and ever expanding. There is a voracious appetite for new and unusual content. Squirrels make the grade for that kind of content. Squirrels are tailor-made for fresh and original sto-

1

rytelling; in fact, they have had stories told about them for hundreds, if not thousands, of years. That's a major factor in why this book has not only focused on current content about squirrels in mass media but also examined the mythology and folklore regarding squirrels. American legends about squirrels seem to focus on their role in filling the gullets of early ruffian settlers with their bounty in stews, burgoos, gumbos and pies. Squirrels are also much appreciated in America for giving hunters and marksmen a good eye for small targets—a useful talent when it comes to fighting in a revolution or surviving a civil war.

Squirrels have also been the subject of folklore and mythology for Europeans as well as the indigenous peoples of continents beyond the tribal lands of the Norse, Gauls, Saxons and Celts. An interesting dimension of the study of squirrel storytelling is the threads of similarity in the tales that are told about squirrels, whether those narratives involve celestial black squirrels eating the sun and causing the dark shadows of an eclipse or gigantic monster squirrels cursed and shrunk to their present small dimensions as a result of crossing the gods. These long-in-the-tooth squirrel narratives have crept into our comics and our video games. Names and storylines can be traced to the mythology of the ancient Norsemen, those brutish seafarers known as the Vikings. New digital technology may be cutting edge, mind boggling, and even miraculous, but the stories conveyed through digital electronics are as old as the Viking warrior who sat around a forest campfire spinning yarns about squirrels a thousand years ago. There's a squirrel in the digital machine, thanks to Vikings of the ninth century.

The McLuhan Factor

No journalist or academic who expounds on mass media can avoid mentioning the guru of communications study, Marshall McLuhan. After all, McLuhan is credited with inventing the word *media*. When this writer began teaching "Introduction to Mass Communications" as a college professor in the 1970s, McLuhan was still in vogue. He appeared in the Woody Allen movie *Annie Hall*, and he often appeared on television news shows to analyze presidential debates, talk about hot and cool media, and remind us that every medium of communication can be classified as an extension of some human sensory input. McLuhan was hot, but he cooled off quickly after his death in 1980. Many critics dismissed him as a charlatan and his theories as gibberish.

Communications professors, who still used McLuhan's ideas in classes, were regarded as outdated oddities. Then we entered the new human epoch of cyberspace. Suddenly, McLuhan and his global village were back in vogue.

The internet and innovative communication technology have had a tremendous impact on young people. High school and college students walk around with iPhones seemingly grafted to the palms of their hands. They've surrendered their privacy, their identity, their physical beings to Facebook and other forms of social media. This all has served to make McLuhan relevant again, but college professors—not so much. It's hard for professors to be relevant—and to get the attention of students in a lecture hall—when there are so many more interesting things coming through the electronic ether for young people via Twitter, Snapchat, Tinder and Instagram. Some professors respond by collecting students' smartphones in a basket before class begins. My answer to this dilemma is simple: squirrels. Students love squirrels. They've grown up with Sandy Cheeks from *SpongeBob SquarePants*, Hammy from *Over the Hedge*, and squirrels like Squirrel Girl in the popular video game *Marvel Super Hero Squad: Comic Combat*.

Students do look up from their smartphones when the lecture hall projector is powered up, delivering images of squirrels jumping on the wide screens behind the classroom lectern. As this study notes, squirrels do well in illustrating multiple McLuhan concepts regarding the mass communications process. A visual presentation of the contrast between newspaper coverage of squirrels and television coverage can be an enlightening exercise for laying out McLuhan's axiom that the medium is the message. It's useful in pointing out the differences in the media treatment of squirrels in McLuhan's hot and cool media. Such a presentation can also serve as a starting point for discussions on whether a communications medium consistently determines or shapes the content of media messages. It will become obvious that every medium seems to possess a hidden taste mechanism that favors some styles and content and rejects others.

The renewed interest in the McLuhan's ideas has prompted new studies and scholarship about his life and work, including Douglas Coupland's engaging biography, *Marshall McLuhan: You Know Nothing of My Work!*[1] Coupland does an excellent job of explaining why McLuhan's critics were so often unable to understand the peculiar jargon and oddly organized ideas that characterized his work. The attention deficit disorder that seemed to afflict McLuhan's thought processes and his intellectual output are far more understandable in the present oversaturated media environment. Of more import, McLuhan's predictions about the global village, the detribalization of Western man, and the tyranny of electronic interdependence have come to pass. All that has driven media literacy teachers to revisit McLuhan's seminal works, such as *The Gutenberg Galaxy*[2] and *Understanding Media: The Extensions of Man*.[3] The latter book provides many of McLuhan's observations on multiple types of media. If McLuhan's observations remain impenetrable half a century later, well, squirrels can always be enlisted to crack the nut of conundrum and decipher the code.

Squirrels are found in our newspapers, television, movies, advertising, comics, cartoons, and games. To take just one example, squirrels have found a nest and a niche in our advertising culture—in unprecedented numbers. There is a reason for this. As McLuhan explained, in the evolving world of electronic advertising, the product matters less as audience participation in the ad increases. Ads targeted to young people are most effective when they provide an iconic group experience. Consider the billions of dollars dedicated to promoting beers, wines and other spirits. Ads are particularly effective with young males when the beer brand trips the collective memory with the shared experience of a squirrel that tried to swipe the beer, or ran the hundred-yard dash to reach the beer, or dribbled the acorn in the soccer match to win the beer. According to McLuhan, the smart electronic advertising of his future—the here and now for us—is all about "the fur and fuzz, the blur and buzz."[4]

There will be critics who try to blur the buzz of this study of squirrels and their function in elucidating McLuhan's mass media ideas. They may declare that the McLuhan connection is an attempt to add some intellectual veneer and complexity to what is otherwise simply a survey of the spectacle of squirrels pervading the mass media. Not to worry—a typical scorecard for McLuhan's own work was that one-half was brilliant insight, one-fourth was questionable hypotheses, and one-fourth was mere nonsense. McLuhan would argue that these are hardly bad percentages in an original and daring exploration. "If a few details here and there are wacky," said McLuhan, "it doesn't matter a hoot."[5]

Introduction:
"Hot" and "Cool" Squirrels

The first animals that we human beings typically encounter in life sport such names as Buddy, Max, Tiger and Fluffy. These animals are primarily domesticated felines and canines that live indoors—that is, pet cats and pet dogs (such as Lucy the Siamese and Coco the Cocker Spaniel). In recent years, the most popular name for these family friends has been "Bella," from a character in the *Twilight* movies and the romance novels on which the movies are based. Untamed animals that live in the great outdoors are different. They generally are not accorded the privilege of being tagged with names like Bella or Coco, Bonnie or Max. Animals in the outdoors are not to be trusted, and they definitely are not going to respond to being called Sophie, Oliver or Shadow. Squirrels in the outdoors will not answer to Nutmeg, Peanut or Nibbles. It just doesn't happen.

Squirrels are the first wild animals that many human beings encounter. Call these crafty, fluffy-tailed rodents by names such as Buddy or Tobey, and they might just flick their tails in a mocking show of contempt. Squirrels may inhabit our backyards, but they don't care a fig about us—and they are not paying us rent. Millions of squirrels inhabit American backyards. Many more squirrels find a home in our majestic purple mountain ranges. And still more scamper about on our fruited plains. So, even if we don't make their acquaintance in our neighborhood, it's still possible that we will become familiar with them in our travels to a local, state or national park. If they are not to be found in our own backyard, they are still among the first wild creatures that many of us meet up with beyond hearth and home.

Google Answers estimates that there are about 1.2 billion squirrels in the United States alone. Squirrels outnumber humans in America by four to one. To paraphrase the late rock legend Jim Morrison of The Doors, we humans may have the guns, but those red, brown and gray squirrels have the numbers. Squirrels have no need for sex education or aphrodisiacs in order

5

to be fruitful and multiply. Successful cohabitation comes naturally to them, and they reproduce at alarming rates. They replace themselves as fast as we humans can trap them, shoot them, devour them or flatten them on highway pavement with two-ton sports utility vehicles.

The ubiquity, resilience, spunk and spirit of squirrels account for their prolific presence in both real life and our mass media and popular culture. Humans generally prefer squirrels as found in the mass media, as opposed to finding them in the garage, in the attic or on a bird feeder. Squirrels show up in our books and magazines, our photo collections and movie selections, our advertising and public relations promotions, our video games and our computer screens. Squirrels have made the jump from the old legacy media to the new social media without a hitch. They have been tweeted, Facebooked, Instagrammed and Snapchatted, not to mention pinned on Pinterest in numbers too great to ignore.

Literally hundreds of squirrel images can be discovered on the Pinterest social media sites. Squirrels have been observed drinking from bird baths, lunching on garden tomatoes and strawberries, scarfing down acorns and peanuts, stealing seeds from bird feeders, nibbling on pine cones, straddling barbed wire, hanging from utility lines, smooching each other, sleeping with each other, battling each other, chasing each other, chattering at each other—the list goes on. There are southern fox squirrels, Siberian flying squirrels, Japanese dwarf squirrels, eastern gray squirrels, northern black squirrels, Van Truan fox squirrels and more.

Squirrels have played a variety of roles in our mass media offerings. They can appear as ruthless villains who will rob us blind or as comedians who leave us laughing—even when the joke is on us. They can be heroes and heroines who save us from the skullduggery of international spies or the disaster of natural catastrophes. They inhabit our popular culture, and it is here that they can actually bear names such as Earl, Cyril, Rocky, Rally, Rupert, Slappy, Skippy and Conker. However, call a squirrel in the backyard by the name of Earl, Cyril, Rocky or Rupert, and they will almost certainly refuse to take notice. They are more likely to oscillate their tails in a most obscene manner or hightail it up a tree to a safe perch high above the ground.

Despite being rebuffed over and over again by real, live, warm-blooded squirrels, we humans continue to incorporate them in our mass media and popular culture. Squirrels are mass-mediated animals. Media maven Marshall McLuhan, sometimes described as "the Dr. Spock of popular culture," would have done well to employ the services of squirrels to illustrate some of his key concepts about mass media. Squirrels inhabit almost all countries in McLuhan's global village. They are perfect fodder for illustrating his theories on what character types work best in hot or cool media.[1] Squirrels in our books and newspapers, on televisions and movie screens, and in video games show us how the "medium is the message." In a cool medium such as television, squirrels are most often portrayed as playful and endearing. They are amusing characters and snappy dressers who can brighten and lighten a nightly newscast. They can model the latest outfits on a fashion show runway or ski in tanks of water at the local RV and boat show. Squirrels coolly perform incredible acrobatic stunts for television audiences. Squirrels are made for TV.

Squirrels do not fare so well in the pages of what McLuhan called the hot medium of print. In newspapers, squirrels are bad hombres. McLuhan theorized that a hot medium, such as a newspaper, constitutes a natural outlet for tales of wrenching conflict between cowboys and Indians, cops and crooks, good guys and bad guys. In newspaper stories, humans are the good guys defending their homes, their bird feeders and their gardens from evil, destructive squirrels—creatures that have little respect for property rights or the emotional well-being of property owners. Vandalism and thievery aren't the half of it when it comes to squirrels. These craven creatures invariably carry diseases, from new strains of rabies to the dreaded Black Death of centuries ago. They can be sick, or sickening, and they will make you sick, according to the newspaper accounts.

Of course, we will never find out about squirrels' propensity for evil within the pages of children's books. The medium is the message—and children's books are most certainly not the medium to find out about sick squirrels infected with the bubonic plague. In these books, youngsters learn that squirrels are fun and frolicsome, but they also have a serious side and can teach important life lessons. Squirrels are fuzzy and friendly; yet they also are purposeful and industrious. They are examples for living an industrious, honest and frugal life.

Squirrels work hard to gather nuts and bury acorns, which they and their families can find and feast upon later in lean times when food is scarce. Wise squirrels think ahead. They are smart enough not to live simply for today. However, they are not spoilsports, and they know how to enjoy themselves. Squirrels and their crazy cousins, the chipmunks, are often jolly jokesters. Squirrels wave their bushy tails and chatter atop bird baths, bird feeders and just about everywhere else a bird might alight. They are high-wire performers that would put the high-flying Wallendas to shame. Squirrel wisdom and squirrel tricks are for kids, and both can be found in books in the children's section of your local library.

If we put down the tiny tomes tailored for tykes and pick up the daily newspaper again, we will find squirrel stories of a dramatically different kind. In fact, we may find it hard to believe that we're reading about the same earthly inhabitants. The legacy print medium, which may still land daily on our doorsteps, takes a decidedly dimmer view of the squirrel species. Squirrels are depicted as pests that will gnaw their way into attics, tear up insulation and build their own homes, where they will procreate prodigiously. When they're not destroying our homes, they're under the hoods of our automobiles, teething on spark plug wires and cables to render our vehicles useless. Stories in newspapers suggest that squirrels are likely to usher in the apocalypse by taking down the electrical grid and darkening the planet, not to mention spreading severe illnesses that can threaten the very survival of the human species.

Before having a nervous breakdown over squirrels, it may be wise to put the scary newspaper down and move on to the cool tales of the television age. On television, we can find squirrels that are not an existential threat to humanity at all; they're actually harmless, handsome and entertaining. They are comic geniuses that can play just about any dramatic role with a little coaching. Among the famous squirrels that have become television celebrities are Tommy Tucker, a true fashion plate who posed for TV cameras in the early years of the visual medium; Sugar Bush, a clothes horse who boasted some four thousand outfits that could make him a pirate one minute or a casino-cruising playboy the next minute; and Twiggy, who found television fame skittering on the water behind a special remote-control Twiggy Speedboat.

This study of mass-mediated squirrels subscribes to the McLuhan's theoretical construct that the medium often determines the message. The hot medium of newspapers picks up stories of squirrels as adversaries and a source of vexation for humankind, whereas the cool medium of television transmits stories of squirrels as entertaining planetary companions and sources of laughter and mirth for humankind. Public relations and advertising media have generally been favorable and accommodating when squirrels are the subject. Both genres of the persuasion industry have found these creatures useful to their purposes in mass communication.

In the field of public relations, squirrels have inspired the mission statements and actual branding of agencies and their work. Squirrels are held up as models in the strategic communication area of public relations because of their athleticism, flexibility and manic commitment to discovery. In the area of institutional communications, numerous sports franchises, municipalities and institutions of higher education have found it useful to adopt squirrels as their mascots, symbols and trademark identities. Towns and villages across the United States have capitalized on their idiosyncratic squirrel populations to assist with marketing and the promotion of tourism. Squirrels are not just inhabitants of the persimmon trees in the town square; they are also objects for sculpture and statues on the village green and in the town square.

Squirrels have a role to play in the advertising media as well. They have been recruited as talent in the service of championing and promoting choco-lates, foodstuffs, and spirits as well as insurance policies, banking and invest-ments. Admittedly, much of the advertising employing squirrels takes a tongue-in-cheek and humorous tack. This advertising has been labeled as "Oddvertising."[2] Years ago, McLuhan predicted that in a growing media-saturated consumer culture, advertising would have to become more witty, novel, eye-opening and smart, while less concerned with the actual selling of a product or service. The ad messaging would become an end in itself— a cultural artifact to identify with as much as the product or service itself. Enter "Oddvertising" and the presence of squirrel talent to help make this unique, cultish sort of advertising succeed.

Public relations and advertising have been open to squirrels and kind to them, but movies have been a mixed bag. Some movies have portrayed squirrels as the noblest creatures in the animal kingdom. Other cinema offer-ings have made them out to be a royal pain in the human posterior and not at all noble. In Chevy Chase's _Christmas Vacation_, a scurrilous squirrel destroys the family holiday when the rude intruder brings down home dec-orations in a chase scene involving an agitated dog named Snot. In _Winter's Bone_, a woodland squirrel is cruelly disrobed and skinned by actress Jennifer Lawrence after she has shot the animal to put food on the table for her hungry siblings. In _It's a Wonderful Life_, an office squirrel is the kindly companion of Uncle Billy and the logical mascot for the savings and loan business in the town of Bedford Falls; however, this pet squirrel is one of many distractions that contribute to Billy misplacing thousands of dollars of customer money— a nightmare for him, the company and citizens of Bedford Falls.

Squirrels may get mixed reviews in conventional feature films in which they appear, but they very often become stars as a result of their performances in cartoons and animated movies. The king of animated cartoon squirrels is the legendary Rocket J. Squirrel, more often referred to as Rocky the Flying

Squirrel, who pals around with a famous moose named Bullwinkle. Rocky is the first in a long succession of cartoon squirrels capable of entertaining both children and adults, serving as an amiable Cold Warrior against foes like Boris Badenov and Natasha Fatale. After Rocky was retired from the television airwaves, a new squirrel arrived to pick up the slack. Secret Squirrel was Agent 000 and much more of a spy than Rocky. Secret Squirrel and his sidekick, Morocco Mole, did their undercover work in the service of their boss, Double-Q of the International Sneaky Service.

More cartoon squirrels came to life on television after Cold War tensions eased. These new squirrels did not have to match wits with espionage agents or take on assigned missions to keep the world safe from sabotage, subterfuge, or sufferin' succotash. These squirrels could be carefree, careless, and occasionally kinky. Slappy and Skippy, two bizarre acorn admirers from *Animaniacs*, achieved notoriety for their squirrelly relationship and screwball shortcomings. Sandy Cheeks, an underwater-dwelling squirrel with a soft spot for sea creatures, attained celebrity status as the friend of a very popular but freakish organism known as SpongeBob in the cutting-edge cartoon called *SpongeBob SquarePants*.

A few squirrels have made the transition from television cartoon roles to appearing as characters in animated movies, although not always with great success at the box office. A movie was fashioned for Rocky, but somehow the squirrel's charm and wit were lost in the translation. Sandy Cheeks made the cut for *The SpongeBob SquarePants Movie*, a film that had an admittedly unremarkable run. More squirrels have found movie glory by jumping from comic strips to the silver screen. Among those fortunate squirrels are Hammy and Surly. Hammy, a crazy red squirrel from the 1990s comic strip "Hammy Over the Hedge," later found a spot in the movie *Over the Hedge* with his talent for weird sounds and constant frustration in trying to find his misplaced nuts. More recently, Surly hit box office pay dirt as the bad boy squirrel in the movies *The Nut Job* and *Nut Job 2: Nutty by Nature*.

Squirrels have scrambled over a lot of terrain in the old, offbeat medium of comics, and some have found a comfortable place on the relatively new media platform of video games. Comic book squirrels include Nutsy, Squirrel Girl, Foamy and a host of squirrel characters from the Squarriors comic book series. Squirrel Girl may be the most successful squirrel to reconstitute herself from the pages of Marvel comic books to a digitized version in games such as *Marvel Future Flight*. Squirrel Girl is sort of a mutant Wonder Woman who can take on all hostile comers with her claws and squirrelly cunning.

Her claws provide a unique advantage in hand-to-hand combat that only a comic character like Wolverine might appreciate. But while Squirrel Girl is a wonder, she has nothing on the video game squirrel known as Conker, who can intimidate opponents with his vulgar utterances, bouts of heavy drinking, and penchant for firing off projectile puke over his shoulder.

Video games constitute a new venue of mass media, and they often make hundreds of millions of dollars in just a few hours after their introduction on the market. The worldwide video game industry is worth more than $100 billion annually, so it's no surprise that squirrels have jumped into the video game fray on all fours. How could squirrels afford to be left out of this kind of action?

Marshall McLuhan was very familiar with squirrels on the college campuses where both he and the squirrels of his time thrived. However, he did not live to see squirrels captured in video game cassettes or online games. Nevertheless, he had plenty to say about games, observations that are relevant to this study. McLuhan noted that games are not just a diversion. Games are an extension of our social selves and a means of learning about the world and our place in that world.[3] Games that are fun and provoke laughter—perhaps a video game about a superhero called Squirrel Girl—can be an essential antidote to the anxiety and tensions found in a highly organized, technological society. And yes, McLuhan stressed, games can be a form of modern mass media.

Before narratives about squirrels entered our mass media and popular culture, there were legends and myths about these creatures. Squirrel stories were told around campfires as part of what McLuhan called the oral culture or the oral tradition. Later, squirrel stories were gathered, transcribed and printed in books, newspapers, and magazines to become a part of what McLuhan called the age of literacy. Finally, we entered what McLuhan called the electronic age of communication, and squirrels became content for analog radio and television programming and eventually the zeros and ones to produce imagery for digital computers, smartphones, and video games on consoles and online.

This study examines squirrel incarnations in all their varied forms on the many popular venues of mass media, from print to electronic. However, the book concludes with a look back at squirrels in American legends and in the folklore and mythology of indigenous peoples. Squirrels are a part of American history, and a few historians contend that they sacrificed so much in the early years of the republic that they should logically be the country's national symbol, rather than the eagle. Squirrels were an important source of nourishment for the colonists and early settlers of America. As small animals, they also provided targets for the early American hunters. Legends about the abilities of squirrel shooters being put to the test against determined foes abound in folklore from the early years of the American experiment.

Squirrel storytelling from centuries ago is now embodied in the popular mythology derived from indigenous peoples. The Wabanakis tell the story of a squirrel of enormous size and temper that was downsized by a divine entity as punishment for his outrageous behavior.[4] Choctaw legend speaks of a squirrel in the heavens with enormous incisors that were sometimes used to gnaw away at the sun. The size of the squirrel's appetite determined whether solar eclipses would be partial or total. Tribal peoples could scare the hungry black squirrel away by making noise, thus sparing the sun.[5] The Inuit and Kwakiutl tribal peoples of North America have similar tales of the sun being devoured by animals in the sky.

The Scandinavians of long ago were a brutish lot and hardly the type of humans to be entertained, intimidated or threatened by small, chattering, fuzzy squirrels. Nevertheless, the Norsemen viewed squirrels with suspicion, seeing them as meddling troublemakers intent on sowing discord with all their antics and noise. The Norsemen, whose lives have been captured in recent times in historical television dramas about Viking raiders and seafarers, did not take kindly to the landlubber squirrels. The Norse Vikings not only killed and consumed the hated squirrels but also told unflattering tales about the animals that crystalized into mythology.

The Norse view of squirrels is captured in a well-known folktale about Ratatoskr, otherwise known as "Drill Tooth." In this tale, the squirrel Ratatoskr runs up and down the tree of life. He tells the eagle atop the tree one story of earthly happenings, but he tells the dragon living below in the roots an entirely different story. Little Ratatoskr is thus intent on causing strife between the two inhabitants of the tree of life. His story provides an apt metaphor for the contents of this book about squirrels in mass media and popular culture. The reader should not be surprised to find that stories about squirrels in our lives change from one branch of media to the next. Every channel or medium offers a different picture, a unique take, on what squirrels are all about. However, don't blame old Ratatoskr for this discrepancy. The fault, dear reader, is not in our squirrels but in ourselves—as creators of a vast and varying network of media and popular culture.

1

Squirrels
in Children's Books

Let's start at the very beginning. It's a very good place to start—at least, according to Julie Andrews in the classic 1965 film, *The Sound of Music*. Andrews, as the character Maria, begins her lyrical lesson for the von Trapp children with an introduction to "a doe, a deer—a female deer." Andrews could have done just as well starting her lesson with a chipmunk, a female chipmunk, or perhaps even a squirrel, a female squirrel. Children love fun facts about squirrels, with their large eyes, bushy tails, and outdoor antics.

There are dozens of books for children that have been used to acquaint youngsters with animals much smaller than that famous doe proposed in *The Sound of Music*. The children's book genre itself dates all the way back to the Victorian era in England, when Lewis Carroll debuted the popular *Alice's Adventures in Wonderland* in 1865. Carroll's acclaimed book allowed young boys and girls to meet a lizard, a caterpillar, a duck, and an eaglet, as well as a dodo and a gryphon. All small creatures, but, alas, Carroll did not include squirrels in Alice's magical menagerie. Squirrels did not catch a break and enter into the panoply of children's literature until the next century.

Beatrix Potter: Early Squirrel Scribe

Squirrels truly owe a debt of gratitude to author Beatrix Potter. They did not get substantial ink in early children's book selections until Potter came along and began writing books for young people. Born in 1866 in an affluent neighborhood of London, a youthful Beatrix Potter played with many pets in her Kensington home. She also enjoyed her visits with her family to the Lake District in the English Midlands, where she observed and painted the local flora and fauna. These experiences paved the way for her to become one of the first illustrators for children's literature, creating the images for her own books. She is most famous for the very first commercial book she put together: *The Tale of Peter Rabbit* (published in 1902). A successful squirrel book about a rascal named Nutkin would follow the very next year. Another Potter squirrel tale about a miscreant named Timmy Tiptoes would be added to her collection in 1911. Before examining her squirrel books, however, it's important to take a look at what Peter Rabbit is all about.

The Tale of Peter Rabbit has captivated children, and young boys in particular, for more than a century.[1] Peter is a mischievous young rabbit—not exactly a wild hare, but certainly a foolhardy fellow willing to take a dare. At the beginning of the story, his mother tells her four children that they can go out and play, but under no circumstances should they consider going into Mr. McGregor's garden, as their father met his demise there and was baked in a pie. Peter's three sisters dutifully follow Mrs. Rabbit's advice, with the fate of their dear old dad weighing heavily on their minds. However, the mischievous Peter decides to take his chances in the garden of delights.

Peter has a good time eating the forbidden garden's vegetables—this is, until he is seen by Mr. McGregor and has to make a mad dash for his life. He escapes, but only after losing his new coat and his slippers. After his terrifying experience, he reaches home, where he collapses on the floor with exhaustion. Mrs. Rabbit is distraught about his health and upset at Peter's loss of his clothes, so she puts him to bed without the benefit of the supper that she has made. However, his three well-behaved sisters enjoy a wonderful dinner of blackberries, bread and milk. *The Tale of Peter Rabbit* has been analyzed as a cautionary tale for youngsters. The moral of the story is that small fry should listen to their parents if they hope to stay out of an oven, a frying pan, or other sorts of trouble (though some critics say there is more to Potter's rabbit story than a simple lesson to obey one's parents).

Although *The Tale of Peter Rabbit* has been deemed Potter's most popular among her twenty-four children's books, the character of Peter Rabbit is pretty one-dimensional: he has an appetite for garden produce that gets him in trouble. In contrast to Potter's rabbits, the squirrels have much more personality and moral complexity. The smart-aleck red squirrel in *The Tale of Squirrel Nutkin*, like Peter Rabbit, barely escapes with his life after taking foolhardy chances and tempting fate. However, Nutkin doesn't simply lose his nice jacket and slippers to a gardener—he loses a major portion of his tail to a menacing, angry owl. In addition, Nutkin intrudes upon the owl's peace of mind—the owl's very sanity—rather than simply trespassing on his valued property.[2]

As the story goes, Nutkin and his brother Twinkleberry, along with a bevy of squirrel cousins, sail daily to Owl Island by making little rafts of twigs and using their tails as sails. It's fall, and the nuts of the island are ripe and ready for harvest. There is, however, one problem: the location of all this abundance is the province of Old Brown, an owl who lives a lavish life in the hollow of an oak tree, standing sentry over the island. Each day, when the squirrels land on the island, they make a pilgrimage to Old Brown's oak tree, where they make an offering to him and humbly beg permission to gather the nuts from his island. However, the impudent Nutkin is not so obsequious. In fact, he's downright impertinent, if not deplorable. He goads and antagonizes Old Brown with silly words, riddles and smart-aleck songs.

At first, Old Brown appears to be indifferent to Nutkin's antics. He seems more interested in the morsels given to him by Nutkin's better-behaved companions. Those offerings include mice one day, a fat mole the next day, and some scrumptious minnows on yet another visit. However, at each encounter, Nutkin cannot resist taunting the master of the island. He dances up and down, recites a riddle, and attempts to goad the owl into answering his odd lyrical queries. Old Brown shuts his eyes and says nothing, but it's clear his patience is being tried. The other squirrels are pleased the owl accepts their offerings, and they quietly go to work collecting nuts in their sacks, while Nutkin dallies and demurs.

On the sixth trip to the island, a day that will live in infamy for Nutkin, he starts his song and dance routine while the other squirrels humbly offer Old Brown the gift of an egg in exchange for permission to gather more nuts. This time Nutkin's

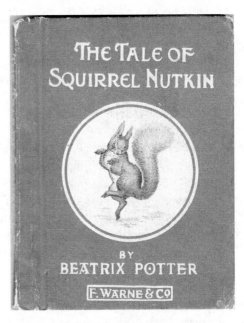

The Tale of Squirrel Nutkin **is one of many classic children's books composed by British author Beatrix Potter. The 1903 tale covers the antics of a mischievous red squirrel named Nutkin and his narrow escape from the clutches of an owl named Old Brown. Though Potter's best-known character is Peter Rabbit, critics found the impish squirrel Nutkin a much more interesting and complex character compared to the famous young rabbit.**

provocative and defiant actions spur a response that sends the other squirrels retreating in terror. Old Brown pounces on Nutkin and soon has him in his waistcoat pocket, where the arrogant little squirrel will stay until Old Brown likely decides to dine on him. Normally, this would be the end of the story, but Nutkin finds an opportunity to make a break for it. He escapes, but only after losing a substantial piece of his bushy tail to the angry owl.

As with *The Tale of Peter Rabbit*, most critics have concluded that the moral of the Nutkin story is that the insolent squirrel got what was coming to him for his uppity behavior. Peter should not have trespassed in Mr. McGregor's garden, and Nutkin should not have teased Old Brown and ought to have been grateful for his tacit approval to gather nuts on his island. Lesser beings need to mind their manners and show respect for authority. Old Brown's forbearance with Nutkin's folly should inspire admiration. Nutkin deserves nothing but rebuke for his offensive actions. This conventional analysis places *The Tale of Squirrel Nutkin* in the category of a cautionary tale for young readers. There are partisans of Nutkin, however, who see the story in a different light.

In a 2015 post on her blog *Channel Light Vessel*, Josephine Gardiner takes the position that the popularity of *The Tale of Squirrel Nutkin* with children is all about the spectacle of Nutkin defying higher authority. It's not about the wisdom of knowing one's place in the animal kingdom and staying obedient. Gardiner writes, "Nutkin is the spirit of irreverence. He ignores the concept of 'respect' and ridicules the owl's complacent authority. He suggests that creativity and play are worthwhile as duty and conformity (he may not work with nuts, but he does invent games). He shows that you can confound and baffle tyrants using words, humor and poetry, and he does it with inspiring insouciance. I can't think of many better 'lessons' for young children."[3]

Gardiner argues that parents who use *The Tale of Squirrel Nutkin* to preach to their children about the importance of obedience and respect are missing the point. Yes, Nutkin is pounced on and captured by the large owl. Yes, Nutkin does lose part of his tail to the master of the island, Old Brown. However, Nutkin's spirit is not so easily extinguished, and he gets loose from the claws and threatening beak of the old owl. What's more, it's Nutkin's name and image that grace the cover of Beatrix Potter's book. The story of Nutkin is one of flamboyant defiance, according to Gardiner, and the lyrical squirrel, who taunts the old owl with creative verses and rhyming riddles, remains one of the most subversive creatures in all of children's literature.

Before moving on to examine other children's books about squirrels, it's important to take a cursory look at Potter's second squirrel book, *The Tale of Timmy Tiptoes*.[4] Timmy is another squirrel who seems burdened with behavioral issues. The other squirrels in the woods suspect that Timmy is a dishonest pilferer of nuts and conspire to address the problem. They imprison the nut-thief Timmy in the hollow of an old tree with the expectation that he will confess to his various nut job heists when he realizes that he is irretrievably trapped. However, Timmy Tiptoes suffers neither loneliness nor despair in the confines of the old tree. A small, striped chipmunk named Chippy Hackee keeps him company and urges him to dine on the many nuts stored in the tree. In time, a strong wind blows off the top of the dead tree trunk and Timmy finds a way to make his escape. He is reunited with his fretting wife, and they hurry home together under her umbrella through the rain (presumably to live happily ever after).

Despite the happy ending, *The Tale of Timmy Tiptoes* actually left Potter's critics extremely unhappy. They pummeled the book as inauthentic and inferior to her previous productions. Among the complaints was that this book was geared to capture American fans and featured American animals that would not be found in the setting of England's Lake District. Also, some obvious domestic discord between Timmy and his wife was deemed inappropriate for a children's book. Then there were the rhymes and riddles employed in the new squirrel book, which were thought to be less creative or connected to the story than in Potter's first squirrel tale about Nutkin. Finally, Timmy and his wife (along with Chippy and his wife) were wearing clothes in the illustrations, but other animals in *The Tale of Timmy Tiptoes* did not have any clothes at all.[5]

More recent authors of squirrel books do not encounter the same degree of scrutiny and criticism leveled at Potter for her story of Timmy Tiptoes. Perhaps this is because Potter's children's books come off as a form of literature that even adults can appreciate. Her illustrations are works of art. Her stories have suspenseful plots and thought-provoking life lessons. Her rhymes and riddles within the stories are creative and meaningful. In more contemporary works for children, squirrels just don't get the Potter treatment. In many cases, the drawings are cartoonish. The language is sparse. The moral of the stories can be superficial or nonexistent. Nevertheless, many of the modern-day squirrel books for kids are comical and intended to tickle tyke-sized funny bones. Sometimes they are downright nutty—even hilarious.

Square, Squeamish, Scaredy Squirrel

The *Scaredy Squirrel* series of books by Melanie Watts portrays the fuzzy creatures as frightened of practically everything—bunnies, beavers, walruses and piranhas. The fearful and neurotic Scaredy Squirrel confronts his fears over and over again. When Scaredy contemplates time at the beach, he decides that he doesn't like the sandy foot traffic, so he builds his own beach with kitty litter. However, kitty litter doesn't quite make the grade of a pebbly beach, so he has to confront his fear of seagulls, sea monsters, jellyfish and crowds to experience the real thing. Scaredy takes the plunge into the real world of sand and sea and overcomes his outdoor fears. Youngsters whose lives are limited by their anxieties or shyness can take a lesson from Scaredy.

Of course, coping with a day at the beach can be a piece of chocolate cake compared to dealing with the darkness of night and the battle to go to sleep. In *Scaredy Squirrel at Night*, the fearful squirrel is desperately afraid of falling asleep because of bad dreams that could be full of dragons, ghosts, vampire bats, polka-dot monsters and more.[6] Wide-eyed Scaredy has a plan to stay awake all night, every single night. Scaredy counts stars, plays cymbals and makes scrapbooks, which certainly wards off any nightmares. However, exhaustion takes its toll and Scaredy comes face-to-face with a horrible horoscope prediction: all his dreams are about to come true.

Scaredy prepares for the worst with his "Bad Dream Action Plan," which includes a fire extinguisher to take out dragons and a fan to blow away the ghosts. *Scaredy Squirrel at Night* offers a bedtime story to make light of kids' fears of the dark. Scaredy makes lists of ideas and plans for staying awake all night. Naturally, the energy he puts into staying awake inevitably tires him out to the point that he nods off. Of course, *Scaredy Squirrel at Night* was first published in 2009, before so many kids were blessed with the blue light of computer tablets. How much harder would it be for Scaredy to fall asleep now if his lists of ideas were composed on a glowing screen?

Richard Fowler's squirrel in *A Squirrel's Tale* is just as anxious and neurotic as the furry ball of fear that inhabits Watts' squirrel books.[7] However, Fowler's unnamed squirrel's mental issues stem from the fact that he can't find his nuts. The squirrel unwisely invades the domain of blackbirds, owls, moles and voles, frantically searching for his nuts. Later he enters what looks to be a bat cave and asks, "Have any of you bats seen my nuts?" The wisecracking bats are less than helpful. When the upset squirrel stumbles upon the web of a spider, the amiable arachnid warns him not to enter the nearby cabin of a woodchopper. The squirrel naturally ignores this good advice but quickly figures out that he is in the wrong place—there is a recipe for squirrel pie on the woodchopper's table.

To escape his predicament, the hapless squirrel exits quickly out of the cabin's window. "Squirrel was so scared, he jumped high in the air and landed in a pile of leaves ... and guess what he found?" asks Fowler, presumably the book's narrator. That's right, he finds his lost nuts. The reader can lift up a flap of leaves on the last page of the book, and there, lo and behold, is an ample supply of nuts. The beauty of Fowler's squirrel in *A Squirrel's Tale* is that there's an actual cutout of a squirrel that can weave in and out of the slots on the pages. The slots provide access to various creatures that can be queried about the whereabouts of the lost nuts. And if the reader loses the original cutout, Fowler has provided instructions on the book's back cover on how to make a replacement squirrel, complete with a tale of orange felt or similar material.

Darn, Busy, Skiing Squirrels

Squirrels are not always scared, squeamish and apprehensive like those portrayed in the books of Melanie Watts and Richard Fowler. Squirrels can also be infuriating, fuzzy geniuses capable of solving any problem that gets in the way of obtaining their food. Just ask Old Man Fookwire in the book series *Those Darn Squirrels!* (written by Adam Rubin and illustrated by Daniel Salmieri).[8] Old Man Fookwire lives on the outskirts of town in a decrepit house on the edge of a forest. He loves all the birds that come his way, because he loves painting pictures of the various species of fowl. However, these birds are not your typical robins and sparrows. There are whirley birds, bonga birds, baba birds, yaba birds and even the occasional floogle bird.

Although Old Man Fookwire loves his odd feathered friends, he is far less fond of the pesky squirrels that come around his place. When Fookwire decides to set up a series of bird feeders to keep his winged warblers from heading south, the squirrels invite themselves into the old man's yard to enjoy the delicious seeds and berries contained in the feeders. The birdseed burglars send Fookwire into a tizzy—hence the title for the book and the subsequent series. When Fookwire sees that his bird feeders have been raided, he shakes his fist at the sky and yells out in frustration, "Those darn squirrels!"

Fookwire tries to devise a plan with a clothesline and the feeders to outsmart the squirrels. However, Fookwire does not realize just how smart his adversaries are. Rubin (the author/narrator) explains that squirrels are the cleverest of all woodland creatures. They can make a house out of a tree and build a bed out of twigs, dirt and spit. The squirrels foil Fookwire's plan, and the war between the old man and the squirrels escalates. When the birds head south and the squirrels seem to win the final birdseed battle, Old Man Fookwire becomes sad and depressed. The squirrels then meet to devise their own plan to address the situation. Their solution to make peace with the old man is to disguise themselves as birds the next time they visit his yard and dine at the feeders. Their plan works. Fookwire is overjoyed and begins painting the squirrels in their bird outfits. He even invites them into his house for a party.

The characters in *Those Darn Squirrels!* (as well as the book itself) get great reviews from book journals and individual readers. Old Man Fookwire is loveable, even though he sneezes dust, hates both pies and puppies, and is generally a grump until the ingenious squirrels turn his attitude around. The squirrels also garner kind words for their brilliance, cheerful dispositions and wonderful plan to charm the old grouch. Children love this book from 2008, as well as the more recent books, *Those Darn Squirrels Fly South* and *Those Darn Squirrels and the Cat Next Door*. Adults may appreciate these books for putting smiles on their children's faces, but adults also know better if they've had any real encounters with squirrels. Battles with squirrels over bird feeders or property rights never really end happily ever after.

In the award-winning series about "those darn squirrels," the fuzzy animals are always ingenious and hilarious, whether they are mollifying a temperamental old man; tripping up a nasty, bird-hating cat named Muffins; or flying south with the birds to enjoy some beautiful beaches and a more tropical diet. It's hard not to be captivated and enchanted by the darn squirrels. It's also hard not to fall in love with some new squirrels that enjoy cruising down snow-covered slopes in *Squirrels on Skis*.[9] This story of the marvelous, manic squirrels on skis is by J. Hamilton Ray with illustrations by Pascal Lemaitre. The book is recommended for young readers who may want to curl up—and chill out—with a cool squirrel story on a snow day when their schools are closed.

Squirrels on Skis begins with an alarming scene of hundreds of squirrels invading a quiet, snowy town on their skis. They rush down a nearby mountain slope and disrupt everything, crowding the city center, jumping from roofs and church steeples, jamming the roads and knocking over garbage cans. The mayor calls a town hall meeting, where the local pest control expert says he can swoop the rodents up into his vacuum device. However, there are objections to using an exterminator, and a reporter, named Sally Sue Breeze, says she will get to the bottom of the infestation and find a better way to remedy the situation. Sally Sue climbs to the top of the mountain and discovers all kinds of shenanigans—the squirrels have been lured into trading their acorns for popsicle stick skis by a devious rabbit. Meanwhile, back in town, the pest control man is preparing his equipment to suck up the annoying squirrels.

Spoiler alert: Sally Sue Breeze and the reformed rabbit start an acorn roast on the mountaintop, and the aroma lures all of the squirrels back to their original nesting area. Sally Sue also arranges for the abandoned popsicle stick factory to become the Bushy Tail Great Ski Chalet. Ski trails are designed and prepared near the chalet, so the squirrels do not have to give up the new sport that they have come to love. The mayor and the townspeople trek to the snowy mountaintop to enjoy hot drinks at picnic tables, where they get an excellent and much more agreeable view of the squirrels on skis. And everybody lives happily ever after. This book is a favorite of parents who are interested in getting children excited about learning to ski, but it has less favorable reviews among pest control experts.

The Busy Little Squirrel is about a furry creature that is less interested in winter sports and more focused on preparing for a hard winter.[10] The leaves are falling, and there's no time left to hop with the frogs or run with the dogs. He can't even take time to accept invitations to nibble at a pumpkin with the mice or to enjoy a full moon with some friendly owls. He has to gather food for the winter. The busy squirrel turns down many opportunities for fun activities with animal acquaintances, but it all pays off when he is at last found fast asleep in his tree hollow surrounded by a lot of goodies. His winter worries are over.

Some parents find inspiration in the lesson that the busy squirrel hopefully imparts for young children. The "busy theme" is a winner for these parents. The squirrel wisely stays focused on his important task, even as his animal friends implore him to play. Author Nancy Tarfuri has created more than thirty books for young children and has won awards for many of them, including *Have You Seen My Duckling?* and *I Love You, Little One.* Another busy squirrel can be found in the bilingual board book by Belle Yang titled *Squirrel Round and Round.* In both English and Mandarin Chinese, this book offers a celebration of the natural world as it takes children through the seasons with one energetic squirrel.

Unlike other squirrel books, *Squirrel Round and Round* lacks amusing rhymes, gimmicky pop-ups and silly tongue twisters.[11] This is not an anthropomorphic squirrel that interacts with humans and displays a lot of personality. This is a basic squirrel in a simple story. The book is focused on a squirrel that traverses the seasons through attractive watercolor illustrations. Birds tend to their babies in the spring; lightning bugs put on a display on a summer night; seeds fly and leaves flutter in the fall; and the squirrel leaves fresh tracks in newly fallen snow with the arrival of winter. Beyond the beauty of the simple images, *Squirrel Round and Round* exposes children to the reality that squirrels are written about all over the world in vastly differing languages.

Name That Squirrel: Cyril, Earl and Mr. Peanuts

In children's books, you can find squirrels visiting the seashore, skiing down snowy hills, reciting rhymes and riddles, playing the piano, and disguising themselves as birds (the bird disguises allow the enterprising rodents to dine at bird feeders to satisfy their voracious squirrel appetites) (photograph by Ursula Ruhl).

Unlike the simple, natural squirrels of Nancy Tarfuri and Belle Yang, Nancy Rose's squirrel in *The Secret Life of Squirrels* is a hyperactive, confident genius.[12] He has given up climbing trees in favor of playing the piano. However, Rose's squirrel, Mr. Peanuts, gets tired of being lonely, so he sends an invitation through the mail to his equally exceptional cousin. Soon the two squirrels are together playing chess, picnicking, camping and telling each other ghost stories. Mr. Peanuts is a classic case of anthropomorphism run amok. However, the book gets rave reviews from readers precisely because Mr. Peanuts and his squirrel cousin do a lot of human things that make them entertaining.

One element in particular

makes this book even more unique than Richard Fowler's cutout squirrel: Nancy Rose's Mr. Peanuts is real and has been caught on camera. Rose employs her camera skills for setup shots used in the book showing the squirrel at work and play. The less than candid camera captures Mr. Peanuts cooking hot dogs and potatoes on his tiny grill. Other shots show him reading favorite books in his library, such as *A Tail of Two Cities*, or pounding away on his piano. After Mr. Peanuts is united with Cousin Squirrel, the author's camera catches them playing chess indoors and putting up a tent for a campout outdoors. The moral of the story is that having a friend makes everything twice as much fun.

The final page of the actual story is followed by two sections that seem a little out of place in a children's book. These sections are titled "Ten Tips for Photographing Wildlife" and "Q&A with Nancy Rose." The photographic advice includes a warning not to take pictures too close to birds' nests and risk scaring the feathered parents away. Also, you are advised to be careful about taking photos of unfamiliar pets and wildlife, nor should a wild animal be asked to pose for you. This begs a number of questions: Just how wild was Mr. Peanuts? Did peanut treats make the difference in getting Mr. Peanuts to pose? Did Mr. Peanuts win the chess match with Cousin Squirrel? Most important, how can *The Secret Life of Squirrels* be so secret if someone is always tailing them with a digital camera?

Of course, some of these weighty questions get answered on the "Question and Answer" pages of the book, where Rose concedes that Mr. Peanuts has been lured into unusual action with alluring bribes of peanuts. Also, Rose admits that she has trained a stable of squirrelly actors and actresses. Mr. Peanuts was her first actor, but there have been several others who have found the limelight, including Nicky, Pisa, Claus and Mittens. Had Beatrix Potter lived in our digital world, how might the stories of Nutkin and Timmy Tiptoes been altered by the tools of new technology? Perhaps an even better question is whether *The Secret Life of Squirrels* is really a thinly disguised manual for adult shutterbugs, rather than an educational children's book.

Moving on from the photogenic Mr. Peanuts and his cousin, it's time to be introduced to two oddly named and traditionally illustrated squirrels known as Cyril and Earl. Cyril inhabits Jo Wright's children's book *Cyril the Squirrel*.[13] Wright, a native of England's Staffordshire, wrote her first book about Cyril for her daughter, who had a habit of filling her pockets with acorns as a toddler when she went out for walks with her mom. Wright's Cyril is frustrated because he keeps forgetting where his acorns are hidden.

He thinks he ought to remember where he hid them all, because he intentionally buried them under something he thinks he can't miss—as it turns out, that "something" is a shining Christmas tree.

The big problem for Cyril is that the tree is not always shining, causing it to become as nondescript as other trees on his stomping grounds. Thus, he loses track of where all the acorns are located—that is, until another holiday season comes along and it becomes apparent where his treasure trove is buried. The summers are especially frustrating, but when the warmth disappears and wintry breezes return, so does Cyril's luck. On one cold winter's morn, the big tree starts glowing, and Cyril is back in business. This is a fun story for humans who know that Cyril had a bright idea all along for his cache of nuts, but it's an idea that's only bright for a certain time of the year.

The book features holes in the pages through which to count Cyril's buried acorns. The text consists of short but entertaining verses of the rhyming variety. Wright's children's book is from the *Cyril the Squirrel and Friends* series. An amazing number of Cyril books have since proliferated like trees from acorns buried and lost by tens of thousands of squirrels. *Cyril the Squirrel and the Nut Thieves* comes to us from Melinda Kinsman, as does *Cyril the Squirrel and the Long Run Home*. B.C. Copland has penned *Cyril the Squirrel and the Lavender Wood Mob*. Jane Evans and Izzy Bean offer us *Cyril the Squirrel Finds Out about Love*. There is also Eugene McCabe and Al O'Donnell's *Cyril: Quest of an Orphaned Squirrel*, and many more.

Cyril has enough squirrel tales for a lifetime (or, at least, for enough bedtimes to get a child well past the kindergarten years). In fairness, children might also wish to enjoy an acquaintance with Don Freeman's *Earl the Squirrel*.[14] This squirrel is a wet-behind-the-ears youngster whose mother wants him to learn how to find his own acorns, as opposed to relying on his human friend, Jill. Earl doesn't even know where to begin with this task, although he does resolve to show his mom that he can find some acorns. Earl's mom believes Jill is spoiling him and helping him too much, especially after Jill gives him a red scarf. Earl wears the red scarf and encounters a grouchy owl and an angry bull in the process of learning about self-reliance and resourcefulness. With the help of his multipurpose scarf, he finally finds his way home with acorns to please his anxious mother.

In the tradition of Beatrix Potter from a century earlier, Freeman experiments with other animals as story subjects for his children's books, including mice, birds and bears. And like Potter, he has experienced varying degrees of success in the creation of useful and amusing stories for youngsters. *Earl the Squirrel* is one of the success stories.

There are many more children's books about squirrels that could be reviewed here. And the multitude of squirrel books available for children dwarfs the number of books written for adult readers. Nevertheless, it's worth taking a look at four entertaining and informative books on squirrels for more mature readers. Among these books are *Squirrels: The Animal Answer Guide*; *Squirrels: A Wildlife Handbook*; *Squirrels at My Window: Life with a Remarkable Gang of Urban Squirrels*; and *Outwitting Squirrels*.

Squirrel Selections for Older Folks

Squirrels: The Animal Answer Guide, by Richard W. Thorington, Jr., and Katie Ferrell, tells us that a groundhog is really a type of squirrel, that squirrels have natural sunglasses, and that the first squirrels showed up on the planet about thirty-six million years ago (although that assertion is up for debate).[15] Squirrels obviously have the jump on humans when it comes to inhabiting the real estate on planet Earth. By most accounts, our ancestors appeared a mere six million years ago. The modern form of human being is thought to have evolved about two hundred thousand years ago, and civilization as we know it is only about six thousand years old. So, this means that squirrels have preceded human civilization by at least 35,994,000 years—probably more. It's no wonder that squirrels seem a bit smug around humans and occasionally take to scolding the naïve newcomers with their incessant chatter.

Thorington and Ferrell cover every aspect of the diverse squirrel family, from the first squirrels of millions of years ago to squirrels of the twenty-first century. According to the authors, 278 species of squirrels inhabit all continents except Antarctica and Australia. They readily share human habitats in most parts of the world, raiding our bird feeders and setting up shop in the attics of our homes. They vary in size from the impish pygmy flying squirrel to the weighty eighteen-pound gray marmot. The authors devote only a paragraph to the role of squirrels in humanity's forms of popular culture, though, as scientists, they can be forgiven for such inattention.

Kim Long's *Squirrels: A Wildlife Handbook* offers more on popular culture and folklore, but it also can be used as an illustrated field guide.[16] Like Thorington and Ferrell's answer guide, this handbook presents an informative portrait of squirrels in their natural habitat and plenty of useful factoids. It examines squirrels' social interactions with early American cultures and their role in localized North American ecosystems. Among the basic questions answered: What do squirrels have for dinner? How do they keep their food supplies intact and safe? What squirrel species are most aggressive and to be avoided at all costs? Can you find any backyard bird feeders that are truly squirrel-proof?

That last question about squirrel-proofing bird feeders is more exhaustively answered in a sometimes silly book titled *Outwitting Squirrels: 101 Cunning Stratagems to Reduce Dramatically the Egregious Misappropriation of Seed from Your Birdfeeder by Squirrels.*[17] The many stratagems that Bill Adler, Jr., provides involve Vaseline, Teflon spray, Nixalite, Perrier bottles and baffled fishing line. He examines methods to "squirrel-proof" bird feeders and property with such devices as spooker poles, water bombs, mirror mazes, rubber acorns, camera flashes and more. Adler's book, which has been released in several editions, and is now three decades old, continues to be a popular manual for those seeking to protect the bounty of their bird feeders from marauding squirrels.

Adler's *Outwitting Squirrels* is definitely more of a popular culture treatment than an adult science book like the answer guides and wildlife manuals available on squirrels and their habits. However, Adler's book, especially in the opening chapters, does offer some serious information on ways to ward off squirrels. His third chapter, titled "Know the Enemy," provides information on the physical capabilities of squirrels, their sex life, their most-feared predators and the foods that they crave. He reveals that every week squirrels eat as much as their entire body weight—or even more. "You try that and see what happens," suggests Adler.

As Adler moves on to later chapters, it becomes obvious that he feels trying to squirrel-proof anything is a losing battle. In the chapter titled "101 Cunning Stratagems," the methods suggested to squirrel-proof bird feeders devolve into farce. Among the techniques that Adler proposes: rent a guard cat; move to southern Florida and enjoy flamingos; paint your feeders to look like owl habitats; take up falconry and keep your falcon untethered; enclose your yard with a twenty-foot Plexiglass fence; dig up their nuts during the winter; import killer bees; and decide that squirrels aren't so bad after all. In his final chapter, "Quitting," Adler throws in the towel on trying to outwit squirrels. He writes, "I think a lot of pro-squirrel people are actually quitters. They are tired of what they consider to be a losing battle ... tired of throwing things; tired of transporting squirrels across state lines; tired of digging moats;

tired of mixing waxy, noxious chemicals; tired of running to the local rent-a-cat. A lot of former birdfeeders turned pro-squirrel would rather take the afternoon off and sleep."[18] Adler's first-hand experiences with anti-squirrel strategies all point to the central quandary of our time: Can humans really outsmart squirrels?

By contrast, Grace Marmour Spruch is not interested in outsmarting squirrels or driving them away from her abode. In Spruch's book, *Squirrels at My Window: Life with a Remarkable Gang of Urban Squirrels*,[19] we learn all about how Spruch developed personal relationships with squirrels named Notchko, Runty, Genius and Sweetie from the window of her New York City apartment. Spruch provides an account from more than a decade of caring for and being entertained by city squirrels.

Spruch and her husband, Larry (now deceased), both physicists, lived very near Washington Square Park in a fifth-floor walkup apartment. One day she discovered what looked like a gray blob in a planter by the window. The gray mass turned out to be the first of many visiting squirrels. Spruch soon began to observe the visitors on a regular basis and record the story of their lives. She discovered that city squirrels do not have an easy life, especially in the cold, dreary winters of the Big Apple. She found the individual differences in her squirrels startling, with their different likes and dislikes, their habits and their mannerisms. She also was struck by their intelligence and even (on occasion) affection. A particularly amazing chapter in *Squirrels at My Window* comes when a visitor she named Sweetie Longtail suffers from malocclusion. Just trapping the skittish Sweetie was an overwhelming challenge, never mind the task of carrying the bouncing cage down a busy New York City street to the veterinarian's office. Spruch's devotion to her squirrel friends is inspiring, a bit eccentric and somewhat dumbfounding. As one appreciative reader observed on the book's Amazon site, "I will probably never have the opportunity in my life to get to know a squirrel so I am grateful for this marvelous account told with scientific accuracy as well as a warm heart."

Squirrels can take heart from their treatment in books, whether in hardcover, soft or electronic form, or in a children's book or an adult genre. They are never demonized in books, as they often are in other venues of mass media. Even when literary squirrels are chastised for some of their nuisance or destructive behaviors, they are still generally admired and even praised for their energy and persistence. Squirrels share some of the same traits as young humans in children's books: they can be shy, forgetful, playful, impish and a bit reckless. Perhaps that is why they make such fitting subjects for children's books. The authors of these books often can find a lesson to impart to youngsters near the end of a wily or rakish squirrel tale.

Most adult books on squirrels tend to be science oriented or more in the nature of guides for observing wildlife. The field guides are especially useful for those with natural curiosity and a set of binoculars or a camera on a tripod. The science books offer facts and details on how squirrels live and survive—though the facts are not always flattering. Nevertheless, on balance, squirrels receive favorable reviews for their attributes in the pages of books for the older set, just as they are treated lovingly in most children's books. Overall, squirrels fare well within the covers of the book medium.

2

Squirrels
Make the Headlines

The squirrel that hops and bops through the pages of children's books is warm and fuzzy—a sympathetic figure. He never snarls, screeches or threatens anyone with a mouthful of sharp, ever-growing incisors. His teeth are never bared. He never causes chaos or destruction and is never more than mildly annoying. He appears to be naïve, as he always expects the best from other earthly inhabitants. He is vulnerable and innocent while graciously encountering other animals that are not as good natured. The benign squirrel of the book medium is a loveable creature. The squirrel in both children's and adult books often prompts amusement and laughter, and occasionally even inspires heartfelt compassion and acts of kindness toward real squirrels.

By contrast, the wily squirrel of the print newspaper medium is an entirely different creature. Contrary to the portrayals found in many hilarious children's books, a newspaper squirrel does not simply gather nuts and pose for delightful art and photo illustrations. In newsprint, the destructive squirrel garners fearmongering stories and wildly disturbing headlines. The newspaper squirrel is an angry little mongrel who is always ready to make the lives of human beings miserable in countless ways. He's a trespasser. He's a destroyer. He's a carrier of viruses that antibiotics cannot address. He's the newspaper squirrel.

From New York to San Diego, from Miami to Seattle, squirrels make headlines for the millions of dollars in damage they cause to human domiciles. Newspaper stories alert us to the myriad threats that squirrels pose to humans—destroying humans' homes, compromising human life-support systems and endangering human health. After all the jolly squirrel tales in children's books, newspaper stories attempt to make us realize that it's time to grow up, to concede that virtually every squirrel constitutes an existential threat. Newspaper stories implicitly and explicitly advise humans to trade in those thin, oversized volumes of squirrel fairy tales for some real news. It's

29

best to close those lovely illustrated children's books and opt for a needed dose of squirrel reality pills with the hard news of the local daily.

Saboteur Squirrels in Your Attic and Beyond

The most common newspaper horror stories about delinquent squirrels tend to hit humans right where they live—at home. Often the stories give

Newspaper stories such as this one, titled "Squirrelly Behavior," note that squirrels cause thousands of dollars' worth of damage to homes, automobiles, and electrical equipment on power line poles. When squirrels make the headlines in newspapers, it's usually because of the destructive behavior that they inflict on the human world (courtesy *Webster-Kirkwood Times*).

squirrels the tabloid treatment, with scary headlines, frightening copy and a message that these animals constitute a 24/7 menace. According to these stories, squirrels are running track on your roof and only making pit stops to chew away your eaves in order to find an entrance into your home. Once in the attic, squirrels tear up the insulation to make their own homes and chew on the electric wires as if they were dental floss. Within a home's walls, squirrels raise their offspring. And when they are not birthing new broods, they are rudely expiring, leaving you desperately trying to locate their corpses and alleviate the rotting squirrel stench. Down the chimney, squirrels take advantage of a convenient route to your kitchen and your family room. In the false ceilings of the finished basements, squirrels leave their acorn shells and tiny feces to decorate the translucent panels for your overhead fluorescent lights.

No one is secure from the plague of squirrels: not the poet, the physician, the farmer, the scientist or the magician. Newspaper accounts tell about the travails of an elderly woman unable to cope with a fraternity of fuzzy animals partying in her attic. Or they tell about the investigation into the plight of the cleaning lady rendered sick and prostrate after finding squirrel feces in every nook and cranny of a home that she was assigned to tidy up. Or they speak of the contractor suing a couple for $90,000 after receiving injuries caused by a squirrel when he entered the home on a remodeling job.[1] And then there is the alarming report of the animal control agent who had to virtually destroy the occupied house in the village in order to save it from an angry squirrel interloper. These news articles may have begun as oddities or human-interest assignments, but they commonly morph into squirrel horror stories.

News about squirrels causing anguish for a grandmother living alone, illness for an unsuspecting housekeeper, physical injury for a contractor, serious turmoil for an upset animal control agent—all of these accounts actually seem rather pedestrian compared to some of the major squirrel scare headlines of our time.

Consider the headlines about what appear to be kamikaze squirrels taking down electrical power supplies all across the country. Consider the headlines about cyber-terror squirrels threatening stock market exchanges and creating financial ruin for American investors. Consider the headlines about squatter squirrels taking up residence in American automobiles, disabling them, and leaving commuters stranded. Consider the headlines about diseased squirrels testing positive for a malady akin to bubonic plague in several states in the American Southwest. Consider the headlines about today's overpopulation of squirrels, an out-of-control species, because mankind no longer finds them suitable game for hunting adventures or for the frying pan.

The disturbing headlines about squirrels harken back to the age of yellow journalism, when newspaper moguls William Randolph Hearst and Joseph Pulitzer competed with each other to see who could publish the most outrageous stories to capture the public's attention. The scare headlines also recall the Roaring Twenties tabloid journalism, when exaggerated news stories and sensational copy were anchored by stacks of inky stepped heads. A prime example is the three-deck headline out of 1929 Chicago: "Crazy Squirrel Is Executed by Police Officers." The tabloid story was picked up by both downstate Illinois and national papers. One account noted, "The little red squirrel that got mad and bit seven persons, and thus described as a red menace, has been executed."[2]

The headlines in newspapers today are somewhat different from those of the yellow journalism era and tabloid journalism era, two low points in the newspaper industry. They mirror the "question heads" and teasers used as "clickbait" on computer screens. These news website headlines on the internet, which are now influencing the way headlines are written for print, are designed to goad and drive readers to open up stories and find the frightening answers to the horrifying questions posed: "Is a Killer Squirrel Virus Loose?" "Should You Be Scared of the Black Death?" "Did Squirrels Shut Down the Market?" "Forget Hackers: Are Squirrels a Bigger Threat to America's Power Grid?"

Suicide-Mission Squirrels: Taking Down the Grid

Many Americans do seem to be aware of just how vulnerable our electrical energy network is to piracy, implosion and shutdown. In his investigative tour de force, *Lights Out,* former ABC *Nightline* anchor Ted Koppel reveals that a major attack on America's power grid is not only possible but also likely. He warns that a shutdown would be devastating, and that this country is woefully unprepared for such an event. Koppel covers just about every threat—cyberwar, electromagnetic pulse attacks, unforeseen solar flare interruptions from an otherwise beneficial sun. There is one proven threat to the electrical power grid, however, that Koppel does not cover: squirrels.

On the evening of November 9, 1965, the lights went out across New York and in six other states, putting more than thirty million people in pitch-black darkness. Carl Bernstein, who would later become famous for his stories on the Watergate scandal, found himself in the dark in New York City. Bernstein decided to write a so-called "new journalism piece" on the blackout experience, which was flighty and farcical, and which failed to grasp the gravity of the situation—a big part of America was literally without power.

Wrote Bernstein, "I was at a friend's apartment ... and the lights fell asleep and I woke up. We looked out the window and—Dig We Must—this crazy, unbelievable scene with half the lights in Manhattan out. Half the lights hell! We made our way up to the roof by candlelight and somebody had stolen the Empire State Building. And the Chrysler Building and Harlem, and Jackie Kennedy's apartment house, and Queens, and Lincoln Center and Temple Emmanuel...."[3]

Bernstein was young and not yet in his crack investigative mode. Had he been driven to seek out the actual cause of the Great Northeast Blackout of 1965, he would have gotten a crazy, unbelievable earful. Several theories for the cause of the power loss involved UFO sightings prior to the calamity. Utility maintenance people pinned it all on some malfunctioning safety relays. Engineers put the blame squarely on transmission line overloads. Scientists talked about cascading power surges and electrical transformer blowouts. No one talked about squirrels.

The situation was much the same with the subsequent Great Northeast Blackout of August 14, 2003. Only this time the impact of the power loss was much more widespread. An estimated ten million people were affected in parts of Canada, with forty-five million people affected in eight states in America.[4] Explanations for the blackout ranged from faulty control room software to overload alarm failures. There was talk about unpruned foliage somehow coming into contact with electric transmission lines. Again, no one talked about squirrels sabotaging the electrical lifelines of North America.

Not until ten years later, when the *New York Times* published an investigation of squirrel sabotage of our electric power grid, did Americans learn the extent of power outages caused by the ever-present, large-tailed rodents. Investigator Jon Mooallem outlined in the *Times* how it now appears that there are hundreds of attacks on the nation's power grid by squirrels. Mooallem's findings pointed to an uncoordinated wave of squirrel "nut job" assaults. However, his cumulative findings did not begin to raise any cries of squirrel conspiracy. Most of the citizenry remained complacent about the squirrel threat. After all, they are just squirrels.

Mooallem documented fifty power outages caused by squirrels in twenty-four states in the summer of 2011. He noted that most Americans make snarky jokes about his squirrel attack analysis, but he stressed that the phenomenon can be deadly serious, not just an inconvenience. The extent of the problem, according to some observers, resembles a squirrel uprising. Mooallem said it's hard for Americans to accept that a single squirrel can disrupt the lives of so many thousands of citizens. When squirrels attack the nation's grid, the results are frightening, if not electrifying.

Among the instances of squirrel sabotage Mooallem cited:

- In Wichita, Kansas, a squirrel attack left 10,000 without power.
- In Clackamas County, Oregon, an attack left 5,000 without power.
- In Roanoke, Virginia, a squirrel attack left 5,000 without power.
- In Rock Hill, South Carolina, an attack left 7,200 without power.
- In Kalamazoo, Michigan, an attack left 2,000 without power.
- In Portland, Oregon—squirrel attack left 9,200 without power.

All across the country, squirrel attacks leave thousands without power. Mooallem refers to these instances of squirrel treachery as P.O.C.B.S. events (Power Outages Caused by Squirrels).[5] Many of his documented P.O.C.B.S. involve high-voltage violence. A solitary squirrel can cause a blackout by simply scampering across electrical equipment and producing an arc between an energized component, such as a cylindrical transformer atop a utility pole, and a grounded piece of utility equipment. Essentially, squirrels create a high-voltage short with their bodies.

When a furry conspirator generates an arc and causes a short circuit, a flash of crackling blue light signals yet another squirrel fatality. The squirrel becomes a high-powered suicide bomber, sometimes igniting and other times exploding. If the charred squirrel cadaver does not fall away from the wires or the electrical equipment, it can cause a continuous fault, a cascading blackout, which means that the lights will go out for miles as the electrical grid is compromised.

As Mooallem explained, the "aftermath can be gnarly. Often, there are burned-out circuit breakers or other costly, obliterated equipment to clean up or replace. And occasionally a P.O.C.B.S. will generate an idiosyncratic storm of ancillary mayhem."[6] Mooallem provides an example of that mayhem when he describes how a squirrel chewed into high-voltage lines near a water-treatment facility, setting off "a chain of improbable events" that forced the city of Tampa to boil its water for the next thirty-seven hours. He also tells of a flaming squirrel that fell from a utility pole near Tulsa, Oklahoma, starting a grass fire across several acres of land.

Since Mooallem published his 2013 squirrel study, squirrel disruptions of electrical supplies across the country have not abated. As this book went to press in 2019, stories about squirrels causing electrical fires and disruptions appeared in headlines from Minnesota, Pennsylvania, and North Carolina. A news dispatch from Morganton, North Carolina, described a squirrel that bit into a high-tension electrical line, causing sparks to fall to the ground and disperse. The sparks led to a grass fire, which spread to a mobile home that soon had flames licking out from every window. The fire was contained, but the home was a total loss. Witness statements about power lines sparking led to the discovery of a squirrel that was a total loss as well. Photojournalists were able to document the squirrel perfidy with photos of the charred animal's body hanging from its clenched teeth on the electrical power line.[7]

Newspapers ask: How long will Americans continue to put up with the serious disruptions and fires resulting from squirrel attacks on the grid? So far, solutions to this problem smack of accommodation and appeasement. For example, one highly publicized remedy is to undertake a massive campaign to bury the nation's power lines. Proponents of burying the power lines point to European countries that have buried their lines, making them safe from summer winds, winter ice and saboteur squirrels. Residents of these countries seldom experience the power outages that Americans do. Opponents of burying the power lines make the point that the costs will be upward of $1 million per mile.[8] And the enormous cost of making our electric grid squirrel-proof will not come close to ending our war with squirrels.

Cyber-Terror: Squirrels Bring Market Collapse

Assaults on the power grid are only one aspect of humans' multidimensional vulnerability to the misanthropic designs of the squirrels. The rodents, after all, have shut down our stock market on several occasions. There is a keen irony in this, as many Americans are said to "squirrel away" a portion of their salaries in 401(k) retirement plans or IRA accounts, especially now that fixed pension plans are becoming a thing of the past. In fact, Americans are urged to behave like squirrels when it comes to both saving up money and looking out for the future. After all, squirrels are supposedly always on the alert for any danger or volatility in their environment. Humans need to take a lesson from the wary squirrels, according to a number of financial institution advertisements. Some of the ads employ squirrel characters in their messaging, telling us that we must be on guard like the squirrels.

Even when they are standing upright and enjoying a few nutty bites in the wild, squirrels will nervously stop to look and listen for predators that may be sneaking up on them. Investment advisers often suggest that squirrels are the classic conservative investors, as they are lean, mean, acorn-burying machines. They eat only what they need, even with opportunities to gorge themselves when nuts are in great supply. They eat what they need and then "squirrel away" hundreds, if not thousands, of acorns for later consumption. Some of those buried acorns are forgotten and inevitably sprout through the ground to become mighty oak trees. Unsurprisingly, oak trees have become symbols of solid investment—thanks, in part, to squirrels.

There is a lot of mythology about prudent and parsimonious squirrels, but, in truth, there is nothing all that wise or solid about these rodents. Squirrels are overrated when it comes to their vigilance, frugality and aptitude for preparing for the future. The myth that squirrels are vigilant and careful is belied by their ample representation among the flattened roadkill littering the nation's rural roads and state highways. Likewise, the myth that squirrels are great savers is punctured by the sheer number of trees that spring up from the many acorns they bury and then forget. For humans, the ultimate irony of squirrels as investment gurus can be found in newspaper headlines about the havoc they have wreaked on the markets—for example, the Nasdaq.

The National Association of Securities Dealers Automatic Quotation (Nasdaq) service has been criticized any number of times for glitches that have halted trading, lost money for investors, and resulted in Nasdaq agreeing to pay the Securities Exchange Commission millions of dollars for technical system breakdowns and poor decision-making. Failure to totally squirrel-proof the system has been part of the problem. The first recorded squirrel cyber-terrorism event came in 1987, when a furry creature touched off a power failure in Trumbull, Connecticut. The back-up systems meant to keep power flowing at Nasdaq's Trumbull facility failed to kick in properly. Millions of shares were unable to be traded. The squirrel lost its life, and reverberations of that death were felt at stock exchanges across the country. Financial papers around the world covered the squirrel's impact on stock trading, and the *New York Times* article was headlined "Stray Squirrel Shuts Down Nasdaq System."[9] This raises the question: How can a squirrel be classified as a stray? When is a squirrel presumed to not be a stray?

Perhaps using the term *stray* to describe the squirrel was intended to reassure investors that this incident was an aberration—the squirrel in question was an abnormal, wandering waif—and such a crime surely could not be expected to happen again in a world of well-adjusted, well-situated squirrels. But a squirrel cyber-terrorism event did happen again. "Squirrel Leads to Second NASDAQ Closing in Seven Years" was the headline anchoring a 1994 Associated Press story about yet another closure of America's second largest stock market. AP reporter Dan Blake cited a utility spokesperson in Connecticut who blamed the incident involving lost power on a squirrel chewing through power lines. The *New York Times* was still reviewing the interruptions almost a decade later with an article titled "Computer Bugs and Squirrels: A History of Nasdaq's Woes," which revisited the disastrous squirrel incidents of 1987 and 1994. The *Times* article asked, "Shouldn't a stock exchange focused on technology be able to prevent technological problems?"[10] Apparently not—at least, not when squirrels are involved.

The newspaper medium has performed a great service with its articles and headlines about squirrels wreaking havoc on community power supplies and shutting down stock exchanges. However, those articles do not tell the whole story about the calamities caused by squirrels. Newspapers have chronicled plenty of other squirrel outrages that have added to the human misery index. Among the injurious phenomena is the mischief of the so-called squatter squirrel, whose antics can appear comical when reported as some isolated incident but multiply to the level of a serious concern when these outrages are taken in their totality.

Under the Hood: Squatter Squirrels

The term *squatter* has most commonly been applied to human beings. A squatter does not own, does not rent, does not even temporarily inhabit a domicile with the owner's approval. A squatter occupies a dwelling or space without legal permission and with little concern for the inconvenience of such irresponsible behavior. Squatting has always been a problem in the so-called underdeveloped world, but it has increasingly become a problem in the developed world as well. With the onset of the global recession in 2007–2008, squatting became far more prevalent in the United States as a result of foreclosures and a general real estate collapse.

Robert Neuwirth, author of *Shadow Cities: A Billion Squatters, A New*

Urban World, estimates that one out of seven people on the planet can now be classified as squatters.[11] Woe betide the human race when one out of seven squirrels are moved to abandon their tree nests, hollows and burrows to become squatters. In fact, growing legions of squirrels are now taking up residence in spaces specifically constructed, and rightly reserved, for human beings. This is not the stuff of Gothic novels or horror movies. Squirrels are "coming in from the cold" in North America to take up residence in the attics, inner walls, rafters and crawl spaces of even the best-appointed, premium homes.

Squirrel squatting causes untold inconvenience and stress for humans. While the problems associated with these furry invaders may seem minor when compared with the destructive practices of the delinquent squirrels that disrupt phone lines, the transmission of electricity and the critical communications necessary to a market economy, squirrel squatting can actually be far more unsettling because it hits so close to home—and that includes the garage, the carport, the driveway, even the street space. These are, of course, the prime locations for a crucial human possession—the automobile.

Squirrels use their incisors to gnaw and tear through eaves and soffits to get into attics and other parts of human dwellings. However, there are other places that squatter squirrels now claim as home—locations that provide easy access and require less work. Squirrels are crawling under the wheels and jumping onto struts, frames and engine mounts of cars. They are finding cozy places to build their nests somewhere between the radiator cap and the window washer tubing behind the engine—smack under the hood. These nests (constructed of leaves, grass, nuts, seeds, patio furniture stuffing and refuse) are not just a problem for auto air filters and carburetors. Occasionally, the squirrel nests catch fire when the autos go mobile, though the reason for the vehicle fires (and the culprits themselves) may elude surprised and distressed vehicle owners.

A decade or so ago, newspaper stories of squirrels' car capers brought incredulous looks and laughter. There was the story of a Volvo owner who became frazzled as error lights flashed and the car ground to a halt, thanks to rodents rearranging the wiring under the hood. There was another story of a Grand Cherokee owner sprinkling cayenne pepper on his engine compartment in an effort to prevent thousands of dollars of additional damage to his vehicle from squatting squirrels. And there was the story about a Honda Element's malfunction light flashing due to a squirrel eating the wires, which turned out to be a totally familiar debacle to the insurance adjuster.[12]

As squirrels become more populous and bolder in their behavior, their actions under our hoods will no longer be isolated occurrences. Instead, there could well be massive SITU (Squirrel-induced Interstate Tie-Up) travel catastrophes. As auto industry writers point out, when squatter squirrel damage becomes epidemic, there will be freeway snarls, shutdowns and perhaps even highway pileups as cars and trucks come to a screeching halt in SITU disasters.[13]

Thanks to what passes for "end-of-the-world entertainment" these days, there's no need to strain the imagination to envision what it would be like to be caught in SITUs. A bona fide SITU would be very much like what happens with an electromagnetic pulse (EMP). An EMP is a high-intensity burst of electromagnetic energy that would disable much of our electronic infrastructure. Disaster movies and dystopian television shows reveal how EMPs—whether emanating from solar flares, satellite transponder ray guns or atomic detonations—would disastrously affect the normal routine of our lives.

In the movie *The Day After*, frantic Americans on their way to Lawrence, Kansas (in an attempt to escape a nuclear attack on Kansas City), are suddenly stopped in their tracks when all cars are rendered useless due to the EMP originating with an overhead atomic burst. In the television show *Revolution*, Americans find themselves in a post-apocalyptic world overrun by warlords and militias after an EMP catastrophe destroys the conventional means of transportation and forever alters life on the North American continent.

The threat of a debilitating EMP attack prompted Congress to establish the EMP Commission in 2001. Known formally as the Commission to Assess the Threat to the United States from Electromagnetic Pulse, this study group reported that an EMP blast is capable of wreaking havoc on our transportation system, as well as our telecommunications and computer networks.[14] The time also may have come for a congressional think tank to analyze the critical harm potential posed by SITUs.

A SITU commission (to be known formally as the Commission to Assess the Threat of Squirrel-induced Interstate Tie-Ups in the United States) would examine the adverse consequences of ignoring the menace of rogue, squatting squirrels. The commission would also be charged with determining the intelligence requirements, interdiction apparatus and all elements of deterrence necessary to stave off a massive SITU event in the United States.

So far, solutions to potential SITU disasters are ineffectual and puny. They include advising vehicle owners to keep their hoods up all night to make sure the engine space is unattractive as a shelter for a squirrel squatter;

spraying the engine with detergents, dog urine or bitter apple spray; sprinkling the engine with peppermint or curry powder, or placing bags of pet hair or stockings full of cat litter in the engine's vicinity along with rubber snakes; and inserting moth balls in crevices along the engine mount.[15] All of these solutions to the squirrel squatter issue would be laughable if they were not so pathetic in light of what may loom ahead.

Is There a Killer Squirrel Virus?

It may be premature to anticipate headlines about the creation of a government Commission to Assess the Threat of Squirrel-induced Interstate Tie-Ups. And it may border on paranoid fantasy to imagine the interstate chaos of multiple collisions caused by car engines damaged by squatter squirrels. However, there is nothing improbable or fantastical about the prospect of squirrels making human life difficult through the transmission of serious diseases. There are plenty of dark headlines that underscore the seriousness of this potential threat. These headlines ask, "Is There a Killer Squirrel Virus?" and "Squirrel Plague Prompts Fears: Should You Be Scared of Black Death?"

Deadly plagues are associated with times past, before the advent of modern medicine. However, contemporary humans are not unfamiliar with the concept of a revival of deadly viruses that could spin out of control. Among the pandemic scares in this new century have been swine flu, bird flu, various mutations of influenza viruses and the frightening possibility of an Ebola crisis. Sometime in early 2014, the world woke up to a spreading Ebola epidemic. Although victims were heavily concentrated in West Africa around Liberia, infected humans began to show up in Western countries, prompting calls for draconian travel restrictions and quarantines. The mounting deaths in Africa started in the hundreds and quickly moved into the thousands. The crisis of this virtually unknown disease unfolded with shocking severity and an exponential mortality rate.

By the end of 2014, exposés began to surface regarding how Ebola was initially transmitted as international medical researchers sought to trace the origins of the epidemic. One of these stories held that the first humans infected were young boys who had been playing in a hollow tree. This hollow tree was home to swarms of infected fruit bats, which bit the boys and transmitted the virus.[16] Shortly thereafter, the youngsters and their mothers were dead of infection, and the disease soon spread through their villages.

Also in 2014, other stories began to emerge about disease-carrying animals. Only these stories weren't about isolated locations in West Africa, but rather about locations in southern California in the United States. In this case, the infected animals were not fruit bats but common American squirrels. While these squirrels did not test positive for Ebola, they did test positive for a disease perhaps even more frightening, and more familiar—bubonic plague.[17]

The plague is a bacterial disease that brought untold suffering and carnage to Europe in the Middle Ages. Also known as the Black Death, this disease wiped out as many as 200 million people and reduced the human population of the Earth by as much as a third. Bubonic plague is spread to humans from rodents, such as rats and squirrels, although it can be transmitted to humans when fleas feed on the blood of sick rats and squirrels and then bite humans.

Deaths from the plague can be agonizing and horrible. Existentialist Albert Camus, author of *The Plague* (1947), based his book on an epidemic that hit North Africa and Algeria multiple times from the 1500s into the period of European colonization. Camus was interested in making philosophical points about the human condition in his novel, but he included graphic (and disturbing) accounts of the plague victims' anguish. In one such account, Camus likens the struggle of a plague victim to the onslaught of a storm full of convulsions, flashes and the raging wounds of heaven: "The fever reached its climax. A visceral cough racked the sick man's body and now he was spitting blood. The ganglia had ceased swelling, but they were still there, like lumps of iron embedded in the joints ... soon his eyes opened less and less often and the glow that shone out from the ravaged face in brief moments of recognition grew steadily fainter. The storm, lashing his body into convulsive movement, lit up with ever rarer flashes, and in the heart of the tempest he was slowly drifting, derelict."[18]

During the pre-antibiotic era, two-thirds of all plague victims succumbed to the disease. Now, about 90 percent of plague victims who get prompt medical attention survive. According to the Centers for Disease Control and Prevention, an average of seven human plague cases are reported in America each year, with most of the incidences stemming from contact with squirrels in the Southwest. Human cases of bubonic plague have been found in Montana, Wyoming, Colorado, New Mexico, and (since 1970) all the states west of those states. As science writer Esther Inglis-Arkell has noted, many people are surprised to hear that the disease still exists, especially within the United States. However, infected people continue to lose appendages and

41

even die from the illness caused by the *Yersina pestis* bacterium, so it must be taken seriously.

"The United States is one of the many countries around the world that technically still suffers from what was once called the Black Death," observes Inglis-Arkell. "Although we're not keeling over like medieval peasants, there are regular cases of bubonic plague that spring up every year in the American southwest. Occasionally, they lead to deaths.. .. [The plague is] incredibly well-known, but still almost unthinkable. No one seriously considers the plague these days, and a few scattered cases throughout an entire nation doesn't mean people will recognize it when it comes."[19]

The chances of an unthinkable plague returning increase with each day that the industrialized world continues to abuse and overuse antibiotics. The plague itself—the plague of medieval times—has not gone away. The fleas that carry the plague have not gone away. And the squirrels that host the disease-carrying fleas have not gone away. Squirrels are identified as plague purveyors by doctors and medical experts treating so-called Black Death cases in the American Southwest. Newspapers have covered these occurrences and usually provide some cautionary notes for readers. For example, they caution humans to avoid hiking or camping near known disease carriers such as squirrels, and not to feed them. They also note that symptoms of plague infection include the sudden onset of high fever and chills. Those who experience a temperature spike and swollen lymph nodes (especially after visiting an area where plague was recently found) should immediately visit their doctor.[20]

Breeding Squirrels: A Population Time Bomb

Newspapers warn us about the threat of plague-infected squirrels. It's a threat that could increase exponentially because of the growing problem of squirrel overpopulation, but also because of the prospect of mass squirrel migrations due to climate change. Stories about a squirrel population explosion have already appeared in the nation's newspapers. These articles explain how squirrels were kept in check in America's early years because hunters valued them for their meat and fur pelts. In the early 1800s, hunters collected squirrels in culling spectacles in which the little animals were rounded up and harvested. Even after the culling events became an anecdote of U.S. culinary history, Americans continued to eat squirrel by the millions of pounds.

Across America, municipal officials have tried to address expanding squirrel populations with cage traps, repellents, customized contraceptives and occasionally buckshot. Many of these approaches have raised the hackles of animal rights groups, according to newspaper accounts. What's more, these squirrel control methods are mostly ineffective, because these rodents are resilient, resourceful and reproduce regularly (courtesy Missouri Department of Conservation).

Well into the twentieth century, America's appetite for squirrel meat seemed innate and unlikely to abate. But a combination of developments in dining after World War II eventually led to a precipitous decline in squirrel consumption.

Among those developments was the advent of frozen foods, TV dinners and fast foods, as well as a general unwillingness to spend the time and energy necessary to prepare squirrels for the dinner table. By the end of the twentieth century, squirrels had lost their primary enemy: humans. Americans were turning up their collective noses at squirrel—whether it was sizzling in a frying pan, tenderizing in a stew pot or browning in an oven. The few Americans who continued to dine on squirrel were summarily dismissed as yokels, rednecks and hillbillies. It was thought that only people with small brains or mental illness would choose squirrel for sustenance. Even worse, misleading stories began to spread that eating wild game (especially squirrel brains) could cause brain illnesses in humans.

Newspaper stories in the late 1990s warned that people who ate squirrel brains, tagged as a popular dish in backwoods Kentucky, should probably have their brains examined. These stories warned that the regional delicacy could be spreading a variant of mad cow disease known as Creutzfeldt-Jakob disease, a transmissible spongiform encephalopathy, which is a progressive neurodegenerative disorder. Stories about the disease threat were later downplayed as exaggerated. However, even the *New York Times* went after the Kentucky culinary tradition of squirrel burgoos in which the carcasses of squirrels killed on the road were supposedly thrown in the burgoo pot without concern.[21] The story also described a ritual of cracking squirrel skulls and sucking out the brains for use in scrambled eggs with white gravy. Needless to say, such stories have played a major role in the declining consumption of squirrel meat.

With Americans no longer hunting, skinning, dressing, frying, and devouring squirrels, the population of the animal family known as Sciuridae has multiplied. The squirrel population explosion is evident from the deepest woods to the backyards of suburbia to county fair campgrounds and inner-city parks. Now newspapers are covering the debate over what exactly to do with too many squirrels here, there and everywhere. The battle lines are drawn. On one side are those humans who see the squirrels as a proliferating pest problem to be eradicated by use of poisons, gases, steel traps, pellet guns and more. On the other side are those humans who believe that squirrels are unique and blessed creatures to be protected. Among the latter group are the animal rights activists who believe that if squirrels are to be reined in at all, the methods must be utterly humane.

So now, across America, harried municipal officials are struggling to contain the squirrel population growth with methods such as immuno-contraception. Communities are spending precious tax dollars to give squirrels vaccines that will halt ovulation in females and testicular development in males. Groups such as the People for Ethical Treatment of Animals (PETA) praise this approach as progressive and cutting edge. They see the infertility shots as a diplomatic solution that should please everybody in the controversy over how to suppress squirrel reproduction. By contrast, critics view the squirrel birth control programs as a mere pin prick in the effort to control squirrels; they favor the more traditional, inexpensive final solution, such as customized toxics, repellents and buckshot. No need to implement expensive contraceptive measures—dead animals cannot procreate either. Newspapers document the battle between the hardliners and the appeasers in the war to contain the proliferating squirrels.

There's no way to predict whether some of the apocalyptic squirrel scenarios garnered from the headlines and from newspaper stories might come to pass. Will squirrels cause even more billions of dollars in damage to the homes of humans as these creatures become more fruitful and multiply? Will increasing numbers of squirrels become culprits in future national and international pandemics? Only time will tell, but it can definitively be said that humankind has been warned.

Another point that can be drawn from this study is that squirrels get remarkably different treatment in moving from the book medium to the newspaper medium. Squirrels are treated kindly and with kid gloves in books. However, in many newspaper stories squirrels are treated harshly and as the villains.

One explanation for the unforgiving treatment in newspapers could stem from the fact that all the weekly and daily publications rolling off the presses depend on advertising to survive. After all, he who pays the piper calls the tune. Pest control companies are important advertisers, spending millions of dollars on newspaper ads to reach readers desperate for protection from nuisance squirrels. They sell squirrel poison bait, squirrel traps, squirrel repellent, squirrel predator decoys, cordless ultrasonic squirrel chasers and similar high-tech devices to ward off destructive squirrels. Obviously, pest control services are not going to look favorably on newspapers that publish articles portraying squirrels as humanity's cute and friendly companions feasting at the bird feeder or nesting in the red oak behind the house. "Squirrel control" copy in advertisements emphasizes the propensity of squirrels to damage houses and cars, to raid bird feeders, and to carry diseases.

At a time when advertising revenue for newspapers is in short supply, it's certainly true that newspaper publishers have never been more sensitive and responsive to the needs of advertisers. Pressure from pest control advertisers, however, is probably not the primary reason squirrels get a bad rap in newspapers as opposed to more positive portrayals in books, especially children's books. Another, better explanation for the discrepancy in treatment comes from media maven Marshall McLuhan, with his dictum that the medium is the message. According to McLuhan, each medium has certain characteristics that make some messages acceptable and other messages totally unacceptable. The medium of a children's book is not conducive to stories about squirrels destroying property or transmitting diseases that can result in sickness or death. Likewise, the newspaper medium has little interest in stories about friendly squirrels that gather nuts for the winter and try to please their mothers.

McLuhan's ideas about "hot" and "cool" media also are applicable here, and they will become even more relevant in this study when moving on to the issue of how squirrels are treated in television and film versus newspapers. The newspaper is a "hot" medium, and thus it prefers "hot" stories and "hot" characters. Newspaper editors know that their medium works best (and attracts the most readers) when the stories are about struggle, drama, conflict and strife—the good guys versus the bad guys. McLuhan was always quick to point out that war is subject matter that works well in a "hot" medium such as newspapers. Hence the popularity of humanity's war with squirrels, which serves as a perfect story subject for newspaper headlines: "Plague Squirrels Found in California" or "Squirrel Attack Leaves 10,000 Without Power." This terrible news about squirrels could affect you and your loved ones next.

Squirrels definitely get bad press in the nation's newspapers. One explanation for the malevolent media treatment of squirrels points to advertising pressures from the billion-dollar pest control industry. Another explanation points to the nature of the newspaper medium and its propensity for running dark headlines and even darker copy about squirrels anchored by the grim headlines. However, a third explanation could be that proliferating squirrels actually do pose a threat to the general welfare of the human species. Extra! Extra! Read all about it!

3

Squirrels for a Television Age

When television came along for regular home use in the 1950s, adding the reception of unprecedented visual information to existing audio transmission, media experts predicted the demise of the legacy media of newspapers and radio. Television sets seemed magical in their ability to receive moving images of programming that included news, entertainment, education, gossip and advertising. How could newspapers or radio survive in competition with this new, colossal electronic appliance? In fact, the old legacy media of radio and newspapers did just fine because they adapted and because they possessed characteristics that the new medium of television did not have. Indeed, daily newspapers had already weathered several decades of the instantaneous communication of radio, and the old print medium was well positioned to continue functioning in the television age.

As Marshall McLuhan pointed out, information presented in newspapers can be dramatically different from that packaged for electronic transmission to television sets. McLuhan coined the terms "hot media" and "cool media" to describe these differences, and he explained that newspapers are a hot medium that package and deliver information in a starkly different manner than a cool medium such as television. Newspapers thrive on content and characters that tend to be "hot." Thus, newspapers are favored by an audience that has a predilection for this type of information.[1]

Media literacy and mass communication professors often struggle to reach students when parsing theories and concepts about messaging—encoders, channels, decoders, feedback loops and more. The challenge of explaining McLuhan's ideas can be even more daunting. Scholars can be frustrated in their efforts to illustrate for students the dramatic differences between one medium of mass communication and another. Educators of mass media would be wise to consider the subject matter of squirrels when attempting to shed light on the inherent bias of various media, especially when comparing the medium of the newspaper to that of television. As noted in the previous chapter, newspapers, as a hot medium, thrive on story content that warns us about the dangers from squirrels as they overrun homes, cause power outages, carry diseases and multiply in numbers that wreak havoc on the ecosystem.

Scary stories about squirrels make for hot news in a hot medium. For example, the *Chicago Tribune* published a story in November 2016 titled "Kamikaze Squirrel Gets Revenge on Alderman Brookins." According to the story by Kim Janssen, the alderman made a fiery speech in Chicago City Hall about the increasing menace of "aggressive squirrels" in the Windy City. Just a few weeks later, a squirrel leaped into the front wheel of the alderman's bike as he was cycling through a park. The squirrel lodged in the bike's spokes, halting its forward motion and sending the alderman over the bicycle's handlebars. The squirrel perished in the attack but left Brookins needing surgery and treatment for a broken nose, a

Rocky and His Friends (ABC) TV Series
1959 - 1961
Shown from left: Rocky J. Squirrel (voice: June Foray), Bullwinkle J. Moose (voice: Bill Scott)
Credit: ABC/Photofest ©ABC

Rentals grand one-time, EDITORIAL use only, unless otherwise negotiated. Please inform us about usage or non-usage as soon as possible. Research fees may apply if no images are used.

Squirrels receive more favorable coverage on television than in newspapers, in part because they are cool and entertaining. One such character in the early years of television was Rocket J. Squirrel. Rocky and his moose friend, Bullwinkle, entertained Americans in an original animated series airing from 1959 to 1964. Rocky and Bullwinkle resided in the fictional town of Frostbite Falls. Talented and witty, Rocky became the most popular televised squirrel in the United States.

fractured skull and five or six teeth that were knocked out in the encounter with the kamikaze park squirrel. Some Chicago readers found this incident funny, especially in light of the alderman's prior derogatory remarks about squirrels, but doctors observed that the injured alderman could have easily broken his neck in the bicycle crash.[2]

Newspapers can't resist the lure of animal stories full of peril, conflict, strife, health hazards and injurious attacks. By contrast, the broadcast media are more attracted to animal stories that are feel-good, glitzy, funny and superficial. Of course, it will be argued that these are unfair generalizations and an exercise in dismissive stereotyping of television broadcast journalism. There is some truth in this allegation, but the reality of these generalizations about TV news and broadcast content is sometimes glaring and quite accurate when it comes to coverage of animals—particularly reporting on squirrels. Broadcast content lulls us into thinking that squirrels are our friends. TV news in particular tends to focus on squirrels for fluffy, heart-warming or outlandish and downright weird feature material. On TV, squirrels are covered as fashion models on the runway, water ski entertainers at recreation shows, and tiny athletes that run the bases at a baseball contest (or even a World Series game).

Whimsical, fuzzy, farcical squirrel stories make for cool news for a cool medium. For example, FOX-6 News in San Antonio ran a story in June 2017 about patriotic squirrels "stealing" American flags for nest-building materials.[3] It was all in good fun, and everybody lived happily ever after. During the week of Memorial Day, an air force veteran in Texas was heartbroken, if not angry, to discover that all of the small American flags in his front yard had been stolen. Little did he know that his neighbor had witnessed the thievery and recorded the nefarious activity. The video revealed that pesky squirrels had ripped the flags free, rolled them into a ball, put them in their mouths, and run off. The squirrels used the flags to help build their nests high in a nearby tree. Neighbors and FOX-6 News viewers marveled at these resourceful squirrels. The cute TV story also brought comfort to the veteran and his family, as they learned that the squirrels had put the ten missing flags to good use for their nest. Like the squirrels in a children's storybook, they were industrious, harmless, amusing and maybe even patriotic. In short, the squirrels were cool.

McLuhan and his many converts to the theory of hot and cool media might argue that there's no mystery in the "bad press" that squirrels get in newspapers versus the more lighthearted treatment they receive on television. As a hot medium, newspapers favor stories about squirrels that prompt humans to pick up the paper to read with alarm about the potential harm that these rodents present. As a cool medium, television favors stories about squirrels that prompt humans to pick up the TV remote and to sit back and have a laugh at the antics of these crazy squirrels. In short, TV news and feature squirrels are as benign and entertaining as the wonderful squirrel characters of the children's storybook genre.

Tommy Tucker: Stuffed, But Not Forgotten

American actress and celebrated star Sarah Jessica Parker once remarked, "You can't be friends with a squirrel. A squirrel is just a rat with a cuter outfit." Parker got it wrong—or, at least, most television media content is at odds with her derogatory assessment of squirrels. Numerous TV media personalities try to befriend squirrels and put them on the air. Media types of the visual persuasion fall all over themselves in an effort to elevate squirrels beyond rat status. This is especially true if the squirrels wear cute outfits—something more stylish and eye catching than what nature bestowed upon their twitchy little bodies. Case in point: Tommy Tucker.

Media professionals—and amateurs—were always ready to make friends with the twentieth-century squirrel named Tommy Tucker, a cross-dressing squirrel that had the camera light bulbs flashing and the film rolling when he was alive. What's more, media practitioners have continued to swoon over Tommy Tucker in his afterlife. Tommy never got to wear his dozens of adorable outfits live for the TV cameras, because he died in 1949, before television took hold as a new medium for the American home. However, plenty of TV reporters have covered Tommy since he was stuffed, preserved and honored as a genuine squirrel phenomenon—a squirrel who paved the way for all television squirrels of the future.

By all accounts, Tommy Tucker was a wayward, infant squirrel without a home until Zaidee and Mark Bullis of the Washington, D.C., area adopted the little fellow in 1942.[4] The Bullis family named the squirrel after the character in the eighteenth-century nursery rhyme titled "Little Tommy Tucker." The rhyme itself is forever enshrined in the classic *Mother Goose Melodies*, where it can be found alongside such favorites as "Old King Cole," "Baa, Baa Black Sheep," "There Was a Crooked Man," and "Goosey, Goosey Gander." With a new home and a new name, this orphaned commoner of the eastern gray squirrel family had a lot to be thankful for—and a lot to live up to as part of the "Little Tommy Tucker" literary lineage. However, Tommy Tucker did just that. He became a media celebrity, touring the country, inspiring wordsmiths and performing tricks—all decked out in women's clothing.

Zaidee and Mark Bullis dressed the wily squirrel in women's clothes, not because of any gender-bender sexual identity issues the animal may have had, but simply because dresses made more sense given Tommy's rather prominent tail. A male wardrobe that always had to account for a bulky tail would require more complex tailoring, as well as more difficulty in getting

Tommy Tucker dressed quickly for his many clothing changes at numerous public appearances. In his early years, Tommy performed in silly stunts at elementary schools, but he soon became a stand-up patriot selling war bonds to defeat the Axis Powers. After the war effort, which included a radio interview with President and Commander-in-Chief Franklin Delano Roosevelt, Tommy Tucker was rewarded with an arranged marriage to a squirrel known as "Buzzy."[5]

The wedding hangover and new life with Buzzy did not slow Tommy Tucker down. Nor did marriage impinge upon Tommy Tucker's penchant for gallivanting around wearing female garb. In fact, the squirrel found fame wearing such ensembles as a casual coat and hat for shopping at the grocery store; a silk-pleated dress for hosting tea parties and polite company; and a Red Cross uniform for public service visits to local hospitals. Although he was male, he had more than thirty different outfits to please crowds. *LIFE* magazine could not resist covering fashion plate Tommy Tucker, giving him a complete gallery of photographs in its pages. *LIFE* noted that the pampered squirrel had both casual dress and a complete ensemble for more formal events. Tommy Tucker was cool TV material even before cathode-ray tubes began to beam images onto screens in America's living rooms.

Zaidee and Mark Bullis made a star out of the blind and hairless baby squirrel after he fell out of a tree in their backyard one afternoon in 1942. The couple acted as parents, publicity agents and talent managers for Tommy Tucker for seven years, but their strange squirrel odyssey came to an abrupt end in 1949, when Tommy died. Although Tommy Tucker's life of fame was over, there was an understandable reluctance to part with the physical presence that had made the squirrel a celebrity for most of his life. The Bullises had Tommy Tucker stuffed, with the intention of having him placed in the Smithsonian Institution. The best intentions sometimes go awry, however, and the Smithsonian did not express much enthusiasm for including the squirrel among such artifacts as Dorothy's ruby slippers from *The Wizard of Oz*, the Kermit puppet from the *Muppets*, or Archie Bunker's chair from *All in the Family*.

According to John Kelly of the *Washington Post*, Tommy Tucker's mounted remains eventually found their way to a lawyer's office in Prince George's County, Maryland, where he was ensconced in a clear plastic cube. At last report, the lawyer's office was still waiting to hear whether the Smithsonian might reconsider taking Tommy Tucker and a steamer trunk containing his tiny dresses. As Kelly wrote in his *Post* column, "I certainly hope the

Smithsonian has room for Tommy and his effects. The collection tells the story of a nation at war, of the heights of celebrity and also of the peculiar mania that affects some Americans, whether they be P.T. Barnum or Zaidee Bullis."[6]

Tommy Tucker was a TV squirrel before there was TV. He often appeared in national picture magazines, an early branch of visual media that has been characterized as a close cousin (if not the forerunner) of the later moving images of television media. Tommy Tucker possessed all the attributes of the squirrels who followed in his claw steps and found a place on television as it became a dominant medium. Tommy Tucker was a picture-perfect squirrel, a performer and a publicist's dream.

Charlie Don't Surf, Twiggy Does Ski

In the Vietnam War movie *Apocalypse Now*, Lieutenant Colonel Kilgore chooses to go surfing in the Mekong Delta amid the chaos of battle. Despite the potential danger from the Vietcong (referred to in the movie as "Charlie"), Kilgore declares that he's not worried, because "Charlie don't surf." Kilgore's actions constitute a bizarre combination of bravado and escapism—a mixture beloved by audiences of war movies. Audiences for Twiggy, the water-skiing squirrel, are similarly swept up in bravado and escapism as they watch Twiggy perform amazing feats in perilous waters. This may explain the aquatic squirrel's appearances in a multitude of feature stories on TV news. More than half a dozen Twiggy clones learned to ski behind special, remote-controlled Twiggy boats at water shows. Twiggy the water-skiing squirrel has become an icon of pop culture and mass media. Charlie may not surf, but Twiggy definitely does ski—and he does it on TV.

Twiggy has performed at boat shows all over the country. Local television news cameras often show up to put together features on the amazing squirrel. According to *TVNewsCheck*, which covers the broadcast industry, the phrase "water-skiing squirrel story" has now joined "if it bleeds, it leads," "man bites dog story," and "all the news that's fit to print" as part of the peculiarly snarky lexicon of the reporting business. A "water-skiing squirrel story" refers to any off-the-beaten-track feature that is not just unusual but also wacky and weird. In a January 2014 article, *TVNewsCheck* reported on how this phrase entered the terminology of the news business through an actual story shot on video for an Orlando, Florida, television station in 1978.

After almost four decades of riding the waves behind a tiny boat, Twiggy the water-skiing squirrel brought his act to a close in July 2018, performing at the X Games in Minneapolis, Minnesota. Twiggy made numerous television news appearances and found fame in the movie *Anchorman: The Legend of Ron Burgundy*, as well as in singer Brad Paisley's music video "River Bank." Twiggy is now immortalized as a bobble-head doll and as pop art on clothing items (photograph by Ursula Ruhl).

As the story goes, Bill Bauman, who was then the assignment editor at WFTV Channel 9 in Orlando, received the suggestion from an agitated man speaking breathlessly over the phone. He was, in fact, an enthusiastic squirrel promoter who identified himself as Chuck Best. Best reportedly said, "I'm down on the southeast corner of Lake Monroe, and I've taught a squirrel how to water ski. I glued two Popsicle sticks together, mounted a little set of handle bars, put some peanut butter on them, and then attached a line to a battery powered boat. I thought you guys might like to see it."[7]

Bauman initially blew off Best's proposal as just one of many wacky calls the station received regularly. However, when a desperate Channel 9 TV reporter called Bauman to tell him that his big story for the evening newscast had fallen through, Bauman directed him to go down to the southeast corner of Lake Monroe and see whether there was anything unusual to cover for the newscast. Bauman was reportedly too skeptical to tell his reporter what he might actually find at that location. The reporter, Ron Comings, discovered a skating rink at the Lake Monroe site, where there were people standing around watching a little remote-controlled boat pulling a squirrel on tiny makeshift skis in loops in a little pool at the rink.

Comings was transfixed, but an hour before airtime the TV journalist had yet to return to the station. There was concern about a gaping hole in the newscast. Just then, the back door of the newsroom flew open and Comings came in shouting about his squirrel scoop on a three-quarter-inch videotape. Bauman recalled crowding into a small editing room to watch the most fantastic feature video, with tight shots of a small squirrel standing up with his hind legs on what looked like water skis. The squirrel's front paws grasped a small stick mounted straight up from the water skis. As the squirrel moved across the water, the video revealed a small boat pulling the him on his skis. It was hard to believe, but TV news staffers were witnessing a water-skiing squirrel. Then Comings announced, "His name is Twiggy."

Twiggy debuted that night on WFTV's 6 and 11 p.m. newscasts. By the next morning, he was booked on *Good Morning America* and made his national debut. That same evening, ABC News anchor Peter Jennings covered Twiggy on *World News Tonight*.[8] The amusing tale of the water-skiing squirrel went national. Chuck Best took Twiggy on a skiing tour across America and the world, with the squirrel water shows taking center stage at literally hundreds of conventions. And at those conventions, the local television station cameras inevitably arrived to cover Twiggy riding the waves in pools, fountains and metal tanks of frothy water.

In November 1997, two decades after Chuck Best made that fateful pitch to WFTV Channel 9 in Orlando, Twiggy's trainer and manager died. Best had a heart attack and drowned during an attempt to rescue his stepfather, who had fallen off Best's boat into the Wekiva River in Central Florida. But Twiggy, the water-skiing squirrel, lived on and was still performing and making TV appearances well into a new millennium. The original Twiggy was replaced by a succession of new Twiggy performers, perhaps as many as nine.

Chuck Best's wife, Lou Ann Best, continued to run the Twiggy franchise and trained and managed the replacement squirrels. After her husband's drowning accident, she fitted every replacement Twiggy with a life vest. She vowed that the Twiggy mission would henceforth be tied to an essential lesson about water safety—wear a life vest. Who knows how many human lives the intrepid Twiggy has saved over the years?

In addition to counseling safety on the water, Twiggy has another legacy: the flippant phraseology and vainglorious vernacular of TV newsrooms, when reporters and editors boast that they have a lead on a silly, goofy, but attention-grabbing feature story—"a water-skiing squirrel story"—that just might come together in time for the 6 p.m. newscast.

Sugar Bush: Raised in the Lap of Luxury

Sugar Bush Squirrel, often described as "the world's most photographed squirrel," carries on the bizarre and outrageous tradition begun by the late Tommy Tucker. Unlike the famous cross-dressing male squirrel, Sugar Bush is a decidedly female gray squirrel. The outfits that she wears come naturally, and they are plentiful. She is Tommy Tucker on steroids in that respect. She has more than four thousand costumes, as opposed to the supply of three dozen that kept Tommy Tucker's many fans in stitches. The woman who keeps Sugar Bush dressed to the nines at all times is Kelly Foxton, a vivacious country and western entertainer who found fame on the Grand Ole Opry and in Las Vegas. However, Foxton sacrificed her own promising future as a performer to the demands of managing the career of a star squirrel.

"You have to have a reason to get up in the morning, and a reason to go to bed late at night. That reason for me is Sugar Bush," explained Foxton in a piece for TLC (better known a decade ago as cable television's The Learning Channel). "Everything I do is around her. She is the star."[9]

On TLC's *My Crazy Obsession*, Foxton's husband, Drew Gardner, joined in on the homage to the squirrel that has obviously completed the couple's lives. Foxton's hubby conceded that Sugar Bush gets most of Foxton's attention. However, as the father figure in this unusual family, he doesn't complain. Gardner added that there really was no room for kids in this picture. Sugar Bush gets more doting and pampering than any children anywhere in any family; as Gardner explained, "it was the right fit for the both of us"[10] to remain childless and be content with the demands of Sugar Bush, rather than have human children competing for their affection. It should be pointed out, however, that despite going childless themselves, the considerate couple did provide Sugar Bush with a notable squirrel sister named Rio.

On TLC's YouTube video about the Sugar Bush Squirrel obsession, the classy two-pound rodent poses for a photo session dressed in a frilly, ruby red dress and matching hat, with a sparkling necklace to accent the ensemble. Foxton controlled the lights and camera, directing the two-pound rodent to look to the left, revealing her best side. Adopted as a baby, the only mother Sugar Bush has ever known is Kelly Foxton. Sugar Bush has never known the thrill of climbing a tree, snagging a tree twig adorned with edible acorns, or snoozing in a nest high above the ground. As the TLC narrator emphasized, Sugar Bush spends her days in a large and comfy custom cage located in a massive photo studio, arranged by Foxton.

Foxton told TLC that fine accessories complement her squirrel's many outfits. Photo galleries of the clothes-horse squirrel known as Sugar Bush abound on the internet. There she can be found dealing cards at a casino, manning a pirate ship, riding a motorcycle in Hell's Angels' attire, and wearing the hat and suit of a private eye. Foxton claims to have published almost six thousand images of Sugar Bush. On her website, Sugar Bush can be seen at her best as a court jester for her illustrated calendars; as a grocery shopper with a cart holding a giant edition of her autobiographical book, *The Sugar Bush Chronicles*; and as a roaming reporter for SSN (Squirrel News Network) seeking an interview with "Alex Tree-beck" on the set of the popular game show *Jeopardy*.

Sugar Bush is a cool squirrel, for the most part, when she sticks to silly shtick and harmless comic routines for television, website and YouTube consumption. However, she is not universally admired, and she has made some viewers hot under the collar with her ventures into politics and foreign affairs commentary. They argue that she should not be posing as the deceased Fidel Castro, or as an exhumed Yasser Arafat, or as a Navy SEAL ready to take out terrorists like Osama bin Laden. Critics say Sugar Bush became a partisan "Swift Boater" for George W. Bush when she criticized the views of Senator John Kerry on the Iraq War and later posed with a noose for hanging Iraqi dictator Saddam Hussein.

Another controversial pose for Sugar Bush was as a jilted Muslim bride in France whose marriage was voided by a French judge at her husband's request. The magistrate dissolved the marital ties after her would-be husband discovered that she was not a virgin on her wedding night. The ruling ended the couple's union, as the judge deferred to Muslim customs regarding virginity in the divorce case. The unhappy squirrel bride in this vignette apparently overheard the sympathetic voices of French countrymen saying, "Our much-cherished secular values are losing ground to cultural traditions from fast-growing immigrant communities."[11]

Sugar Bush makes no bones about being an all-American, Christian kind of squirrel who is happy to don clerical garb and deliver heartfelt sermons on how to get right with the world and the Lord. Sugar Bush has no truck with secularists who espouse a separation of church and state. The right reverend Sugar Bush displays the state constitution preambles of America's fifty states, many of which invoke "the favor and guidance of an Almighty God." Despite being a bit preachy when she takes on the role of the Reverend Sugar Bush, the holy squirrel should get some credit for promising to offer sermons "to lift your spirits and brighten your day" without ever asking for money to sustain the fellowship of her followers.

In addition to the critics who argue that Sugar Bush would be wise to avoid political or religious controversy, there are those who argue that Sugar Bush should be liberated from the demands of being held captive to cameras and life in the public spotlight. Partisans for the squirrel's liberation have posted comments on the TLC YouTube site where Kelly Foxton and Drew Gardner celebrate the phenomenon of their domesticated squirrel—a squirrel that has become a spectacle. Writes one observer, "A squirrel is a living being, yet they seem to treat her as a doll. The fact she has to stay in a cage when pet squirrels can roam free speaks a lot. Poor Sugar Bush. I hope she can live a fun life someday." Writes another, "You love that squirrel so much that you keep her in a prison cell. More like you are a selfish human who thinks nothing of imprisoning a harmless squirrel for your own self-satisfaction. People who truly love their animals don't cage them because they want that animal to be free. Cages are jail cells. I can't stand self-centered people like this." And yet another writer remarks, "This is so bizarre. This lady has serious fear of abandonment issues. She should go to the shrink."

In spite of the naysayers and the objections from some animal rights activists regarding the squirrel's captive life, Sugar Bush remains an icon with many fans, and she gets plenty of positive media coverage. Kelly Foxton told the *Washington Post* in 2013 that Sugar Bush loves all the clothes and attention, and it's no different from happy dog owners who enjoy dressing up their proud poodles. Poodles and squirrels love the pampering, Foxton insisted.[12] She conceded that getting the squirrel to climb a hill with a cross to re-create the crucifixion of Jesus Christ could prove difficult, and she also admitted that some people might find the exercise sacrilegious. However, Sugar Bush's role as a cleric and preacher has received rave reviews from religious people.

Another indication of the squirrel's popularity is the success of the 2015 book, *The Sugar Bush Chronicles: Adventures with the Most Photographed Squirrel*. This book covers the superstar squirrel in her travels from the Crescent City of New Orleans to the land of the pharaohs in ancient Egypt.[13] The volume includes photos and commentary on the most extensive wardrobe ever assembled for a squirrel. Reviewers find the book adorable, humorous, tasteful and perfectly suited for young children. Squirrels have certainly come a long way in the book world since Beatrix Potter wrote and illustrated her children's books on Squirrel Nutkin and Timmy Tiptoes. And Sugar Bush is a multimedia squirrel with cool television savvy that would have been unthinkable for an unruly creature like Nutkin.

Squirrels on TV Sports: Rally and Friends

Televised sports have long championed squirrels, and not just because they are mascots for a number of college and university sports teams. Beyond a campus presence, squirrels have found their way into professional sports and Olympic competitions. Not even a rude squirrel incident at the 2018 Olympics in PyeongChang, South Korea, could drive a wedge between the television sports media and the little devils.

The dangerous squirrel caper happened during a preliminary run in the 2018 Winter Olympics ladies' snowboard parallel giant slalom.[14] A rogue squirrel chose to scamper across the snowy course just as Daniela Ulbing of Austria was negotiating a tough snowboard racing turn at a high rate of speed. Ulbing veered around the squirrel at the last second in a dramatically close call, missing it by a rodent's whisker.

The potential collision became the talk of not only those attending the Olympic games at Phoenix Park in South Korea but also an international television audience. Twitter users went into meltdown mode over the incident, and the narrow miss with the squirrel remains a popular presence on YouTube. There were few remarks by television sports journalists on the potential harm that the squirrel could have caused the Austrian snowboarder. The squirrel went unscathed on that account as well.

Squirrels are not just surprise intruders at the Olympic Winter Games. In October 2011, the entire population of the Midwest metropolis of St. Louis became entranced with a mass-mediated creation known as "Rally Squirrel." Every arm of local, regional and national sports media participated in promoting the fantasy of a good-natured squirrel bringing luck to the St. Louis Cardinals in post-season play. Otherwise hard-nosed and serious baseball fans willingly submitted to a sort of mass hypnosis over a televised squirrel, spending their hard-earned dollars on Rally Squirrel paraphernalia like there was no tomorrow. Rally Squirrel eventually was even credited with winning the World Series for the Cardinals.

The baseball diamond delirium began on October 4, 2011, when a gray squirrel decided to take the outfield in Busch Stadium during Game 3 of the Cardinals' contest against the Philadelphia Phillies in the National League

Go Cardinals!

*Running for their **11th** World Championship!*

Rally Squirrel became a very popular character in St. Louis, Missouri, during the 2011 National League Division Series between the Philadelphia Phillies and the St. Louis Cardinals. The gray squirrel ran across home plate during a baseball playoff game and captured national media attention. Later, the unofficial baseball mascot was credited with helping to win the World Series for the Cardinals against the Texas Rangers (courtesy St. Louis Cardinals).

Division Series. The insolent rodent caused a short interruption in the sixth inning of play as it scampered down the third baseline with Ryan Theriot of the Cardinals at bat. The Cards lost that game to the Phillies by one run with a score of 3–2.

Despite the loss, the Cardinals came back for a win on October 5 in Game 4 of the series. The so-called Rally Squirrel came back for that game as well. This time the squirrel took the field in the sixth inning as Phillies pitcher Roy Oswalt was delivering a pitch to Skip Schumaker of the Cardinals. Play was not suspended, but the squirrel caused a major uproar when it crossed home plate just as the pitch was being delivered. It then jumped into the stands, but the damage had been done, according to Oswalt. He protested that his pitch, which was called a ball by umpire Angel Hernandez, should not have been counted. Oswalt said he missed the strike zone because the squirrel had messed up his concentration.

Oswalt was joined in his anger over the squirrel—and the umpire's refusal to nullify the ball awarded to Schumaker—by a very upset Charlie Manuel, manager for the Phillies. Manuel argued unsuccessfully with Hernandez that "no pitch" should have been called. Manuel was so disturbed over the situation that he later insisted he would have shot the trespassing squirrel right there if he had been in possession of his gun.[15]

The Cardinals' win in Game 4 sent the series back to Philadelphia. Manuel presumed all the squirrel nonsense at Busch Stadium in St. Louis would not be a problem at the Phillies' Citizens Bank Park. He was quickly proven wrong. Near the warning track of the park, Oswalt was again accosted by a squirrel right before Game 5 commenced. The Phillies' fans contributed to the squirrel nonsense by hurling a stuffed squirrel into the St. Louis bullpen. Instead of being upset by the would-be taunt, the Cardinals' pitching staff decided to turn the squirrel mayhem to their advantage. Dominican pitcher Octavio Eduardo Dotel picked up the stuffed squirrel and vowed to keep it as a sort of lucky charm.[16] It worked. The Cardinals defeated the Phillies in Game 5, and Dotel resolved to keep the squirrel close by all the way through the World Series.

Dotel later taunted the Phillies' fans, telling the sports press that they must have been unaware that throwing the stuffed squirrel was a mistake. The squirrel brought the pitchers in the bullpen good luck. Indeed, after putting away the Phillies, it appeared to bring them a successful National League Championship Series victory over the Milwaukee Brewers on October 16. After that 12–6 victory, Dotel and his Cardinal teammates made a toast to the stuffed squirrel and sprayed it with champagne in the post-game locker room celebration. The Cardinals went on to defeat the Texas Rangers in the World Series, with a final win on October 28 in Game 7 by a score of 6–2.

No one can prove that a squirrel, or a team of squirrels, conspired to help the St. Louis Cardinals win the World Series in 2011. However, there's no question that the Cardinals got a morale boost—and also cashed in—on the squirrel phenomenon. After the first appearance of a squirrel in Game 4 against the Phillies, a Rally Squirrel Twitter account was activated and by late October had almost thirty thousand followers. By October 5, the day after its initial appearance, musician Randy Mayfield had composed a Rally Squirrel theme song, which ended with the lyric "Go crazy, folks, here comes the Rally Squirrel!" Some fans swore that they played the song through every subsequent game all the way to the World Series final.[17]

Although it could be argued that Rally Squirrel did the most damage to opposing teams in the October 5 game with the Phillies, the Cardinals enlisted the squirrel's help throughout the 2011 post-season. Two days after defeating the Phillies, official Rally Squirrel T-shirts were flying off the shelves of St. Louis stores by the thousands. A week later, a performer in a Rally Squirrel costume participated in a team rally before the October 12 game with the Milwaukee Brewers. In addition, forty thousand Rally Squirrel towels were distributed for fans to wave during that game with the Brewers, whom the Cardinals defeated by a score of 4–3. Additionally, the Rally Squirrel performer assisted the Cardinals' traditional costumed mascot, Fredbird, with the task of sending out T-shirts to the fans in the stands at Busch Stadium in between innings. The real squirrel on the field during the early playoff games was quickly overshadowed by a much larger, costumed squirrel at pre-game rallies and at the actual post-season contests that followed.

What's more, Rally Squirrel has been immortalized. His televised game appearances from 2011 now are readily available on YouTube. He also appears on a special-edition Topps baseball card. The card captures the pant leg of Cardinals player Skip Schumaker with the nearby Rally Squirrel hustling across the batter's box. It's a reminder of the infamous squirrel controversy at home plate in Game 4 with the Phillies. Perhaps the ultimate compliment to Rally Squirrel is his presence on the 2011 St. Louis World Series rings. And, of course, sports writers have further immortalized the story of Rally Squirrel in their books about the series.

Sports television was extremely kind to Rally Squirrel and the Cardinals. Only a few newspaper articles asserted that the interruption of professional baseball games by squirrels might not be such a good thing. Critical articles also have stressed that the squirrels present liability issues, whether on the field or in the stands with the fans. Squirrels, after all, can scratch, bite and chew when they feel anxious or frightened. It's not such a great idea to have them in the midst of fifty thousand fans packed in the tight seats and narrow aisles of a stadium. During the 2011 post-season, the Cardinals' stadium operations staff of set traps and caught at least four squirrels, never knowing whether the actual Rally Squirrel was captured. The squirrels were released elsewhere, and there was never a thought of exterminating them. After all, the Cardinals' manager during the successful 2011 season was Tony LaRussa, an outspoken animal rights activist.[18] Treating squirrels as unwanted pests to be eradicated would not have been good publicity for the St. Louis Cardinals organization—and it would not have been very cool for television either.

Squirrel Takes a TV Pee

Visual media's infatuation with squirrels cannot be dampened even by a reporter enduring a good soaking from squirrel urine on live TV. Such incidents go viral on YouTube, as viewers somehow find it all "adorable" and even humorous. Rodents, such as rats or squirrels, are known to relieve themselves when angered, stressed or frightened. The visual media take it all in stride, portraying squirrels as talented pets with human traits. The television reporter who endures a good soaking from an uppity squirrel inevitably writes a soggy social media post, dismissing the humiliating squirrel peeing encounter as "all in a day's work."

Such was the case in a squirrel incident involving reporter Kelli Rippin of WZTV, FOX-Channel 17, in Nashville, Tennessee. Rippin was covering a clone of the original Twiggy, the water-skiing squirrel, at the Nashville Boat Show. During the event, the domesticated squirrel took time out from water sports to climb aboard Rippin. However, the squirrel was not in the mood to cooperate for the TV cameras or an interview. After finding a place in the reporter's hair, Twiggy decided to make some news for himself, which garnered a headline in the television shoptalk magazine, *TVSpy*. The January 2015 headline pulled no punches about what happened to the TV anchor and reporter: "Twiggy the Waterskiing Squirrel Proves Love of Water Sports, Pees on Reporter."[19] However, this story did not make the WZTV evening broadcast, despite some interesting footage of the mishap.

The remarkable video of the inconsiderate squirrel is available on the web as well as in the *TVSpy* January 9, 2015, edition. Rippin at first protests the squirrel's messing with her hair and suggests that this is not the normal manner in which she coifs her tresses to get ready for a day's work. After a few moments of musing over the hair mussing, Rippin wonders out loud whether the squirrel has begun to pee on her. Her worst fears are confirmed by a nearby observer, and the camera zooms in on her back to reveal a few rivulets on the back of her red dress. The offending squirrel is promptly removed, and Rippin appears to laugh off the temporary embarrassment. Later that ignominious day, Rippin tweeted about the squirrel's accident to her Channel 17 followers: "This is television, people." And, of course, the best-laid plans for a carefully crafted television feature story can go a little haywire when a squirrel is the story subject.

A website known as "the dodo," which is tailored for animal lovers and those dedicated to the humane treatment of animals, did not take this squirrel escapade in stride: "While there may be no harm done, aside from a soiled dress, there's a chance little Twiggy was trying to send her (WZTV's Rippin) a message. Rodents, like rats, are known to pee when frightened or stressed— so it's entirely possible that Twiggy really wasn't having such a great time after all. And while the squirrel's owner, Lou Ann Best, insisted that Twiggy 'is really quite happy with her life,' there are plenty of animal experts who might disagree."[20] Stephen Messenger of "the dodo" quotes wildlife experts who emphasize that, unlike typical pets and companion animals, squirrels lack the instinct to rely on others for food, protection or companionship. The adult squirrel is primarily a solitary animal unsuited for living with others, according to Messenger's sources.

These observations are reinforced and expanded upon by Phyllis DeGioia, the editor of *Veterinary Partner* and *VetzInsight*. DeGioia provides a laundry list of insights on why squirrels do not make good pets and are not really our friends, drawing on the wisdom of wildlife rehabilitator Sandra Sutherland for her most salient points: Squirrels do not possess the bite inhibition reflex of domestic pets. If the first thing that occurs to them is to bite, there is no countermessage to say that biting may be a bad plan. Squirrels also do not possess the chew inhibition reflex of domestic pets. If something looks tasty, it will be tasted. This includes wallpaper, drywall, furniture, and anything else that might be handy. Then there are those sharp nails on the end of a squirrel's four paws, which are designed to pierce bark so as to claw up and climb trees, but which will also completely rake and shred human skin.[21]

If Kelli Rippin had consulted a veterinarian like DeGioia or perhaps the National Wildlife Rehabilitation Association for some basic background information on squirrels before doing her story, perhaps she would not have been so unpleasantly surprised when Twiggy became entangled in her hair and peed on her neck and back. According to Sutherland, squirrels will poop and pee as they run around a house or other human enclosure. Squirrels will also hang on to the sides of their cages and purposely aim their poop and pee onto the floor. Squirrels clean themselves and are determined to keep their own areas neat and clean. They don't care a fig about the condition of a human's space.

Of course, as a cool medium, television is primarily interested in cool squirrel stories—stories about a squirrel crossing home plate at a playoff baseball game, or a squirrel dressed up as a minister to give a Sunday sermon, or a squirrel jumping a wave on skis behind a tiny motor boat. TV is not generally interested in telling us that the best reason not to own a squirrel is that they are wild animals and deserve to be free. That might make for an interesting newspaper story or a provocative editorial, but television news is not so interested in interviewing veterinarians who advise that attempting to raise a baby squirrel as a pet will likely be disastrous for everybody involved. That would probably make for some preachy TV and would not be cool for a medium that's known to be cool.

4

Squirrels in
PR and Advertising

Squirrels are not simply story subjects for books, newspapers and television programs. These nutty creatures are sometimes called on to tell the story themselves as part of the strategy of the public relations world. Sometimes squirrels will interrupt public information operatives and press relations spokespersons to offer sage advice and wise counsel. Such was the case in October 2017, when Kellyanne Conway was distracted from her spokesperson duties in defending President Donald Trump during an interview with CNN's *New Day*. Conway stopped the interview to exchange greetings with a squirrel on the White House lawn.[1] She also noted that the squirrel was far less noisy than the lawnmower used to care for the White House grounds. This presidential press relations incident with the White House lawn squirrel is forever captured on YouTube and went viral at the time of the interview with Alisyn Camerota of CNN.

Sometimes squirrels play more passive roles in the apparatus of public relations, institutional and marketing communication. The famous Rally Squirrel, which emerged as a mascot for the St. Louis Cardinals during the 2011 post-season baseball play, was enlisted for a variety of public relations functions. During the period leading up to the Cardinals winning the World Series against the Texas Rangers, Rally Squirrel appeared at a press conference for a prestigious health care center and the Cardinal Glennon Children's Foundation. Press relations operatives announced that Rally Squirrel was taking on duties as the mascot for a fundraising drive for the Cardinal Glennon Children's Foundation. The sales of Rally Squirrel T-shirts alone raised more than $200,000 for the charity in less than a week.[2] Squirrel public relations capabilities can be measured in dollars and cents in such instances.

Squirrel communication talents also have been drawn upon by a number of American towns to put their best paws (squirrel paws, that is) forward. Towns have championed their abundance of albino squirrels, capitalizing on the unusual creatures as an attraction for tourists. Black squirrels in a number of college towns have been used in much the same way, along with serving as sports team mascots and public relations spokespersons. Squirrels can fulfill these public relations functions because the television media (as detailed in the previous chapter) have downplayed their negative attributes and emphasized their more likeable aspects. Despite some convincing evidence to the contrary, squirrels are portrayed as happy-go-lucky, fun creatures—even positive role models. As a result, they are recruited for media and public relations activities to both entertain and inform the public.

In fact, squirrels are even used to trumpet the miracles that effective public relations can perform. After all, squirrels themselves are sometimes referred to as rats that only succeed through good public relations. They have overcome their status as lowly rodents thanks to the efforts of dedicated media handlers. Media mavens have transformed squirrels into television stars, movie talents and video game characters.

Rally Squirrel became the unofficial mascot for the St. Louis Cardinals during their successful 2011 baseball playoffs and World Series. Based on a real squirrel that invaded the playing field at Busch Stadium, Rally found a niche for public relations purposes. The sale of Rally Squirrel T-shirts raised more than $200,000 for a St. Louis children's hospital (courtesy St. Louis Cardinals).

Some public relations firms have devised strategic communication strategies based on a cursory study of squirrels. These companies have released guidelines for clients on how to achieve optimal messaging and brand identification, based on lessons that can be learned from characters in the squirrel family.

Public relations communication is the art of promoting image and generating favorable media coverage. Advertising communication is the art of promoting products or services that will sell through effective media messaging. Squirrels have found a place in both public relations and advertising.

However, squirrels are present in far greater numbers in advertising. There are so many product areas where squirrels can fit the bill and make the sale: candy bars, toothpaste, dessert plates, eyewear, salted peanuts, oranges, pizza, wings, yogurt, shoes, calendars, and even poison for squirrels and gophers. There are also many service areas in which squirrels have been enlisted to sell people on the idea of using mass transit, attending festivals, participating in job fairs, practicing safe driving, utilizing library services, visiting movie events, enrolling in colleges and much more.

Squirrels are increasingly sought out for a genre of advertising known as "Oddvertising." Ad creators capitalize on the idea that oddities are remembered. An ad in which a squirrel drives a sports utility vehicle or sits down to a platter of hot chicken wings gets remembered. Oddvertising is all about avoiding the hard sell and amusing the potential buyer with a bizarre situation. The more absurd the advertisement becomes, the more effective it will be, especially with attention-challenged younger audiences who demand edginess and seize on subliminal messaging, creative scripting and imaginative scenarios.

"Today, as marketers strive for more traffic and buzz on the internet, contemporary Oddvertising has become so strange that if you're not dabbling with some form of weirdness in your advertising—or, heaven forbid, get caught 'selling' in a commercial—your efforts are going to be little more than white noise," declares Mike Johnston, an advertising creative and advocate for Oddvertising. "If no one is talking about your Oddvertising, you're clearly not pushing far enough."[3]

Today's phenomenon of odd advertising naturally brings to mind the ideas of the media phenomenon of yesteryear, Marshall McLuhan. Because of the advent of the cool medium of television, McLuhan predicted that at some point, the impact of a creative advertisement would overwhelm the actual product or service. This does not mean that the consumer will ignore or forget the product or service. On the contrary, the consumer will purchase the product or service precisely to have an association or identification with the unique and clever advertisement.

"TV experience favors much more consciousness concerning the unconscious than do the hard-sell forms of presentation in the press, the magazine, movie or radio. The sensory tolerance of the audience has changed, and so have the methods of appeal by advertisers. In the new cool TV world, the old hot world of hard-selling, earnest-talking salesmen has all the antique charm of the songs and togs of the 1920s," wrote McLuhan in *Understanding Media:*

Extensions of Man. He went on to say, "Ads (now) are not meant for conspicuous consumption. They are intended as subliminal pills for the subconscious in order to exercise a hypnotic spell."[4]

Numerous examples of Oddvertising using squirrels can be found in the archives of advertising agencies and on ad posts on YouTube. A 2008 Super Bowl advertisement employed the talents of a squirrel to sell Bridgestone tires. The Bridgestone tires advertisement illustrates McLuhan's point about the need for a cool communications experience for consumers in the modern era, rather than the old hot world of fast-talking salesman armed with lots of product details.

Let's begin by noting that a tire is simply a tire for most consumers. A pitchman can talk about tread life, speed ratings and traction factors—and put a consumer to sleep rather quickly. Introduce a cute squirrel about to be mowed down by a speeding car, however, and the prospective tire buyer suddenly becomes engrossed with what looks to be a certain calamity for the squirrel.

The 2008 Super Bowl advertisement for Bridgestone tires begins with idyllic, nature music as a plump acorn falls from a tree and lands intact on a country road. A curious squirrel spies the acorn and scampers from his favorite rock to retrieve the nutty prize. Suddenly, the roar of an oncoming automobile drowns out the lovely background melody. A flattened squirrel seems to be the inevitable outcome. The endangered squirrel looks up into the grill of the fast-approaching vehicle and lets out a blood-curdling scream.

What makes this advertisement particularly odd, and cool at the same time, is that the squirrel's scream is only the beginning of a concerted reaction. The squirrel's high-pitched scream is followed by the cries of a raccoon, an owl, a rabbit, a mouse, a turtle, a deer, an emerald insect, and a chipmunk threesome. Even the female passenger in the car (presumably the driver's wife) gets in on the noisy action. All this screaming elicits a dismissive smirk from her husband, who simply steers the car around the squirrel, confident in the knowledge that his Bridgestone tires will grip the road and save the day. After swerving to avoid the squirrel, the car continues on to its destination, and the grateful animal holds up his acorn and hops away. All is well. And the advertisement's narrator calmly pronounces, "For drivers who want to get the most out of their cars, it's Bridgestone or nothing."[5]

For the purposes of this study, the question that has to be asked—and answered—is: Why are squirrels used to make ads snappy and memorable, and to take on the mundane job of selling products within the advertisement? Why are squirrels the right characters to bring frivolity, joviality and amusement to advertisements? At least part of the answer is that humans have been conditioned by their visual media (especially television) to view squirrels as outdoor companions and as sources of mirth and good-natured fun. This is why squirrels have unwittingly gnawed their way into the hearts of public relations practitioners and the creative professionals of the advertising field.

Squirrels as Strategic Communicators

The public relations industry has been in turmoil in the twenty-first century because of the rise of digital communication and social media. Industry firms feel an increasing need, if not a compulsion, to integrate all the social media tools and digital platforms available to disseminate client messages. Companies also demand a 24-7 public relations presence because a crisis can arise at any time, day or night, in the new digital environment and may necessitate an immediate response. As a result, public relations professionals increasingly refer to their work as "strategic communications."

The PR industry has suffered a number of self-inflicted wounds in recent decades. In some cases, public relations professionals have not reacted quickly enough in crisis situations that threaten a company's reputation, image, messaging or brand. Firms also have been to slow to evolve and to discover new ways of doing things in a markedly changed media ecosystem. Some firms have been tarnished by ethical lapses ranging from deceptive practices to conflicts of interest to being intentionally slow to correct erroneous information distributed to the media.

In all the confusion over the digital revolution and the challenge to core ethical values, strategic communicators have looked everywhere for direction. And squirrels have been found to have lessons to impart for these media communicators, according to John Castanga, head of the Quicksilver Edge Strategic Communications agency. Among those lessons: "Find and Discover New Nuts" and "Climb and Stretch Without Fear." Many strategic communicators are sympathetic to the Castanga approach, because they have learned that everyday reality impinges upon public relations, truth can be a difficult nut to crack and Mother Nature cannot be fooled.

Castanga contends that observing the lifestyles and habits of squirrels can provide useful knowledge for public relations and marketing communicators. As a backyard kind of outdoorsman, Castanga has studied how squirrels are good role models for public relations professionals. Among other things, he has observed that they never give up. Squirrels are always relentless in their battles for the best sunflower seeds in bird feeders that are meant for the local avian population. Whether it's hot or cold outside, they are ready to make their claim to edibles and to pile up a dependable supply.

In his essay, "What Business Can Learn from Squirrels," Castanga argues that public relations operatives and marketers must protect their nuts—that is, they must protect and tout assets, values and ideas that make up the foundation of their enterprise. Effective communication professionals must be willing to find and discover new "nuts." Castanga advises his industry colleagues that "every squirrel understands that it will never survive by being satisfied with the nuts it knows. Discovery is part of the survival business of being a squirrel and it should be yours, too. A great PR partner can help your business discover what you may not find on your own."[6]

Squirrels thrive on urgency, as should strategic communicators. Part of addressing that urgency is a willingness to stretch, ignore boundaries, push the envelope and not always rely on what has been done in the past. Castanga explains that "squirrels take measured, successful risks…. Their athleticism at making good on their mission carries a lesson for all of us. We need to be fearless about discovering new things. We should all be willing to take leaps of faith in ourselves, challenge old assumptions and processes."[7]

Castanga concludes his study of squirrels and strategic communications with this apt advice: "Make Noise and Proudly Wave Your Tail." He contends that success breeds success, and therefore organizational triumphs should be trumpeted both internally and externally. After all, whether it's called public relations or strategic communications, it's all about blowing your own horn, hitting the right notes on your trumpet and creating lots of chatter in between. Chatter like a squirrel. Wave that tail like a squirrel. "No one will notice your success or your worth unless you take pains to signal what you are and what you bring to your business environment. Squirrels are irrepressible. You ought to be irrepressible too…. Sitting on your nuts today won't grow you an oak grove tomorrow."[8]

White Squirrel Claims to Fame

When you're a very small town lost somewhere in Illinois farm country, how do you become a tourism mecca for people many miles away in Chicago, Indianapolis, St. Louis or Louisville?

Well, if you are fortunate enough to have a population of rare, albino squirrels, then the answer is obvious: make noise and proudly wave that white squirrel's tail (so to speak). Olney, Illinois, has a white squirrel monument in its downtown. It conducts a squirrel parade and what is tagged as a "Squirrel Scamper" event for kids. It has numerous squirrel happenings, and townspeople help visitors learn all about Olney's interesting inhabitants as well as when and where to get the best look at them. The rural Illinois town with a population of 8,500 residents proudly positions itself in tourism PR materials as "The Home of White Squirrels."

Olney provides visitors with a detailed, historical account of how the famous albino squirrels came to make Olney their home. According to one hypothesis, a hunter named William Yates Stroup was out hunting squirrels in the woods near his home in the southern part of Olney Township. He saw a gray squirrel run into a nest, so he raised his weapon and shot into the den. The mother squirrel was killed, and two pure white baby squirrels were knocked out of the nest. Stroup was so surprised that he put the babies into his game bag. Back home, he turned the albinos over to his sons,

Olney, Illinois, promotes itself as the home of the white squirrels, and visitors to the town can visit a giant statue of the town's favorite creature in Bower Park. However, visitors must be careful in navigating their vehicles to get downtown because there is a heavy fine for hitting a white squirrel. The white squirrel is protected as public relations gold for Olney (courtesy of Olney & the Greater Richland County Chamber of Commerce).

who raised them and fed them milk from a spoon. The tiny squirrels thrived, and that fall Stroup took them into town and gave them to the Jasper Banks Saloon, which displayed the young squirrels in the window to attract business.[9]

Stroup's albinos were released from captivity in the saloon when the Illinois state legislature passed a law restricting the confinement of wildlife. The squirrels then found their way to the home of Thomas Tippit and were released in Tippit's Woods. Tom Tippit, Jr., and his brother were horrified when the male white squirrel left the cage and soon was attacked (and killed) by a large female fox squirrel. Fourteen-year-old Tom ran into his house, got a shotgun and returned to the site of the massacre to shoot the fox squirrel as it was about to tear the white female apart. Tom saved the life of the albino mother, who produced a litter of pure white squirrels. Thus, the Olney albino squirrel colony was firmly established.

By 1941, there were about eight hundred white squirrels in the town and surrounding area near Olney. However, their numbers began to decline, and in the mid–1970s John Stencel of Olney Central College began a study of the unique animals after receiving a small grant from the Illinois Academy of Science. A squirrel count began to be held each fall, and as the number of squirrels continued to drop, concerns were raised. At one point, the population of white squirrels dipped below one hundred. The Olney City Council amended an ordinance that prohibited dogs from running at large to also include cats, as the felines were deemed to have a deleterious effect on the white squirrel population. City clerk Belinda Henton obtained a permit to rehabilitate wildlife from the Illinois Department of Natural Resources, and Olney residents were then asked to contact Henton whenever they found abandoned or injured white squirrels.[10]

The Olney Chamber of Commerce and the town's citizens know how valuable the squirrels have become to the identity of their town. The city council has passed a number of measures for the squirrels' protection. The population is estimated at about 200 today. The white squirrels are guaranteed the right of way on all public streets. Drivers of vehicles in the town are forewarned that if they drive over a white squirrel, a fine of $750 will be levied against them. Walk into any business in downtown Olney, and the proprietors will offer you advice on where to go to see the white squirrels in action (and also request that you exercise caution on your drive to the city park or elsewhere to see the albinos).

If an actual albino squirrel is not in sight, the town has plenty of other evidence that the Olney white squirrels are the town favorites. Shops in Olney have albino squirrel apparel, playing cards, Christmas ornaments, coffee cups, camping mugs, commemorative plates, garden stakes and garden flags. There are stuffed white squirrels, ceramic white squirrels, white squirrel salt and pepper shakers, and white squirrel wine bottle stoppers. There are silver-finished white squirrels holding chestnuts, acorns and pine cones. White squirrel posters and postcards declare the white squirrel to be the treasure of Olney. Olney police officers wear white squirrel badges on their shoulders, and the logos for the City of Olney and the Olney Chamber of Commerce are not complete without the insignia of the white squirrel.

Other small towns in America have to be jealous that they do not have the rare white squirrel as a public relations icon for their communities. However, there are a few other places that do claim the white squirrel as belonging to them. Marionville, Missouri, contends that it is the original breeding ground for white squirrels and insists that Olney kidnapped a couple of its squirrels to become a faux white squirrel town. According to the article "White Squirrel Wars" in *Roadside America*, officials in the town of Kenton, Tennessee, claim they have had white squirrels the longest, as a traveling gypsy caravan bestowed the creatures on the town in 1869. Brevard, North Carolina, has declared itself the real "Home of the White Squirrel" and throws an annual White Squirrel Festival around Memorial Day. In the "Great White North," the town of Exeter, Ontario, has a song and a video for its Great White Wonder.[11]

Black Squirrel PR Squabbles

White squirrels are employed for PR purposes to attract tourists to towns like Olney, Illinois, and Marionville, Missouri. Black squirrels do the same thing to represent college towns like Kent, Ohio; Rock Island, Illinois; or Albion, Michigan. Black squirrel public relations boosters can also be found in Council Bluffs, Iowa, and London, Ontario. Even Chicago brags about its small herd of black squirrels when not touting its Bears, Cubs and Blackhawks. Like white squirrels, black squirrels are a rare subgroup of the acorn lovers that have congregated in a bevy of small hamlets and a few large cities, and they have become the darling of college towns. Several colleges have jettisoned their former mascots and embraced the black squirrel as the king of the hill on their academic turf.

At one time, black squirrels were not just residents of a few favored enclaves in North America. In fact, jet black squirrels were once dominant, and eastern gray and fox squirrels were in the minority. This change in squirrel fortunes can be blamed on the arrival of the Europeans. Black squirrels thrived when America's old growth forests were dense, dank, and dark. Their dark color was an advantage in the heavily shaded forests because it allowed them to blend in with their surroundings and hide from predators. When the Europeans arrived in the sixteenth century, they began taking down the tall timber in woodlands, and deforestation spelled trouble for the black squirrels. To add serious injury to the insult of deforestation, the Europeans began hunting the black squirrels for their pelts and meat. As sunlight streamed through the thinning forest canopy, black squirrels became easy targets. In this newly changed, lighter habitat, the gray squirrels assumed the privilege of being less conspicuous than black squirrels in the gunsights of hunters.

Black squirrels have retained their advantage in Canada and in northern states where there are still heavily forested areas in which to thrive. Beyond having better survival odds through being able to hide in darker environments, their dark fur allows black squirrels to retain heat better than other squirrels, thus increasing their tolerance for cold temperatures. Black squirrels prosper in habitats where the light is dimmer, although they certainly also do well in areas where humans look out for their needs because they are treasured for their public relations value. Just as albino squirrels get special treatment with protective ordinances in the few towns where they flourish, black squirrels also tend to be the beneficiaries of favorable arrangements in the limited number of towns where they have found a home. Here the law is on the side of the black squirrels.

One of these squirrel-friendly hamlets, which hosts a sizeable contingent of black squirrels, is Council Bluffs, Iowa, where it's possible to be fined for merely annoying a squirrel of the ebony persuasion. An ordinance protecting the squirrels has been on the books for decades, and it is illegal to throw things at black squirrels in Council Bluffs or to repeatedly threaten or scare them. Council Bluffs has been a haven for black squirrels going back to the 1840s, and the town has long had a practice of "Black Squirrel Boosterism." Several other cities have aggressively touted their black squirrels in their public relations as tourist destinations, including Marysville, Kansas; London, Ontario; and Battle Creek, Michigan.

Marysville, Kansas, bills itself as the "Home of the Black Squirrels," and given all the activities the town hosts in honor of its favorite creature, Marysville deserves that moniker more than any other American town. Marysville has been promoting a special Black Squirrel Night for almost half a century. The town has named the black squirrel as its official mascot, honoring it with a Black Squirrels on Parade event. Twenty-one painted and decorated black squirrel statues were unveiled in 2016, and the town also has two five-foot, fiberglass black squirrels designed by Topeka artist Patty Kahn. In 1987, the "Black Squirrel Song" became Marysville's official anthem, with such lyrics as "Lives in the city park / runs all over town / The coal black squirrel will be our pride and joy / Many more years to come!"[12]

The beloved "Black Squirrel Song" gets a workout at the annual Black Squirrel Night in the fall, when the town goes crazy over its amazing mascot. Often celebrated in conjunction with Halloween, this event will typically feature costume contests, hayrides, entertainment by dancers and singers, raffles, food booths and, of course, a parade. A plethora of folklore exists on how the black squirrels came to live in Marysville. Local historians share stories about how the squirrels escaped from a circus that came through town, or about how they were left behind by a traveling gypsy caravan. One legend holds that a traveling carnival, which was headquartered in Marysville, kept black squirrels for a sideshow event. A boy who became excited by the squirrels opened their cage, and they hopped out to take refuge in a wooded area of Marysville—and the rest is history (along with the propensity of the squirrels to be fruitful and multiply prodigiously).

There are also stories about how other towns have sent representatives to come to Marysville to "borrow" some of the black squirrels in the middle of the night, all so that they might accrue the many public relations benefits of becoming a black squirrel town. Black squirrels came to Hobbs, New Mexico, via a highway ride from Marysville in the 1970s, but the plan for the town in the American Southwest did not quite come together. *Roadside America* notes that when the squirrels were turned loose in Hobbs with much fanfare, they were promptly torn to shreds by the local red fox squirrels.[13] The red fox squirrels just were not having it. Marysville is much more protective of its black squirrels now and will take pains to never again "lend" any of its carbon-colored critters to another locale.

Battle Creek, Michigan, sports its own legends as to how it became a black squirrel town. The town (which is better known for Kellogg's cereal characters such as Tony the Tiger, Katy the Kangaroo and Emily the Elephant) boasts a population of black squirrels that have a connection to the giant cereal company. The late Will Keith Kellogg, the founder of Kellogg Company, brought black squirrels to Battle Creek from Europe.[14] His mission was to have them proliferate and crowd out and destroy the red squirrel population, which he despised. Living in a northern state with cold winters and many wooded areas, the squirrels not only prospered in Battle Creek but also were exported to a number of other Michigan locations.

American cities have attracted tourism dollars to their coffers by promoting their rare black squirrel residents, but college campuses and college towns have gotten in on the action as well. Black squirrels are used as sports mascots and inspirations for names for various college facilities. Among the college towns and campuses capitalizing on the black squirrel phenomenon are Kent, Ohio (home of Kent State University); Albion, Michigan (Albion College); Rock Island, Illinois (Augustana College); Haverford, Pennsylvania (Haverford College); Bronxville, New York (Sarah Lawrence University); and Wooster, Ohio (College of Wooster).

Kent State University became a black squirrel refuge when ten squirrels were delivered to the campus after being trapped in Canada for export across the border. (Allegedly, a grounds superintendent brought the black squirrels to campus after he fell in love with the creatures on his travels through Canada

Not only have squirrels been enlisted for public relations purposes in towns blessed with white or black squirrels, they also have become part of the promotional efforts of college campuses. Universities that have capitalized on their campus squirrels include Albion College in Michigan, Haverford College in Pennsylvania, and Sarah Lawrence College in New York. Students at Kent State University in Ohio pass by black squirrel statues on their way to class and participate in the Black Squirrel Festival (courtesy Kent State University).

in the 1950s.) The original squirrels have since multiplied into several hundred omnipresent, bustling bushy-tailed rodents. In 2009, President Lester Lefton and his wife, Linda, gifted a statue of the Kent State Black Squirrel to commemorate the school's upcoming centennial celebration, set for 2010. The squirrels have been a fixture on campus for more than half a century, and the statue should mark their presence for another fifty years in the student center on campus.[15]

Students and faculty at Kent State University haven't always been pleased with the squirrels, which have sometimes chewed through screens to get into classrooms. For the most part, though, relations with the black squirrels have been amiable. As an illustration of this friendly coexistence, the college holds a Black Squirrel Festival in the fall as a tribute to the growing squirrel population. This festival is not the only example of how the squirrels have advanced campus life and the image of the university in northeast Ohio. Businesses in Kent and campus organizations have adopted the black squirrel in logos, titles and branding. There is also the Black Squirrel imprint for trade titles published by Kent State University Press. It's possible to read one of those books while imbibing a brew from Black Squirrel Brewing Company and listening to Black Squirrel Radio on the internet. Black Squirrel Radio is no joke—the station is supervised by the Kent State Journalism and Mass Communication faculty.

In Albion, Michigan, the number one quirk listed in the "Top Ten Quirks of Albion College" is black squirrels.[16] Students find the squirrels to be in-your-face and aggressive, even to the point of securing perches in trees, from which the impish squirrels throw acorns at students as they walk along the college's sidewalks to their classes. Over the years, students have expressed the desire that the black squirrel become the college mascot. In 2011, these hopes and dreams for a furry mascot came true. The administration blessed a college plebiscite that selected a black squirrel as the official mascot over candidates that included a British knight and a British king. Some students (those disappointed in the outcome of the vote) called the new mascot "a joke" that might inspire them to transfer to another college.[17]

Haverford College in Pennsylvania and its students were known as the Fords for much of the school's existence, but a growing population of black squirrels on campus changed all that. The student body now has acquired the unofficial nickname of the Haverford College Black Squirrels. However, new students to Haverford are surprised to find that the creatures are not to be found anywhere when stepping off campus. There are no "townie black squirrels." On campus, it's a different story. The creatures are said to have become so popular that student athletes are proud to carry the name "Haverford College Black Squirrels" into their battles with other colleges.

The trend toward embracing black squirrel inhabitants on college campuses has attracted plenty of media attention. And that, after all, is part of the public relations function of acquiring and cultivating a mascot, an identity, a brand. Augustana College in Rock Island, Illinois, has received print and digital publicity for the students' Black Squirrel Productions and the ten black squirrel statues on campus.[18] Sarah Lawrence College has likewise received print and digital publicity for the bookstore selling stuffed black squirrels as the college's informal mascot.

The College of Wooster revels in its obsession over its black squirrels. Located near the Wooster campus is a bed and breakfast named after the campus black squirrels. We know about the College of Wooster and its connection to black squirrels because it has also received print and digital publicity for that relationship.

There are times when a cigar is not just a cigar, and a black squirrel is not just a black squirrel. This fact has been proven by towns and college campuses that have recognized their black squirrels as public relations gold. The essence of good PR is having someone else talk about your brand rather than you. The idea is to have a tourist talk to another person about a visit to a city that is a "home of black squirrels" or to have an enrolled student talk to a potential enrollee about a fun college campus where the mascot is a black squirrel. Another, larger goal of branding and public relations is to encourage visibility and wide recognition. This goal drives the act of promoting a unique and imaginative brand through all venues of strategic communications. Sometimes a black squirrel is not just a squirrel but also an image, an icon, a brand and a recognizable symbol.

Squirrels Seal the Ad Deal

Squirrels are used to advertise candy bars, beer, insurance, banking services and more. A squirrel risks life and paw in a Bridgestone tire commercial. In a Hall's throat lozenge advertisement, a cheerleading squirrel finds a reinvigorated voice within the bustle and noise of a sports stadium. In a Geico car insurance advertisement, squirrels seem to be congratulating each other for their role in a car accident. Obviously, the advertising business can go a little nutty in recruiting characters from the squirrel world as the needed talent for advertisements. However, squirrels are only suitable for a certain kind of advertising, which has been tagged by some professionals as "Oddvertising." Oddvertising is built around the concept that weird and odd messaging gets remembered by target audiences.[19]

Students of advertising learn that audiences for targeted messaging get divided by demographics and psychographics. Targeting for demographics involves the practice of segmenting audiences by income level, gender, ethnicity, educational attainment and other social characteristics. Obviously, advertisements for items found at a Macy's or Nordstrom's department store are going to be targeted for a different demographic audience than the ads for items at a Dollar General or a Dollar Tree. The messaging will be different, and the media used to convey the tailored messages will most likely be different as well.

Using psychographic segmentation to target advertising messages can be much more nuanced and sophisticated. Targeting for psychographics involves the complex practice of segmenting audiences by values, lifestyle, personal identity and self-image. Obviously advertisements for items found at stores devoted to individualized recreation and outdoor gear are going to be targeted to a different psychographic audience than ads for items found at stores offering team sport trademarked apparel and indoor merchandise reflecting team loyalties. As with demographics, the messaging, along with the media used to convey these messages, will be different depending on the intended audience.

Advertising agencies and their marketing experts may devise their own criteria for breaking down target audiences using psychographic segmentation. After all, psychographic benchmarks change with shifting cultural norms and fluid lifestyle modes. One popular psychographic system profiles consumer audiences under psychographic headings such as "thinkers," "achievers," "believers," "experiencers," "strivers" and more.[20] Believers, for example, tend to be traditional, with conventional loyalties to religion, family, community and the nation. By contrast, the so-called experiencers seek excitement and innovation, and they are unconventional in their need to explore new possibilities and ways of doing things.

Squirrels in advertising are unlikely to appeal to those classified in the more conventional psychographic profiles, but they may be perfect for "experiencers" and "strivers" looking for trendy, unconventional products and experiences. This may explain why squirrels are the talent used in advertisements for movie comedies, zip line vacation spots, new energy drinks or organic foods. Squirrels are not likely to make the cut as talent for advertisements for motivational books, creation museums or wedding gifts.

Squirrels are heavy favorites to be recruited as talent for advertisements promoting beers, ales and other spirits. Social drinking is all about having fun and enjoying a few laughs. Excessive drinking results in what might be described as "squirrelly behavior," so squirrels are natural candidates for ads promoting alcohol consumption. Squirrels appear in liquor ads in the United States, Canada, Ireland, England, Germany and several other European countries. Advertisements for American brews using squirrels tend to be rudimentary, with most of the emphasis on visuals and branding slogans. However, European advertising for spirits tends to capitalize on the cuteness of squirrels and their adaptability for tricks and witty storylines.

Smithwick's Irish Ale, an Irish red ale-style beer originally brewed in Kilkenny, has used a versatile squirrel to provide a tour of its brewery while serving as an advertisement for its product. Now posted on YouTube, the sequence begins with the rodent emerging from its nest in the brewery and passing by a photo of the founder on its way to the brewery's electronic control panel. After getting the operation started, the squirrel finds matches to light the flames under the copper kettles. He then gets the famous ingredients together, including the hops, the yeast, the wheat and more. At the end of his work, the squirrel taps a brew sample, toasts the founder, and takes a drink, as the advertisement narrator notes, "After generations of brewing, you know how to craft the perfect spirit. Experience—it's what you do with it that counts."

An advertisement for Carling Black Label beer features a determined squirrel intent on negotiating a suspended obstacle course to get to his nutty reward. The music of *Mission Impossible* accompanies the squirrel's various acrobatic feats. The squirrel climbs a tall pole, slides down a rope from the pole's high platform, makes a series of harrowing jumps from platform to platform, and then traverses more rope and chain lengths to get to his prize. Two owls watch all this action and bob their heads in fascination. Wise old owls would prefer not to engage in such risky behavior. At the end of the squirrel's successful mission, one owl turns to the other and sagely remarks, "I bet he drinks Carling Black Label." The message is that anyone who drinks Carling Black Label, even a squirrel, is capable of accomplishing impossible missions.

Anheuser Busch (AB InBev) of St. Louis is located in prime squirrel country, and although the giant Clydesdale horses are the animals that pull beer wagons and rank high when it comes to branding, the brewing giant could not avoid using squirrels for a number of the advertisements promoting its best-selling product Bud Light. Squirrels appear in an ad from its expansive "Real Men of Genius" genre, as well as a Bud Light piece featuring a squirrel and a talking dog. Bud Light also employs a squirrel named Walter in an advertisement tailored for young male jocks and fraternity brethren. In the ad, as four fellows sit down at an outside table to imbibe Bud Light, the leader discovers that he is one beer short. He informs the wimpy odd-man-out that he's sorry, but there just aren't enough to go around. The head honcho of the brew fest then tells all of his buddies that he is going inside the house to retrieve some nachos, but not before advising his squirrel, Walter, to keep an eye on his Bud Light. No sooner does he disappear in search of the nachos than the wimp decides he can abscond with that briefly abandoned Bud Light. As he reaches for the beer, Walter jumps up, forces him to the ground, and proceeds to jackhammer his head with an acorn clutched in his paws. The scene ends with the wimp meekly wondering whether he can have a nacho and Walter chattering to warn him to stay clear. The narrator upstages Walter to conclude the piece with these words: "Refreshingly smooth Bud Light. Always worth it."

Advertisements using squirrels as talent often lean toward the sophomoric and ridiculous. A promotion for Air Action Vigorosol chewing gum exceeds all expectations on that score. The ad begins with a woodland squirrel perched on a large tree branch, watching with horror as a forest fire approaches. An ominous voice declares, "Nothing could stop the forest fire ... except maybe a miracle." As desperate men work in a bucket brigade in a futile effort to extinguish the fire, the squirrel steps forward. He unpacks a few sticks of Air Action Vigorosol gum and begins to chew his way to the miracle that will stop the encroaching forest fire.

This is no ordinary chewing gum, and this is no ordinary squirrel. The Air Action Vigorosol cools down the squirrel's insides, and he promptly aims his backside at the fire and releases a mighty, lengthy, noisy, freezing fart. Never mind that farts are known to be hot and flammable—once the extended methane bomb is dropped on the forest fire, a cold wind freezes everything. The raging flames disappear and a forest winter scene emerges, complete with sparkling snow and ice. A startled bullfrog sits on a frozen lily pad on the hardened lake surface and seems to croak, "What (happened)?" Cheers emerge from the now cool and tranquil woods, and the humble squirrel hero retreats to his tree burrow. The narrator ends the tale of the scary forest fire with this pronouncement: "And, oh, how the people rejoiced.... A fresh air explosion."

On the YouTube site, this squirrel ad garnered hundreds of thousands of views, as well as many skeptical comments. Several viewers questioned whether the minty chewing gum would be a smart purchase if it actually caused such a load of abdominal gas.

Squirrel talent for a Sears advertisement begins when a proud husband surprises his wife with a scene of squirrels cutting coupons by the fireplace in their comfy home. As the squirrel crew cuts out coupon after coupon from magazines and newspapers, he tells his wife how he trained the pesky varmints and how they are destined to save "a ton of money." The admiring wife praises him for his brains, but that seems to trigger the squirrels' leader to call for an open revolt against the sweatshop conditions. Soon the squirrels are turning over their tiny worktables and setting fires. The ingenious husband is knocked in the forehead with an acorn, and then a squirrel latches onto his face to inflict pain. His frantic wife begins to bop the squirrel and her husband's head with a handy golf club, which only seems to inflict more pain. A spokesman for Sears then interjects to explain that there's a better way to save at Sears with online or in-store coupons. A chattering squirrel follows and points to a click button on the screen that will reveal the coupons for big savings at Sears.

An advertisement for a Carlsberg energy drink employs a curious squirrel who is tricked into drinking some of the marvelous tonic (poured into the bottle's cap by a prankster in a soccer jersey). The squirrel no sooner laps up the brew than he is inspired to demonstrate his best soccer moves with a bouncing acorn. The agile squirrel dribbles the acorn from paw to paw, balances it on his nose and performs a flip and a goal kick, which has his fans cheering and laughing. The ad concludes with a simple declaration: "Carlsberg Sport—sport inside."

Squirrels seem to be the obvious choice for advertising bank services in Britain. This is precisely because squirrels are highly motivated in their efforts to save acorns for times when food may not be so plentiful. In an Abbey Bank ad, a squirrel in a red cape shows just how to maximize interest with a super savings account. Elsewhere, a Bankwest squirrel advertisement features a squirrel bank president sitting at a sprawling desk in his plush office. He reassures a potential investor that his institution knows quite a bit about "squirreling away" savings at an impressive rate of interest. The furry bank executive makes a joke to the prospective investor inquiring about how big the nuts are that will be invested, and then he looks a little sheepish—for a squirrel. The final message of the advertisement: "Happy banking! An initiative from Bankwest."

Squirrels also perform well as advertising talent for Nestle Clusters breakfast cereal. In the cereal advertisement, a beautiful damsel sits outside on a nice day and savors a bowl of Nestle Clusters. A narrator explains how the clusters are made with crispy wheat flakes, a variety of nuts and a touch of honey. All the while, a hungry squirrel spies on what is happening below him. Finally, he can no longer restrain the impulse to get in on the action. The squirrel swings down from a rope vine and, with a Tarzan yell, swipes the clusters from the beauty's breakfast table. The message is obvious: "If you like nuts, you'll love Nestle Clusters."

It's easy to see why talented squirrels are the right choice for advertisements aimed at the psychographic categories of "experiencers" or "strivers." The "strivers" are said to be those who seek memorable, fun activities. They value achievement, whether in the sports world or in the arena where money can define success. They are similar to the "experiencers" in that they want to push the envelope and get a taste of what's new in life. However, the experiencers are not as inclined to value money as an index of success; they want a taste of what is novel and different. After a lengthy session of observing squirrels used in advertisements posted on YouTube, it is plain to see that the squirrels themselves can easily be categorized as both "experiencers" and "strivers." The assertive rodents conform to the psychographic descriptions for the profile matchups in advertising—and perhaps in real life as well.

Squirrels Hang with TruckNutz

Perhaps the most outrageous squirrel, best known among pickup truck owners afflicted with an outrageous need for attention, is the fuzzy mascot for a company selling vehicle accessories known as TruckNutz. The upright squirrel, aptly named "Nutz," plays a highly visible role in marketing plastic model testicles for autos, trucks and motorcycles, shamelessly peddling plastic scrotums for attachment to trailer hitches or other contrivances located near vehicles' back bumpers.

Trailer hitch TruckNutz are oversized vinyl testicles, and they come in white, red, blue, black, green and brown. David Ham, founder of the company in Santee, California, says the one-pound, eight-inch, flesh-colored Truck-

Nutz have always been his biggest seller. The light-emitting-diode-lit faux testicles (which are packaged in a semi-clear scrotum) also have been very popular. These can be custom-wired to a vehicle's brake lights, which can help grab the attention of anyone riding too close to the vehicle's tail at night. They can also be easily wired to a trailer hitch electrical plug if wiring them to the brake lights is too much of a hassle.

Trailer hitch nuts are just one of the many items offered with a testicular theme. Other products include 16-inch Monster Truck Nuts, 4-inch Biker Balls for motorcycle enthusiasts, 2-inch Keychain Nuts, Chrome Novelty Nuts, and Antenna Pals. Other popular items added to the testicular repertoire in 2007 are the so-called adhesive add-ons, which include the Lipstickers. These consist of red lipstick smackers that adhere to any set of balls (though they are alleged to work best on the chrome Monster Truck Nuts). Some unhappy customers have complained about their bumper accessories being stolen from the trailer hitches. Ham contends that an ounce of prevention can save a pound of nuts, and as he has never heard of local law enforcement solving a nut case, he began selling special lock devices.

Ham has introduced products called Nut Lock, the Nut Shackle and Nut Straps (though he discontinued the straps when he found the materials he imported from China to be inferior and not up to the task of preventing nut heists). He has also been a victim of some thievery himself when it comes to his nuts. Ham alleges that competitors have been ripping him off with knock-off products. Apparently he never got patents for his items because he never imagined that anyone would want to go into his type of business and also never envisioned that it would become so popular. To add insult to injury, competitors selling car, truck and motorcycle cojones began using Ham's squirrel mascot Nutz to advertise their wares. The bushy, upright and particularly well-endowed male squirrel has been showing up everywhere on the internet.

"That squirrel with the saggy nuts was used on just about all the websites that ripped off my ideas," Ham says. "I retired that squirrel from my business about 2006, but I was the one who actually hired a graphic artist to come up with a squirrel who could sell the nuts. The squirrel has been popular in his own right with customers."[21] Indeed, Nutz adorns T-shirts, coffee cups and posters. He always appears with his slogan: "Hang in there!" And he is always standing upright, revealing what looks to be an enormous set of testicles.

In fact, a male squirrel standing upright is the perfect mascot and a noteworthy salesman for a business marketing Monster Truck Nuts and Chrome

Novelty Nuts. Male squirrels commonly have a scrotum that is 20 percent of their body length (excluding the tail). Other portions of male squirrel genitalia, including the penis, are disproportionately large when compared to body length.[22] Biologists and experts on squirrels note that the oversized testicles indicate the need for a large production of sperm to increase the odds of their genes surviving into the next generation. Since female squirrels will usually mate with several different males during estrus, nature has designed males to maximum advantage in the competition to make sure it is their sperm that fertilizes the female's eggs—to make sure that they sire the next generation of squirrels, and not their inferior rivals.

5

Movie Madness
Squirrels in Cinema

No animal in the rodent world has received as much press (as well as time on the silver screen) as the hyperkinetic squirrel. Of course, there is that animated mouse known throughout the world as Mickey, but he's a Disney cartoon character and a far cry from the real thing. It's also true that rats can boast of movie stardom thanks to a character named Ben. However, squirrels ultimately have more star power, and also more frequent cameo roles as stars of Hollywood fare. Squirrels are troublemakers, but they get more favorable treatment and far more positive roles in front of the cameras than their pernicious cousins, those rapacious rats.

In the troubled and turbulent history of humankind, rats have not exactly been a great friend to humanity. In cities, suburbs and the country, wherever humans settle, rats tag along or are soon to follow. Rats form their own cities beneath our metropolises and find homes beneath our farmlands. They enjoy living in our squalor, taking up residence in our fetid sewers, and dining in our dirty alleyways. They poison our food. They bite our babies. They spread plague and other diseases. On occasion, they will eat people alive. They constitute a perfect living nightmare in black and white. By comparison, squirrels are downright dreamy, thus explaining why squirrels get a good reception in Tinseltown.

Two of the more sympathetic movie portrayals about rats, *Willard* and *Ben*, don't do rats any favors on the public relations front. The rat named Ben draws some admiration in the 1971 horror movie, *Willard*, because he becomes the vengeful ally of a young social misfit. The troubled Willard is constantly humiliated at work and eventually fired by a cruel boss named Martin. Bloodthirsty rodent Ben is more than willing to guide his fellow rats to help Willard get revenge upon his boss. Ben and his rats swarm onto Martin and kill him on Willard's command. However, by the movie's end, Ben turns on Willard, who wisely never completely trusts the homicidal rat.

The 1972 sequel, *Ben*, has the same thematic progression as the original. Danny Garrison is a lonely youngster who befriends Ben, the leader of a colony of rats. Ben becomes the shy boy's best friend and protects him from bullying. However, things go south when Ben's rat compatriots become violent and deadly. Police resort to destroying the murderous creatures with flamethrowers, although Ben escapes and makes his way back to Danny. In the end, young Danny tends to the injured Ben in order not to lose a friend—and presumably to ensure another sequel. The saving grace for this movie is the theme song performed by the late Michael Jackson and preserved on Jackson's 1972 album aptly titled *Ben*.[1]

If only Michael Jackson had lived to immortalize squirrels with a sympathetic theme song for the movies in which these more human-friendly animals found notable roles. Squirrels in movies are mostly harmless and certainly much more trustworthy than rats, even if they occasionally cause a ruckus. Many of the squirrel cinematic characters are quite memorable. Who can forget the friendly squirrel on the shoulder of Uncle Billy, the hapless fellow in *It's a Wonderful Life*, who accidentally loses the money at George Bailey's savings and loan business? The squirrel helps make Uncle Billy loveable, even though he nearly drives Bailey (played by Jimmy Stewart) to commit suicide by jumping off a bridge. Then there's the irascible squirrel in another Christmas classic, *Christmas Vacation*, in which the trouble-making animal comes close to driving Clark Griswold (played by Chevy Chase) to the brink of insanity. And let's not forget the dancing squirrel in *The Great Rupert*, an entertaining squirrel and the major portion of a vaudeville act that includes toe-tapping footwork to an accordion.

Actually, more people are going to remember the squirrels in *It's a Wonderful Life* and *Christmas Vacation* than will remember Rupert the Squirrel in the 1950 classic featuring comedian Jimmy Durante. That's because the two Christmas movies get a workout on television every holiday season, while the Jimmy Durante movie has yet to catch on as a December staple. However, the common thread in all three movies is the desperation of the main characters, who are mired in various money crunches—to say nothing of the appearance of squirrels in all of these films.

In *It's a Wonderful Life*, the money trouble stems from Uncle Billy misplacing the money of George Bailey's savings and loan business, and the threat that the community bank of Bedford Falls will go bust and fall into the clammy hands of the miserly Henry Potter. In *Christmas Vacation*, Clark Griswold's expectations for a Christmas bonus are crushed, along with his hopes of providing his family with a swimming pool for the summer. In *The Great Rupert*, vaudeville performer Louie Amendola has fallen on hard times, resulting in his entire family being strapped for cash. Squirrels figure in the narratives of all these desperate lives, as their sad stories finally move to redemptive conclusions with formulaic "happily ever after" endings.

All these stories harken back to the earliest themes of the movie industry, featuring anxiety-ridden underdogs who endure a series of setbacks until the very end of the story, when cash—manna from heaven—comes to the rescue. Media analyst Marshall McLuhan contends that these early themes were the doing of Hollywood tycoons who were true believers in the redemptive power of cash. Corporate owners, executives and producers of Hollywood knew that a major portion of their audience consisted of struggling immigrants in search of hope and a better life. These movie customers were looking for stories that put security, prosperity and the American Dream within their reach.

According to McLuhan, early movies were an astonishing visual process by which the real world was wound up on a spool in order to be unrolled "as a magic carpet of fantasy."[2] This was all made possible by a spectacular marriage of old mechanical technology with the new technology of electronics. "The film pushed this mechanism to the utmost mechanical verge and beyond, into a surrealism of dreams that money can buy," McLuhan tells us in *Understanding Media: The Extensions of Man*. He expounds further: "The Hollywood tycoons were not wrong in acting on the assumption that movies gave the American immigrant a means of self-fulfillment without any delay."[3]

Jimmy Durante's The Great Rupert

The Great Rupert follows the classic formula of the early film era, which McLuhan talks about in his analysis of the various extensions or outlets of mass media. Jimmy Conlin plays Joe Mahoney, a vaudeville performer, who is told that his act with the talented squirrel, Rupert, is a bore and a loser. Nobody cares. Mahoney abandons his little stage companion squirrel when the hard times hit. However, Rupert turns around and saves the day for his boss and the desperate Amendola family when the curious squirrel discovers a large hoard of cash and gets it into the right hands. The plot reflects the intuition of those early Hollywood moguls who sensed that audiences were looking for a light at the end of the tunnel in their own troubled lives.

Early in the movie, it's easy to see why Joe Mahoney thought he had a winner in his stage act with the tiny, tap-dancing squirrel Rupert. Joe lets Rupert know he is "the talk of the town" and will soon be performing before large crowds. He implores the attentive squirrel, "You won't let me down, will you, Rupert? You'll do everything just like I told you?" Rupert's tiny head is barely visible under a Scottish beret; nevertheless, he nods a hearty "yes" and begins a little jig. Rupert puts one leg out, then another. Joe plays his accordion and sings a song about Rupert with such lyrics as "He jumps a rope gracefully, and you ought to see him climb a tree." The two entertainers have their song-and-dance rehearsal well under way when Phil Davis, a talent scout who books shows, walks through the door and scowls at what he sees.

Davis offers his assessment of the squirrel act, and he does not mince words: "You mean, that's it? A squirrel?" He recalls Joe's past act with a lion and wonders how Joe has been reduced from work-

One of the first notable movies to boast a squirrel in a starring role was 1950's *The Great Rupert*, featuring comedian Jimmy Durante. In this movie, Rupert is a failing vaudeville squirrel performer that eventually saves the day for several humans down on their luck. To this day, Rupert and other movie squirrels have inspired gifts of squirrel nutcrackers, squirrel apparel, squirrel welcome mats and squirrel door hangers (photograph by Ursula Ruhl).

ing with a fearsome lion to a minuscule squirrel. "Joe, look, a lion is a big savage beast. He's vicious, ruthless, a bloodthirsty killer from the faraway jungles of deadliest Africa. But a little pipsqueak thing like a squirrel that anyone can see any place at any park, any time, is just a ... besides, he's so small they'd never see him from the balcony!"

Depressed and demoralized, Joe Mahoney has no job and no money, and he is forced to abandon his best friend in the town of the Dingle and Amendola families. Having lost his mentor, it seems that Rupert will have to find companionship with other squirrels and start residing in a tree. However, Rupert uses his wits to work his way into the home of Frank and Katie Dingle and their son, Pete, settling down in the rafters and walls. The enterprising Rupert literally makes a bed in a stack of cash that the skinflint Frank Dingle hides behind his wall molding.

The plot thickens when the destitute Amendolas and their daughter, Rosalinda, rent an apartment from landlord Frank Dingle right next door to the Dingle clan. Right away young Pete Dingle has an eye for Rosalinda. After all, Rosalinda is played by Terry Moore, who was a starlet in *Come Back, Little Sheba* and spent some time in actual life as the wife of Howard Hughes. In addition, Pete is played by the handsome Tom Drake (better known as "the boy next door" whom Judy Garland sang about in *Meet Me in St. Louis*). Tongues had to be wagging in movie houses when this couple got together for scenes in *The Great Rupert*.

However, the real gossip in the movie begins when the impoverished Amendola family suddenly comes into a lot of unexplainable cash. Rosalinda's mother had prayed to the heavens for some money to buy shoes for her poor daughter. At this point, Rupert begins to throw Frank Dingle's dollars through a hole in the house wall, and they float down upon the grateful Amendolas. Their prayers are answered. The Amendolas pay off all their debts. They splurge on themselves. They help the town's businesses. All this spending raises suspicion, so that the FBI, IRS and local police swarm the Amendolas' home. In the end, they all have a laugh. No one goes to jail—not even the squirrel responsible for throwing around all the cash. Everybody lives happily ever after.

Reviews of *The Great Rupert* are all over the map. Some critics think the squirrel gets too much face time; others think he deserves more. Some find the whole scenario amateurish and unbelievable, from the antics of the squirrel to the idea that the beautiful Rosalinda, played by Terry Moore, could be sired by the hilarious and homely Jimmy Durante. Many reviewers lament that *The Great Rupert*, which was subsequently renamed *The Christmas Wish*, did not take full advantage of its potential to be a moving Christmas story and a seasonal favorite. More holiday decorations on the set, along with a good rewrite of the script to capitalize on Christmas lore and magic, could have made this movie a contender with *It's a Wonderful Life* and *Christmas Vacation*.

Realistically, however, squirrel admirers have little to complain about when it comes to *The Great Rupert*. Rupert gets to show off his talents at

The Great Rupert is based on a story by Ted Allan, which was published as a children's book under the title *Willie the Squowse*. The squirrel in *The Great Rupert* plays music and tap dances. Rupert's head is often barely visible under his Scottish beret, but he still manages to dance a jig in his plaid kilt.

the beginning of the film, and he rebounds from the humiliation of being called a pipsqueak animal, a twerp that pales in comparison to the beasts of the jungle. Rupert ends up sleeping in a bed of cash and makes a lot of people happy when he begins distributing it. He also gets a few laughs at his antics and has the privilege of having the film named after him. Of course, it's true that Rupert has a shoddy, fake stand-in at times that looks like a corpse. For the most part, Rupert is played by a live squirrel—except when he is played by a stuffed squirrel that is manipulated by slow-motion animation to look real. Among other things, the stuffed squirrel is pulled across a busy street with an attached wire. (Given how many squirrels are flattened daily by encounters with autos, the fur-and-blood squirrel who played Rupert surely had cause to be grateful that the risks were taken by a stuffed stand-in.)

Squirrels Are for Christmas

National Lampoon's *Christmas Vacation* and the earlier Christmas classic, *It's a Wonderful Life*, both feature noteworthy squirrels. The squirrel in *It's a Wonderful Life* is lucky to appear in one of the most critically acclaimed films ever made. Celebrated director Frank Capra referred to this film as his personal favorite of all the movies he made.[4] Jimmy Stewart, Donna Reed, Lionel Barrymore and Henry Travers all deliver memorable performances in this seasonal favorite, but the amiable squirrel's contribution to this holiday mainstay also deserves mention. The squirrel can be counted among the many pets of the bumbling Uncle Billy, who is employed by his nephew George Bailey's savings and loan business in Bedford Falls, New York.

Bailey, played by the legendary Jimmy Stewart, presumably employs his blundering Uncle Billy out of family obligation, if not the kindness of his heart. However, Billy has a role at the bank well above his pay grade, and he fouls things up royally when he misplaces a large sum of the bank's money. That crucial mistake puts the bank on the edge of insolvency and sets off a chain of events that finally lead Bailey to contemplate suicide on Christmas Eve. His family is spared a tragedy, and Bailey is saved from self-destruction, only through the intervention of a strange fellow named Clarence Odbody. Clarence happens to be an angel, second class, who is back on Earth to try to earn his wings. If he can save the despairing Bailey, he can make it back to Heaven with a pair of wings and first-class status.

Uncle Billy has endured his share of criticism for causing the savings and loan crisis in Bedford Falls, a calamity that even Heaven could not ignore. He has been accused of having a drinking problem and obsessing over his pets. He engages in this tomfoolery rather than minding the savings and loan's assets, which are so critical to the average citizens of Bedford Falls. A critique by Peter K. Rosenthal, film reviewer for *The Onion*, offers a satirical and withering assessment of the character of Uncle Billy. Rosenthal hammers Billy for paying undue attention to the pets in his office, rather than caring about the fate of his nephew's business patrons.[5]

Uncle Billy and his squirrel have been immortalized, not only because the movie is shown countless times during the Christmas season but also because they are the subject of questions in trivia contests year-round throughout America. What pets did Uncle Billy own? In most cases, the squirrel is readily identified as one of at least three of Uncle Billy's pets in the trivia competitions on the subject of movies.

With all due respect to Uncle Billy's pet squirrel, the squirrel in *Christmas Vacation* is considerably more famous. This movie squirrel, which almost destroys the Griswold family's holiday, is easily the most popular merchandised squirrel in the history of cinema. Best-selling squirrel shirts are emblazoned with such logos as "Griswold Squirrel Removal," "It's a funny, squeaky sound," and, of course, "SQUIRRRRRRELLL!!!" Sweatshirts and sweaters feature a smug squirrel sitting in the Griswold Christmas tree or a frantic squirrel running roughshod over a fallen Yuletide tree. Coffee mugs and travel tumblers are decorated with the Griswold Family Squirrel. A company called Trendsetters offers a delicate, hanging, painted glass plate with the Christmas squirrel jumping though the "O" in "JOY." Hallmark offers a glistening Christmas ornament showing Clark Griswold with the squirrel clinging to his back. For the baby at Christmas, there is a movie squirrel pet toy, a colorful squirrel baby bib and an infant creeper.

This cornucopia of Griswold Family Christmas paraphernalia is all the more impressive when one considers that the squirrel ultimately logs less than four minutes in the movie, but these are obviously memorable minutes that combine to make a vintage Christmas squirrel tale. The movie itself consists of a series of holiday vignettes that many Americans find familiar, beginning with the family search for the perfect Christmas tree, although Clark Griswold (played by Chevy Chase) takes the hunt to extremes. He drags the family out into the country on a perilous drive and leads his wife, son and daughter on an epic walk through deep drifts of snow. They locate the right tree, only to discover that they haven't a saw or an axe to chop it down. They pull it out by the roots and somehow wrestle it onto their car. The tree turns out to be far too large for their suburban Chicago home, but that does not deter Clark from squeezing and squashing it into his living room.

The Christmas tree fiasco kicks off a series of events that culminate in Clark blowing his stack and coming to the disheartening realization that his efforts to have "a fun, old-fashioned family Christmas" are for naught. Among the disasters that lead him to that disappointing conclusion: a struggle to cover the exterior of his house with twenty-five thousand twinkling lights fails multiple times and even puts his life in jeopardy; a throng of obnoxious and argumentative relatives crowd into his house, including the strange family of Cousin Eddie (played by Randy Quaid); and a Christmas Eve dinner featuring a smoldering, overcooked turkey is interrupted by family shenanigans that leave poor Clark Griswold's eyes bulging wide with disbelief.

The most traumatic setbacks for Clark in his mission to have "a fun, old-fashioned family Christmas" can be attributed to animals that invade his holiday space. The uninvited Cousin Eddie not only has his wife, Catherine, and kids, Rocky and Ruby Sue, in tow but also brings his hunting dog, Snot, to the Griswold family get-together. Snot is a Rottweiler with a slimy sinus condition. He also has a little "Mississippi leg hound in him" (a nasty horn-dog habit that the dog displays on occasion). Additional bad habits that Snot manifests include raiding the kitchen trash, gnawing on turkey remains underneath the dining room table, and noisily yakking up bones that get caught in his throat and can't be digested.

A family cat also causes trouble for the Griswold family as they strive to have a merry holiday gathering. During dinner, the fluffy feline goes to work chewing on the wires of the Christmas tree lights, pulling the plug out of the wall socket. When Clark plugs the lights back in, the surprised cat becomes the victim of a noisy, fiery electrical short and literally burns through the floor, leaving an outline of itself that smolders in the destroyed piece of carpet. Clark is flabbergasted, while Cousin Eddie finds the whole incident an opportunity for some choice wisecracking. "If that cat had nine lives, she just spent them all," Eddie remarks. He then makes another astute observation: "fried pussy cat."

In addition to the cat snuffed out by its own curiosity and the Rottweiler with the boorish manners mirroring those of his master, there's a third animal that rips apart the Griswold family Christmas convocation at the seams. That would, of course, be an invasive squirrel. When the first tree in the living room is destroyed, Clark chops down a fir tree down in his yard and drags it into the house. A squirrel hitches a ride in the tree, unbeknownst to the Griswold clan. As they sit around the tree and enjoy the approach of Christmas, Aunt Bethany thinks she hears a strange noise coming from inside the house. "Do you hear it? It's a funny, squeaky sound," she observes. Her skeptical husband, Uncle Lewis, responds that she is so old and deaf, she wouldn't hear "a dump truck driving through a nitroglycerine plant."

Clark also senses that there is something wrong. Something is stirring and making odd sounds. When he spreads the thick branches to look into the Christmas tree, the unwanted intruder jumps out at the flustered master of the house. Chaos ensues. For a time, the squirrel cannot be located until it is found clinging to the back of Clark's red Santa suit. This is when the famous cry—"SQUIRRRRRRRELLL!!!"—is heard, at which point the pillaging Rottweiler gets into the act. Snot literally crashes through the wood panel of the kitchen door in his quest to capture the wily squirrel. The assembled family can only watch helplessly and in horror as the frightening chase noisily moves from room to room.

Snot growls and snarls and leaves a trail of destruction as he pursues the squirrel up the staircase to the second floor, back down the staircase and over the dining room table. At one point, the squirrel jumps up on a shelf of the china cabinet; in reaching for the small chattering prey, Snot knocks down the entire cabinet and all its contents. Snot is hot on the squirrel's trail when he heads toward the front door, where Clark is ready to open it and let the two beasts out into the front yard. By some strange happenstance, the Griswolds' next-door neighbor Margo Chester (played by Julia Louis-Dreyfus) is at the door, ready to knock and give Clark a piece of her mind for all his disturbing Christmas upheavals. Unfortu-

Two Christmas season movies with squirrels in the cast are It's a Wonderful Life from 1946 and National Lampoon's Christmas Vacation from 1989. Christmas Vacation in particular has spawned gag gifts such as mugs, pillows, stuffed squirrel dolls and T-shirts featuring Chevy Chase's character, Clark Griswold, and the squirrel that brought ruin on the Griswold family Christmas (photograph by Ursula Ruhl).

nately for her, when Clark opens the door, the squirrel jumps out onto Margo's chest, and then Snot jumps at the squirrel, knocking Margo down. Clark conveniently closes the door on all the mayhem outside and declares to the family, "Gone!"

The squirrel scene in *Christmas Vacation* has inspired the creation of countless keepsakes and funny souvenirs. The scene also has been reviewed multiple times to determine the source of its popularity, with one analysis insisting that parents relate to the uproar in the movie because the squirrel reminds them of their own children. Some points of similarity between the wild squirrel and the young brood at home: they both speak in languages that are mostly unintelligible; they leave the floor and the dining room table a total mess; and they're completely quiet one minute, then the next they are jumping on their parents' backs and taking away their breath. (These examples of parallels in behavior and demeanor are just for starters.)

Christmas Vacation and *It's a Wonderful Life* have both become television-watching traditions. Families have bonded over these two movies for decades now, whether on cable, video, DVD, or new digital transmission options. No matter how it is viewed, who can forget the angel, Clarence Odbody, trying to earn his wings by saving George Bailey? Who can forget Cousin Eddie trying to explain Snot's "Mississippi leg hound" problem to the frazzled Clark Griswold? Who can forget Uncle Billy's pet squirrel? Finally, who can forget the crazy squirrel making a funny, squeaking sound in the Griswold family Christmas tree?

Winter's Bone *and PETA Protests*

Jennifer Lawrence achieved stardom as Ozark teenager Ree Dolly in the dark film *Winter's Bone* (2010) about life in a southwest Missouri town suffering from economic devastation and the meth crisis that afflicts so many rural areas. Ree's mother is mentally ill and basically beyond hope. Her criminal father, Jessup, is on the run from the law for cooking methamphetamine. Young Ree struggles to keep what's left of the family from completely unraveling. She bravely attempts to care for her two younger siblings, but she gets some bad news when the sheriff informs her that Jessup put their home up for bond and now has disappeared. Ree then takes up a dangerous mission to find her father. The ragged household that she manages is in jeopardy, and its fate is in her hands. Her outlaw kin's code of silence puts her own life in danger as she desperately seeks to uncover her father's whereabouts.

Winter's Bone won critical acclaim and several Academy Award nominations, including a Best Actress nomination for Lawrence. The film, directed by Debra Granik, also won the Grand Jury Prize for dramatic film at the 2010 Sundance Film Festival.[6] Despite all the awards and accolades, however, the movie seemed to receive the most ink for the controversial scenes in which Ree shoots and skins a squirrel to feed her twelve-year-old brother, Sonny, and six-year-old sister, Ashlee. Several of the squirrel skinning scenes posted on YouTube have received thousands of hits. They show the grim reality of youngsters struggling to feed themselves in backwoods America when their wayward parents can no longer provide for them.

In the clips, Ree enlists her siblings to help hunt for squirrel to put on the table. Little Ashlee is the first one to spot a squirrel, and as Ree takes aim through the rifle sight, Ashlee pulls the trigger. Later the three of them are shown at a rickety picnic table with their bounty, and Ree asks whether they want the squirrels fried or stewed. Perhaps the film clip that leaves the most viewers squeamish is the one in which they all grab the squirrel's coat and pull down the furry skin to reveal the meat. Ree then asks Sonny to help gut the squirrel so it can be prepared for a meal, but he, apparently repulsed, replies that he does not want to do it. Refusing to let him off the hook, Ree tells him that in this life, "there's a bunch of stuff you're going to have to get over being scared of."

The squirrel cleaning and gutting scenes not only disgusted Sonny but also horrified movie audiences and animal lovers. The cleaning episode outraged People for the Ethical Treatment of Animals (PETA) members, who were appalled that the scene was real and not simulated. As a Kentucky girl who knows a little bit about what happens in mountain country, Jennifer Lawrence viewed all the hubbub and reaction over squirrels as crocodile tears at best. She was curt, terse and to the point in rebuffing PETA. Later the *New York Post* suggested that Lawrence might have been channeling her famous *Hunger Games* character, Katniss Everdeen, when she went on the offensive against PETA. (In the later movie, released two years after *Winter's Bone*, Katniss hunts animals—including squirrels—for survival, an exercise that prepares her for the later competitions that require her to slay her peers for the entertainment of corrupt government elites.) Lawrence showed little patience for the complaints about her squirrel gutting in *Winter's Bone*. "I should say it wasn't real, for PETA.. .. But screw PETA," Lawrence told *Rolling Stone*.[7]

Despite the tough comments from Lawrence, the animal rights organization backed off a few notches, remarking that the actress was young, barely out of her teens, and would wise up about the plight of animals, especially squirrels, as she got more experience in the real world. "She's young and the plight of animals somehow hasn't yet touched her heart," said Ingrid Newkirk, president of PETA. Newkirk also referenced Henry David Thoreau for the blog *Gothamist*, noting that the famous nature writer said, "The squirrel you kill in jest, dies in earnest." Then she added, "We are told that this squirrel was hit by a car, but when people kill animals, it is the animals who are 'screwed,' not PETA, and one day I hope she will try to make up for any pain she might cause any animal who did nothing but try to eke out a humble existence in nature."[8]

Lawrence eventually conceded that the squirrel episode did bother her and that she was sickened when a friend of her brother taught her how to skin a squirrel. She said that when he cut into the squirrel, she had to go into the house and cry and let him complete the job without her. PETA subsequently eased up even more on Lawrence, stating that she was bound to have a healthier respect for animals in the future. With regard to the "Screw PETA" remark, the People for the Ethical Treatment of Animals released a statement: "That was just a throw-away remark and we have our bet on Jennifer ending up joining the ranks of other young celebrities like Natalie Portman, Lea Michele, and Kellan Lutz, who are using their influence to help animals."[9]

All the tender feelings on behalf of the gutted squirrel must have been a bit amusing for the folks in southwest Missouri, where squirrel hunting, killing and gutting are a normal part of life. Indeed, they may have wondered why there was not more sympathy expressed for Ree Dolly's father, meth cooker or not. In the movie, Ree gets bloodied up for snooping into her father's whereabouts. She finally is led to a pond, where she finds her daddy's submerged remains in the cold, murky water. After her discovery of the corpse, his hands are cut off with a chainsaw, and Ree takes them to the sheriff. She tells him that someone left the severed appendages on her porch, thus proving that her father is no longer on the lam.

Ree's actions save the family home, and she receives a portion of the cash bond that was put up to try to keep her father from jumping bail. Ree has good news for her brother and sister, assuring them that she will never leave them. However, they are definitely not out of the woods, and it's likely that they will all be hunting, killing and gutting squirrels together in the future. After all, a dinner of squirrel meat, whether fried or stewed, is still regular culinary fare in some parts of the Ozarks. PETA's concern for the fate of the squirrel in *Winter's Bone* is not a major consideration for hungry folks in the Missouri backwoods.

Anchorman 2 *Presents a Skiing Squirrel*

Television news is an easy mark for comedy and satire. Will Ferrell's *Anchorman* movie series has plenty of fun taking on the romantic intrigue, bloated egos, senseless industry competition and superficial news of the broadcast business. Lampooning "eye-witless news" is not exactly a formidable challenge. Shallow stories and shallow personalities abound in the real world of TV news, as well as in the television sitcoms and movies that satirize what goes on in the newsroom. It was bad enough in the 1970s, when television news stations only had to compete with each other. Now they must compete with cable news, bloggers, websites, Twitter, Snapchat and other forms of social media. It's a continual downward spiral to reach the lowest common denominator in the search for ratings and holding onto a fickle audience for news.

Two landmark movies of last century that take aim at television news are *Network* (the famous 1976 film based on Paddy Chayefsky's masterpiece screenplay) and *Broadcast News* (a 1987 film directed and produced by James L. Brooks). In *Network*, an older news anchorman named Howard Beale gets wind that he's being pink-slipped, and he threatens to shoot himself on live television. Instead, he gives his audience an angry evening news tirade, which turns out to be a huge ratings boost for his TV network. Beale's unhinged stunt allows ambitious producer Diana Christensen free reign to devise more bizarre news programming that optimizes profits and also minimizes any adherence to traditional journalistic standards.

In *Broadcast News*, a mercurial, high-strung news producer finds herself romantically attracted to a telegenic airhead anchorman, even though she detests his lack of journalism ethics and his superficial approach to delivering the news. It would make more sense for her to reciprocate the love of her best friend, a talented and serious news reporter who struggles in front of the camera. However, love is neither logical nor sensible. In the end, everything blows up for all three characters in this newsroom triangle. *Broadcast News* has some good lessons about the pitfalls of office romances. This movie also reveals how journalists wrestle with tough questions about what constitutes news and how it should be presented responsibly.

Holly Hunter plays Jane Craig, an ambitious news producer with prickly ethical standards, who reveals her concerns about maintaining quality journalism early in the movie. She gives a lecture to colleagues at a conference on the state of TV news, in which Craig denounces the dangers to democracy when real news is replaced by fluff and amusing feature material. She is met with yawns, and some in the audience even walk out on her. Craig makes one last attempt to drive her point home by showing a tape of an inane domino exhibition that every network ran instead of covering something serious. Suddenly, Craig's audience takes an interest, applauding the feature story of rows of cascading dominoes. Craig plaintively observes that, of course, a domino display can be entertaining, but it's not news.

The endless collapsing dominoes story featured in *Broadcast News* serves as a metaphor for the collapse of American journalism standards over the years. This scene can also be a metaphor for how the concern over those declining standards has played out in cinema portrayals. In 1976, the concern was shrill, with *Network* revealing how television news will put on anything provocative to hold audiences, even a deranged and ranting anchorman posing as a prophet. In 1987, the concern was muted and plaintive, with *Broadcast News* revealing how television news will resort to the most trivial feature fare to hold audiences, even stacks of falling dominoes. In 2013's *Anchorman 2: The Legend Continues*, there is no longer any real concern about quality broadcast journalism—concern is futile and passé. As with the first movie, *Anchorman: The Legend of Ron Burgundy* (2004), any concern about quality news itself is laughable, certainly not to be taken seriously. And *Anchorman 2* reveals how television news will stoop to attracting and holding viewers with anything—even a performing squirrel.

The *Anchorman* movies have breaking news, industry competition, tremendous egos, romantic triangles in the newsroom and more. What they don't have is any serious exploration of ethical issues in broadcast journalism. Being farce, these movies present television news as farcical. Nonetheless, the very serious Newseum in Washington, D.C. (in collaboration with Paramount Studios), offered an exhibition relating to the sequel with a display of props and other items from the films of the broadcast news anchorman, Ron Burgundy.[10] In addition, *Anchorman 2* has a squirrel and some newsroom conversation about squirrels.

In *Anchorman 2*, Ron Burgundy (played by Will Ferrell) sits at his anchor desk and presents the news. Behind Burgundy sit his colleagues, tossing a football back and forth (much like pundits and commentators do regularly today on the FOX Cable News set). Burgundy prepares his audience for "a Channel 4 news exclusive" caught by his "lucky cameraman who happened to catch an unusual aquatic daredevil." The star squirrel then entertains the nightly news audience, perched on his water skis and pulled by a tiny boat. A close-up shows the squirrel's bushy tail skimming the waves as he circles the water several times. Burgundy laughs and tells his news audience, "His name is Nutty the Squirrel, and he's three years old. How about that? That squirrel can water ski!"

The truly ironic aspect of the cinematic TV news segment about Nutty is that there is absolutely nothing ironic or satirical about featuring a skiing squirrel on TV news. Been there, done that. Reality trumps fantasy. The skiing squirrel has appeared on dozens of real television news programs around the United States. It's not even necessary to paraphrase Burgundy: "Our lucky cameraman happened to catch an unusual aquatic daredevil.... His name is Twiggy the Squirrel, and he's three years old. How about that? That squirrel can water ski!"

As detailed in chapter 3, in 1978, Twiggy the actual, original waterskiing squirrel made television news history in Orlando, Florida, with a debut on WFTV's 6:00 and 11:00 p.m. newscasts. Within hours, the daredevil squirrel was booked on *Good Morning America* and entertaining a national audience. That same evening, ABC News anchor Peter Jennings covered Twiggy on skis on *World News Tonight*.[11] Twiggy's caretaker and publicity agent took him on a skiing tour across America and the world, with the squirrel water shows taking center stage at literally hundreds of conventions. At those conventions, the local television station cameras arrived in droves to cover Twiggy riding the waves. So, who needs a seemingly endless colorful cascade of dominoes falling in multiple rows for the nightly news? Who needs the proverbial "man bites dog" story to grab the attention of a listless audience? Just get that squirrel. Put a water-skiing squirrel on television news, and prep the smiling anchorman: "How about that? That squirrel can water ski!"

Flesh-Eating Squirrels: Horror's Future?

On the heels of the cult success of *Sharknado*, an apocalyptic horror film in which bloodthirsty sharks rain down from whirling tornadoes, it was only a matter of time—probably mere nanoseconds—before ideas for a *Squirrelnado* movie were generated. The movie has yet to be produced, but the merchandising is already under way, as well as spinoffs, such as the proposed *Squirrels*. The trailer for *Squirrels* offers the tacky tagline: "Hold On to Your Nuts."

Investors in these movie franchises might want to hold on to their dollars. If squirrels were the kind of animal that could star in a horror flick, wouldn't they have found a place on the silver screen a long time ago? Enough scary animals to fill all the decks of Noah's Ark have already been featured in movies made with the sole mission of scaring humans to death.

Horror movies that draw on the worst of nature (better known as creature features) have never really picked up on the threat posed by rampaging squirrels. As of this writing, there are no gargantuan squirrels that have emerged from nuclear testing sites ready to satisfy their ravenous appetites by gorging on human flesh and blood. Mad scientists have not accidentally spawned bloodthirsty squirrels ready to suck the life from the necks of little children. Unsuspecting hunters in the darkest woods have not been swarmed by a mutated throng of crazed squirrels eager to gnaw through their rosy cheeks to dine on human tongue. Girl Scouts at a pajama party in the suburbs have not succumbed to armies of rabid squirrels sweeping down the chimney and crashing through the windows.

Forget the idea of carnivorous squirrels—human movie buffs have already eyeballed frog monsters from hell, giant tarantulas, humanoid turkeys, abnormally large hermit crabs, shocking electric eels, prehistoric piranhas, leviathan squids, devil monster stingrays, giant snails, giant cuttlefish, giant horseshoe crabs, giant lobsters, an enormous octopus, super vampire bats, behemoth cave bears, monstrous sloths, atomic apes, feral dog packs, wolf-like canines, cloned saber-toothed felines, man-eating lions, enormous Bengal tigers, flesh-eating feral pigs, corpulent razorbacks, ape-like aliens, blood monkeys, gargantuan gorillas, beast-like apes, terrorizing rats, killer rats, brain-eating rats, scratch-fever rats, genetically engineered rats, graveyard shift rats, rogue white buffalo, zombie beavers, returning woolly mammoths, elephants gone berserk, giant rabbits, and abnormally large shrews (among others). Where are the abnormally large squirrels?[12]

What about sharks? The roll call for monster sharks can go on forever. Stupendous sharks roam the deep and swim in the shallows. There are giant two-headed sharks, five-headed sharks, sharks that fly in tornados, radioactive sharks, abnormally large sharks, prehistoric snow-dwelling sharks, tiger sharks, undead great white sharks, killer albino sharks, great-jawed sharks in 3-D, prehistoric goblin sharks, raging sharks, toxic sharks, slithering sandbar sharks, sharks of the Ozarks, global swarming sharks, swamp sharks, spring break sharks, sharks in women's prisons, trailer park sharks ... but where are the abnormally large squirrels?

Even loathsome lampreys get screen time, while squirrels languish. Barely evolved insects are firmly established in the movie kingdom, while squirrels receive nothing but stinging rejection. Among the insect stars are naked jungle ants, bone snatcher ants, killer fire ants, deadly bee swarms, savage monster bees, giant flies and maggots, mutant mosquitos, mosquito-human hybrids, alien cockroaches, mutant cockroaches that can start fires, three-headed moths, giant death's head hawk moths, king killer moths, wasp women, black swarm moths, prehistoric rhinoceros beetles, giant praying mantises, giant grasshoppers, assorted giant bugs, and mutant plague locusts. Has anyone seen the abnormally large squirrels?

So far, as of this writing, the crazed, carnivorous cinema squirrels exist only in abbreviated movie trailers. A 2014 movie trailer for a proposed squirrel horror movie opens in a lovely wooded suburb with a grandmother declaring it to be a "beautiful day" to her perky little granddaughter. Grandma spots a squirrel in the tree, and she invites the youngster to grab a morsel from her goody bag and feed the squirrel. The squirrel gets excited and hops back and forth in anticipation, and the child looks back to her grandmother, who smiles with approval.

However, when the precocious little girl turns back to the squirrel, it leaps onto her face and begins biting her with great ferocity. Grandma, the squirrel and the little girl wrestle on the ground together, until finally Grandma gets a grip on the animal and hurls it against a tree. At that point, offended squirrels race in from all directions to converge on the trees above the terrified humans. They have assembled for an attack—and Grandma lets out a blood-curdling scream.

At last count, the YouTube trailer for the squirrel horror movie had collected about seven hundred thousand views over four years and had yet to morph into an actual movie. Perhaps the fly in the ointment is that squirrels simply are not terrifying. They don't have what it takes. They don't have the bulk of flesh-eating feral pigs. They don't have the spindly, hairy legs that carry a gigantic tarantula. They don't have the slashing, giant claws of behemoth cave bears. They don't have the jagged, stabbing barbs of angry stingrays. They don't have the impenetrable shells of abnormally large cockroaches. They don't have the steely, penetrating eyes of agitated, beast-like apes. Squirrels are anxious little balls of fur that frantically bury acorns (and, more often than not, forget just where they have stashed their treasures).

Live squirrels that have found roles in the movies discussed in this chapter are relatively docile creatures and, when faced with danger, are more likely to run than to confront their adversaries. After losing his dancing role in a vaudeville act, the squirrel in *The Great Rupert* finds another way to ingratiate himself with humans and to help them as well as himself. Uncle Billy's pet squirrel in *It's a Wonderful Life* is as benign and bumbling as Billy himself. The *Christmas Vacation* squirrel only causes household mayhem after being forced to flee for his life as a nasty Rottweiler snaps at his tail and chases him from room to room. The squirrel in *Winter's Bone* involuntarily sacrifices his life for the good of Ree Dolly and her siblings. And in *Anchorman 2* a squirrel finds his way onto television news for a furry feature piece, thanks to his entertaining performance on water skis.

Live squirrels are rather benign and usually friendly to humans in the movies in which they have found stardom. Animated squirrels that inhabit the world of cartoons and movies are pretty much on a par with their real-live counterparts in cinema. They are entertaining, harmless and primarily helpful to humans. Consider Rocket J. Squirrel, the clever companion to loveable moose Bullwinkle, who continually saves the day for the United States (and in a very humorous way), fending off the scurrilous schemes of those who would do harm to humankind.

Animated movie squirrels have been on the same warm and fuzzy wavelength as Rocky, although the squirrels in the recent *Nut Job* movies have had their acorns roasted by any number of movie reviewers. Animated fellows in the *Nut Job* movies are by no means horror movie squirrels, but they have been heavily criticized for inhabiting very thin story plots and being involved in scenes with a little too much violence for children. After all, animated squirrels are mostly for kids and should be appropriate for their young audience. They should not be monsters. Critics argue that they have a responsibility to behave more like the storybook squirrels going back all the way to the golden age of children's book author Beatrix Potter.

6

Cartoons and Animated
Movie Squirrels

Squirrels have managed to channel themselves into virtually every medium of mass communication. They have found a prominent place in between the covers of children's books for more than a century. The bushy-tailed rodents squeeze their way onto newspaper pages and into the headlines with some regularity. Squirrels squander precious TV time as news directors decide to make room for their antics on evening broadcasts. They squeal and chatter with delight when they become stars of the movie industry. And it doesn't stop there. With the help of cartoonists who transform them into jet-propelled flyers, secret agents, slapstick comedians and more, squirrels have a long track record of work in animation. Animated squirrels, whether on television or in movies, become talkative and quick-witted, often assuming the voices of big-name movie stars. They have even been converted into digital forms of media, making them accessible on a variety of electronic platforms. There is no nook, niche or cranny of media technology that squirrels haven't squirmed their way into—much to the edification, entertainment and exasperation of human audiences.

One of the first great cartoon squirrels was an amiable Cold War hero named Rocky Squirrel, who entertained millions of baby boomers in their early years, which coincided with the early years of television. Also known as Rocket J. Squirrel, the high-flying Rocky helped foil the schemes of villains Boris Badenov and Natasha Fatale, who worked in the service of "Fearless Leader," a dictator presumably modeled after a Russian autocrat such as Nikita Khrushchev. Indeed, *The Rocky and Bullwinkle Show* aired at the height of the Cold War, from 1959 to 1964, a period when America was at odds with Khrushchev's Soviet Union over atomic bomb tests and missiles in Cuba. These were the years of fallout shelters being constructed in high-end suburbs, with the prospect of atomic mushroom clouds on the horizon as warning sirens wailed. These were the years of "duck and cover," when children in grade schools learned to hunch under a classroom desk and to not look into a glowing sky if there was a flash as bright as the sun.

Perhaps it was comforting for American children and parents to know that at least there was an extraordinary squirrel that had their backs in a war of wits with Russian spies. It also had to be reassuring that the precocious cartoon squirrel Rocky had a know-it-all friend in a moose named Bullwinkle. An interesting side note from that time: When Rocky's creators showed up at the White House gate with petitions for statehood for "Moosylvania," they were turned away.[1] No one likes being snubbed, but this was truly a matter of bad timing. President John F. Kennedy had his hands full with the frightening discovery that the Russians had installed atomic missiles in Cuba that could vaporize U.S. cities in a matter of minutes after being launched. If Rocky and Bullwinkle had been on the case, perhaps the most dangerous nuclear weapons crisis in the atomic age could have been averted before we came "eyeball to eyeball" with potential catastrophe.

Rocket J. Squirrel had a good run on television as a clever cartoon character that teamed up with a friendly moose. However, his much-anticipated animated movie, *The Adventures of Rocky and Bullwinkle*, was not so successful. Despite the dismal box office results, the many fans of Rocky the Flying Squirrel transformed the 2000 movie into a cult film.

In the same year as the Cuban Missile Crisis, Agent 007 came onto the cinema scene to take on Russian espionage. The first movie covering the exploits of Agent 007, *Dr. No*, was released in 1962 and established the James Bond spy series as a film franchise that would have staying power into the next century. The amazing cinema success of Agent 007 inspired more than 20 movie spinoffs in the espionage genre within a few years. In the realm of animated, undercover squirrel cartoons, NBC debuted *The World of Atom Ant and Secret Squirrel* as a primetime special in 1965.[2] Secret Squirrel got his own show in 1966. Designated as Agent 000, the wily rodent employed a variety of gadgets to deter all archenemies, including an arms collection in his trench coat and deadly devices stored inside his ever-present fedora. Secret Squirrel, like Rocky Squirrel, was good for the kids (and not all that bad for the parents raising them in an uncertain age).

Jump ahead to the 1990s, when the Berlin Wall had fallen, the Soviet Union and its KGB spy network were in disarray, and peace in our time looked like a real possibility. It also was time for some of the best Hollywood minds to be enlisted in creating lighter cartoon comedy fare. Enter Slappy Squirrel and Skippy Squirrel, who emerged when Steven Spielberg and Warner Brothers collaborated to produce their children's offering of *Animaniacs*. The success of the cartoon series can be attributed to a formula involving youthful wit, screwball comedy and clever pop culture references.

The cartoon episodes covered subjects as varied as history, geography, astronomy and social studies. Slappy Squirrel, often characterized as grumpy, had reason to be a bit grouchy when facing such enemies as Walter Wolf. The old girl did find companionship in a tree with her young, chipper nephew Skippy Squirrel. Innocent Skippy idolized his crabby aunt Slappy, despite her shortcomings and scratchy demeanor. Slappy inspired sympathy because of her trials, tribulations and forbearance with Skippy's numerous emotional outbursts. Despite a downer duet of a grouchy aunt squirrel and an unpredictable nephew squirrel, *Animaniacs* achieved the distinction of being listed among the "60 Greatest Cartoons of All Time" by *TV Guide* in 2013.[3]

Any squirrel that can land a role on a television cartoon series called *SpongeBob SquarePants* is bound to be one strange creature. The underwater rodent named Sandy Cheeks lives up to the definition of profoundly weird in a mind-boggling way. *SpongeBob SquarePants* is the brainchild of marine biologist and animator Stephen Hillenburg for cable television's Nickelodeon. The cartoon follows the adventures of SpongeBob and his unusual friends, including Sandy Cheeks, who all live in the underwater city of Bikini Bottom. The highest-rated series to ever hit the Nickelodeon airwaves, the media franchise is estimated to have generated $13 billion in merchandising revenue.[4] The children's show began airing in 1999 to popular acclaim and within five years had inspired a feature film (released in 2004).

The SpongeBob character is an animated sea sponge that works as a fry cook at the Krusty Krab fast-food restaurant. He has the shape of a square-like kitchen sponge that often sports a large smile; protruding from that sponge are spindly legs attached to small feet outfitted with children's shoes.

SpongeBob's best friend is a pink starfish named Patrick Star who lives under a rock, while SpongeBob resides in a submerged pineapple. SpongeBob's many neighbors under the sea include Squidward, an unhappy octopus that just happens to work as a cashier in the Krusty Krab. Squidward is temperamental and dismissive toward SpongeBob and Patrick because he regards them as totally immature. Sandy Cheeks, by contrast, happens to be a fine underwater friend for SpongeBob. Sandy excels in scientific understanding and karate, and she wears a deep dive suit and helmet in order to survive in SpongeBob's habitat of 100 percent humidity. Originally from Texas, this lady squirrel lives in Bikini Bottom because she is involved in a science project funded by three landlubber chimpanzees. All of this makes sense in the cartoon world of *SpongeBob SquarePants*.

Animated squirrels have been shown to jump from cartoons to the movies with skills that parallel their ability to jump off tree limbs and onto roofs. *Over the Hedge* is a 2006 computer-animated film based on a comic strip by United Media. A DreamWorks Studio production, *Over the Hedge* achieved fame for the many creatures given voice by some of the most famous names in the movie business, including William Shatner, Wanda Sykes, Nick Nolte, Gary Shandling, Bruce Willis and Steve Carell.[5] One of Hollywood's highest-paid actors, Carell can take credit for the weird sounds that emanate from Hammy the crazy red squirrel. Carell is perfect in providing the voice works for Hammy, who is forever trying to find his misplaced nuts (a frequent double-entendre gag). When he's not looking for his nuts, the impish squirrel is squealing for his coveted cookies. Hammy's short attention span, combined with his love of nuts, makes this squirrel a credible cousin of the tree residents who act out in real life.

Two more animated movies featuring nut-loving tree residents—squirrels that again take on the voices of Hollywood superstars—are *The Nut Job* in 2014 and its sequel, aptly titled *The Nut Job 2*, in 2017. Both films garnered less than stellar reviews but managed to make millions of dollars at the box office even with relatively high production costs. Both benefit from star-studded voiceovers for the major animal characters, including the obnoxious lead squirrel named Surly. The 2014 movie includes the voices of Will Arnett, Brendan Fraser, Gabriel Iglesias, Jeff Dunham, Liam Neeson and Katherine Heigl. Many of these voices return in the 2017 movie. *The Nut Job 2* also benefits from a new member of the cast, Jackie Chan, who joined the action as a gang leader and one tough street mouse.[6]

The Nut Job is all about the antics of a trouble-making purple squirrel operating in the fictional town of Oakton. This squirrel was first seen in 2005 in a short animated film by director Peter Lepeniotis called *Surly Squirrel*. In *The Nut Job*, Surly accidentally destroys the winter food cache of his buddies in Liberty Park, a mistake that gets him banished to the mean streets of Oakton. Once Surly stumbles upon the town's nut shop, he figures out a plan for redemption that involves stealing the nuts from the shop for his friends. However, at around the same time that Surly and his team break into the nut shop, a group of mobsters is perpetrating a bank heist—and then all hell breaks loose.

Rocky Squirrel: Cold War Hero

The amazing aerial acrobatics of Rocket J. Squirrel inevitably raise the question: Can squirrels really fly? Rocky Squirrel, the loveable character in the 1960s cartoon *The Rocky and Bullwinkle Show*, manages to fly straight up like a guided missile, does loops in the sky like a stunt pilot, and then manages to land vertically like a British Harrier Jet. Squirrels with flight capabilities do actually exist in real life, and there are several varieties, ranging from the large, woolly flying squirrel of Afghanistan to the diminutive pygmy squirrel of the island of Borneo. However, all of the world's "flying squirrels" might be better labeled as "gliding squirrels." They are built in such a way that they appear to have wings when they spread their limbs, and these furry wings allow them to glide. In Missouri, a species of flying squirrel has been known to glide as much as 140 feet, but other flying squirrels around the globe have been known to glide almost three times that distance.[7]

Rocky Squirrel puts real flying squirrels to shame with his unique abilities, and he probably would never have been as entertaining as a cartoon hero if he had debuted as Rocky the Gliding Squirrel. Rocky is jet-propelled and, when in flight, sometimes leaves a streak of gray or a contrail, as jet aircraft are wont to do. Rocky also is a supersonic flying squirrel, which means he occasionally flies at speeds as high as 768 miles per hour. This results in a sonic boom caused by shock waves when he flies through the air faster than the speed of sound. When a sonic boom occurs, Rocky disappears and a giant "BLAM!" fills the cartoon sky. It's a good thing that Rocky always wears a protective aviator cap, much like the iconic, brown specimen worn by the original trans-Atlantic flyer Charles Lindbergh. However, Rocky's blue-green cap appears to be better equipped than Lindbergh's, as it sports aviation goggles. Of course, it also should be noted that Lindbergh never had a sidekick like Rocky's friend, the moose named Bullwinkle.

Rocky's flying abilities and aviation gear can be witnessed every time the lengthy musical opening theme plays for the start of another episode of *The Rocky and Bullwinkle Show*. The initial episode of the cartoon adventure series begins when scientists at the Slick Observatory gaze through their telescope at the moon to prove there is no life there. However, they are shocked to find a moose and a squirrel waving back at them from the moon's surface. The two creatures take off for Earth in their strange spacecraft, and when they land they are mistaken for moon people. The squirrel then introduces himself as "Rocky the Flying Squirrel," and he explains that both he and the moose are from Frostbite Falls, Minnesota. The scientists quickly realize that these two creatures are earthlings and have the secret formula to a jet fuel that can take mankind to the moon and back.

So, what is the secret formula for the jet fuel? It's actually Bullwinkle's grandmother's recipe for mooseberry fudge cake. Bullwinkle discovers how powerful the recipe is as a jet fuel when he lights his baking oven. Powered by the fudge cake batter, the oven takes off and lands on the moon. Rocky and Bullwinkle have to build their own rocket ship, fueled by another layer of Grandma's cake, so they can journey to the moon and retrieve it (after all, they still owe two payments on that oven). When the squirrel and moose return to Earth, the American government puts Rocky and Bullwinkle to work trying to duplicate the rocket formula. It's tough to do that, however, since the written recipe was torn in half during the explosive moon events. Bullwinkle laments, "I know how much, but not what of…." Meanwhile, the squirrel and the moose become targets for Boris Badenov and Natasha Fatale, who are intent on sabotaging the U.S. space program and the magic rocket fuel. They plot to deliver a crude bomb in a gift package to the boys, but the scheme literally blows up in the face of the clumsy Boris.

Many, if not most, of the episodes of the squirrel Rocky and his friends revolve around the floundering schemes of villains Boris and Natasha, who work in the service of "Fearless Leader" (presumably a Russian dictator). The show's Russian connection is thinly disguised, with the two scoundrels and their autocrat leader hailing from the fictitious state of "Pottsylvania." Badenov and Fatale are constantly pursuing the adventurous flying squirrel and the foppish moose. Sometimes they're after "moose and squirrel" because they've accidentally stumbled upon an amazing rocket fuel formula. In other episodes, they are after the boys for reasons that involve less international intrigue—for example, they just want to steal Bullwinkle's life savings from his paper route that are stuffed in his bed mattress.

In the mattress episode, Bullwinkle decides he can be an irresistible actor and must take his mattress full of life savings and head to Hollywood. The wise squirrel, Rocky, tries to talk him out of it. However, Bullwinkle is convinced that if he learns to be an actor with an "ultry sultry" stare, he will turn women to jelly. So, Rocky decides he must join his movie-struck friend on the trip to California. Boris and Natasha decide to head to California as well in an attempt to divest the moose of his life savings. Rocky eventually helps protect his best buddy from the worst.

Just detailing the squirrelly plots about Rocky, a jet age aerial ace, does not do justice to the ingenuity of this show. Although the animation is amateurish, the writing is exceptional. The show employs puns and word play on a masterful level. There is the moose bragging about his MIT education credentials after graduating from the Moose Institute of Toe-Dancing. And then there is that humbling moment when Bullwinkle is given a scholarship to Wossamotta U. The puns are always there, even when the plot lines are not. Consider the story of the jewel-encrusted ship that is eventually uncovered as the "ruby yacht" of Omar Khayyam. Consider an episode in which the squirrel admonishes the moose for reading a classic book titled *Maybe Dick*, about a legendary wailing whale. Bullwinkle learns that Maybe Dick was "big enough to swallow a whole ship—maybe. He could swim faster than any vessel in the sea—maybe. And he had been seen by sailors whose reputations for sobriety were beyond reproach—maybe." Rocky, however, is skeptical of all the claims about the wailing whale.

The Rocky and Bullwinkle Show was groundbreaking for many reasons, including the easily accessible inside jokes about the series itself. These hilarious quips were made by the actual characters on home TV screens. They would sometimes muse about how they hoped their program didn't get cancelled before the next episode. They would jest that advertisers might not be too happy with sponsoring the content of a particular episode. These irreverent comments were strictly for amusement and not a bit self-conscious. In no way were they meant to be taken seriously. It was all part of the fun. Rocket J. Squirrel was always inviting audiences to come along for the fun as a friend, not a huckster seeking ratings.

Rocky may be the most famous, influential animated squirrel of all time. Baby boomer Steven Spielberg, who had more success in Hollywood than Bullwinkle, has said that he turned on *Rocky and Bullwinkle* with his parents watching the show over his shoulder. They laughed in places he couldn't comprehend. He was impressed that a cartoon show could be shared and enjoyed with parents.[8] Matt Groening of *The Simpsons* said the squirrel and moose inspired his fantasy to grow up to have his own cartoon show.[9] Ray Bradbury, science-fiction writer and cartoon buff, said that any history of animation cannot leave out the squirrel and moose. According to Bradbury, they were unique because their cartoon show was witty and assumed you had a brain in your head.[10]

An amazing team of anthropoids, now passed on, made the animated squirrel and moose possible. Cartoonist Alex Anderson drew the boys. Jay Ward and Bill Scott brought them to life in scripts. June Foray, the queen of animation, provided many of the voices in the show, including that of the squirrel and the "dahlink" character of Natasha Fatale.[11] Unfortunately, attempts to revive Rocky and his friends and their brand of humor in the movies fell flat. In 1992, a feature film, *Boris and Natasha*, was less than stellar and easily forgotten. A 2000 live action remake for the cinema, *The Adventures of Rocky and Bullwinkle*, again proved that the original incarnation was not so easy to duplicate.

James Bond, Move Over for Secret Squirrel

Not too long after Rocky the Flying Squirrel disappeared from television airtime, a new squirrel appeared that answered to the moniker of Secret Squirrel. Secret Squirrel and his fez-wearing sidekick, Morocco Mole, faced many enemy agents determined to trip them up, just as Rocky and Bullwinkle were constantly harassed by the likes of Boris Badenov and Natasha Fatale. Secret Squirrel and Morocco Mole fought other enemy agents with a vast array of spy gadgets, including a machine gun cane and a collection of guns. NBC introduced the sleuth squirrel with its *The World of Atom Ant and Secret Squirrel* as a primetime special in 1965.[12] A year later, Secret Squirrel got his own show, and, as the cunning Agent 000, he took his orders from his secretive boss, Double-Q of the International Sneaky Service. Just like Agent 007 in the James Bond movies, Agent 000 had a number of archenemies, such as Yellow Pinkie (a parody of the Goldfinger villain out to eliminate the film hero James Bond).

Secret Squirrel does not have the suave demeanor or disarming wit of a seasoned master of espionage such as Agent 007. He typically enters the

Secret Squirrel landed his own television cartoon show in 1966 as the intrepid Agent 000. Secret Squirrel served as a cartoon parody of the popular spy genre movies that took off in the 1960s. Those secret agent movies included the James Bond films as well as the *Pink Panther* movie offerings. The bumbling Secret Squirrel had an interesting arsenal of weapons, but he was no James Bond.

headquarters of the International Sneaky Service headquarters wondering what his next assignment might be when he meets with his agency chief. When he asks the chief how he should find the bad guy that he is instructed to capture, the chief tells him to look the bad guy up in the phone book. Secret Squirrel confesses that it's this kind of wisdom that qualifies his boss to be chief, while he is a mere agent in the field.

Secret Squirrel may not have a lot of intellectual acumen or keen powers of observation, but he does have a super car that flies and can be folded up into an attaché case. Secret Squirrel is also equipped with the sort of weapons appropriate for an agent in triple figures, even if they are all zeroes. He has a squirt gun in his watch to extinguish the fuses on any bombs thrown his way. He has a hat that hides a cannon and a coat that is bulletproof. Inside his coat are four arms of choice: a zip gun, an atom gun, a secret ray gun, and a laser blazer gun. He also sports a cane that can be utilized as a machine gun. This is not a squirrel that you want in your backyard, but Secret Squirrel is more interested in international travel than hanging out in your trees. He has a set of disguises that allow him to travel incognito through all the world's capitals. However, his personality is not exactly exciting or cosmopolitan.

If Secret Squirrel is often found wanting in the personality and clever dialogue department, his sidekick and driver, Morocco Mole, is even more one-dimensional, with his knee-jerk line that he repeats mechanically every time the duo's car pulls up to the International Sneaky Service headquarters: "I shall wait good, like a faithful friend should." He might as well be mouthing a cigarette slogan. He's totally subservient and warns the narrator of the cartoon (and presumably the audience) that it is not permitted to converse with him, because he is the important driver of the Secret Squirrel mobile. Nevertheless, Morocco Mole does play a useful role in stating the obvious when his squirrelly superior gets into trouble. For example, when the squirrel gets blown up early in a cartoon episode, the mole cleans up the mess and explains that Secret Squirrel is "always a slow starter" when he gets put on a case.

In a typical episode, Secret Squirrel must travel to the island home of the demonic Yellow Pinkie to bring him back to the International Sneaky Service headquarters and justice. However, Yellow Pinkie outsmarts the squirrel over and over again. He deflects a beam from Secret Squirrel's laser beam gun with a mirror and blows up his opponent. The squirrel appears to have nine lives, as he revives and returns to Yellow Pinkie's domain via a rocket belt, only to land in the patented squirrel squisher. The persistent Secret Squirrel is crushed like a pancake, but he returns to the fight once again with his freezer squeezer gun. This time Secret Squirrel's weaponry does the trick, as Yellow Pinkie is "put on ice" in a frozen block that is taken back to headquarters. "What an agent, what a squirrel," begins the long, laudatory song to conclude the episode.

Secret Squirrel was a cartoon parody of the spy movie genre, which ran from the James Bond films to *Our Man Flint* movies to the *Pink Panther* series. Some of the more memorable titles of Secret Squirrel episodes included "Five Is a Crowd," "Cuckoo Clock Cuckoo" and "Double Ex-Double Cross." In "Five Is a Crowd," Dr. Dangit creates five robot duplicates of Secret Squirrel to commit serious crimes and to frame the real squirrel. Secret Squirrel follows the imposters to Dangit's hideout and turns them against their creator. In "Cuckoo Clock Cuckoo," Secret Squirrel receives a mission from England to recover London's Big Ben clock, which was stolen by a giant determined to transform the iconic timepiece into a monster cuckoo clock. In "Double Ex-Double Cross," Secret Squirrel and Morocco Mole investigate the petrified population of Okey Dokey Isle, where the two partners encounter the scoundrel responsible for the petrification crime: Double-Ex.

According to Deirdre Sheppard of Common Sense Media, parents need to know that the Hanna-Barbera created Secret Squirrel promotes using violence and keeping secrets as methods of solving problems—not the best behavioral model for young audiences. Guns and bombs are used frequently, and all of the weaponry is glamourized right from the opening credits. In addition, Secret Squirrel's bulletproof vest does an incredible job of protecting him from attacks, which could mislead youngsters into thinking that guns don't cause serious injury and death.[13] On the positive side, the show is futuristic and can open the door to a discussion about law enforcement, spies and espionage, and how officials protect citizens: Is Secret Squirrel a good example of law enforcement? How do his duties compare to the tasks of a real secret agent? Why does he rely so heavily on weapons? What is the difference between a detective and a secret agent? How does it make sense to pick a squirrel for the role of a secret agent—and what about the mole that serves as his driver?

TV's Animaniacs—*Spielberg's Screwball Squirrels*

The animated furballs Slappy Squirrel and Skippy Squirrel were born in the 1990s when movie director and producer Steven Spielberg, along with Warner Brothers, collaborated to produce a successful television cartoon called *Animaniacs.* In theory, the cantankerous Slappy Squirrel could not have been born in the 1990s because she is described as an octogenarian in all profiles put together on the many characters from *Animaniacs.* She would have to have been born before 1920 to be eighty at the time of the show. In any case, she could not be an eighty-year-old squirrel because the animals never, ever survive into their eighth decade of life. In fact, most squirrels are lucky to live past their first year. Squirrels that live to adulthood seldom die of old age; instead, they fall prey to raccoons, hawks, and highway traffic. Wild squirrels that make it past the one-year mark rarely live longer than six years, while the maximum age that wild squirrels reach is about twelve years old.

Perhaps the cranky, elderly Slappy Squirrel has such an unusually long lease on life in *Animaniacs* because she cares about her appearance and her health and is such a snappy dresser. Slappy likes to wear a green hat decorated with a yellow flower, though her floral is a bit floppy. She stays flashy with her purple eyeliner, while she sports a pink purse and green umbrella that she finds useful for bludgeoning other characters. Slappy has a good mind and memory for an octogenarian. She outsmarts her foes and gets her revenge with exaggerated cartoon violence, often while recalling her past film appearances in more youthful days. She sometimes remarks on how her enemies remind her of famous cartoon characters when they were very young. Her impish nephew, Skippy, loves to hear the yarns of his old Hollywood aunt.

Perhaps Slappy Squirrel lives so long because she finds such wonderful companionship in her tree house with her attentive nephew Skippy Squirrel. Innocent Skippy idolizes his crabby aunt, despite her crusty and ill-tempered demeanor. Skippy provides an eager audience for all her stories of past cartoon lore, though she does have some rough edges and a tough New York accent. However, Skippy is no picnic himself when it comes to the personality department. He is overly sensitive, emotional and prone to outbursts that Slappy must contend with on a regular basis. An example of this emotional trauma comes in a cartoon episode in which Skippy watches the movie *Bumbie* (a parody of *Bambi*) and cries his eyes out when little Bumbie loses his mother to violence.

When Skippy begins crying uncontrollably in the movie house over the death of Bumbie's mom, Slappy is awoken from her movie snooze and must try quiet down her nephew as theater patrons become annoyed. Aunt Slappy tries to explain to the little critter that it is only make-believe—that it's all acting. Slappy tries to impress the lesson that "no one ever really gets hurt in cartoons" by handing a droopy-eyed dog an exploding bomb, having the pup run over by a train, and then having a flying house land on top of him. Skippy is only momentarily assuaged, as he breaks down into a fit of crying that is probably more familiar to human moms than squirrel moms (or aunts).

In "Soccer Coach Slappy," the amazing octogenarian auntie squirrel finds that little Skippy is getting continually clonked with the soccer ball. After taking a second hit in the face, Slappy makes a comment about how no one has been hit in the kisser this much since Milton Berle. Then Slappy advises her nephew to consider taking up badminton: "I hear it's very exciting, once your medication kicks in." Skippy is oblivious to his aunt's humor as he stumbles around the field with stars circling his head. Finally, Slappy finds a place for Skippy where he can do a lot of good in deflecting soccer balls off his face—as a goalie. Skippy ultimately wins the game by blocking a ball from going into the goal with his battered face. Skippy wails and cries and yelps in pain, but the game announcer and crowd go crazy, as Slappy Squirrel's hapless nephew has saved the game.

The all-time classic episode of the squirrel twosome comes when Aunt Slappy is trying to find out what band is on stage when they both attend a rock concert together. The vaudeville routine titled "Who's on Stage" may be even funnier than the original "Who's on First" sketch by comedians Abbott and Costello. The squirrelly pair go back and forth as Slappy tries to determine which band is making music on the stage ("The Band," "Who" or "Yes"). Slappy appears to lose her mind as she asks Skippy who is on stage fifty different ways, and he answers fifty different times, "Who." When she finally rephrases the question as to what band is on stage, Skippy replies that "The Band" isn't on stage until later, which only revives the conundrum of who is on stage.

The cartoon cast of *Animaniacs* drew inspiration from celebrities past and present—from early television comedians to contemporary rock bands to writers' family members to authors and scriptwriters not involved in the show. Sherri Stoner reportedly created Slappy when another writer and friend of hers, John McCann, made fun of Stoner's previous career in TV movies, which always featured her playing troubled teenagers. When McCann joked that Stoner would be playing troubled teenagers when she was fifty years old, the seed was planted.[14] Stoner developed the concept of Slappy's character as an older person acting like a teenager. She especially liked the notion of a senior cartoon character because an aged cartoon star would know the secrets of all the cartoons of yesteryear and would have the dirt on them. It all sounds a little squirrelly, but Stoner's old gray squirrel lady, Slappy (with the help of her nephew), has helped make *Animaniacs* one of the top TV cartoon series of all time.

Sandy Cheeks: Weirdest Squirrel of All

Most humans would love to possess even a fraction of the incredible number of attributes of a squirrel named Sandy Cheeks, one of the mainstay starlets in the television cartoon series known as *SpongeBob SquarePants*. Sandy Cheeks is a squirrel who wears a diving helmet and protective gear for living in the underwater city of Bikini Bottom. She is a math and science genius, as well as an inventor of high-tech products. Among this squirrel's inventions are a teleporter, a spacecraft, a cloning device and a submarine that can become miniaturized and travel inside a person's body. Sandy is extremely athletic, exhibiting skills ranging from karate to sand boarding to using a lasso to catch or shatter objects from a great distance. She is an outstanding western singer and guitar player. She is also into bodybuilding and developing huge muscles that will scare away anyone attempting to cause a hassle. Sandy is a proud Texan dedicated to living out the motto "Don't mess with Texas." She is one smart, talented, intimidating squirrel—don't mess with Texas, and don't mess with the Lone Star State Squirrel.

Sandy Cheeks was born to Mom and Daddy Cheeks along with her twin brother, Randy, in the great Texas town of Houston. As an adult, she found a position with a company called Treedome Enterprises, which sent her underwater to live down in Bikini Bottom to study sea life. In the episode titled "Chimps Ahoy," viewers learn that Sandy Cheeks works for a trio of chimpanzees up on the surface, named Professor Percy, Dr. Marmalade and Lord Reginald. Fans of Sandy Cheeks speculate that she was sent to research how U.S. atomic testing in the Bikini Atoll after World War II affected the sea animals. At the beginning of her new life in Bikini Bottom, she meets SpongeBob SquarePants while fighting a large monster clam. She also meets Patrick Star, another transformative character in *SpongeBob SquarePants*. Other characters in the unusual underwater neighborhood include Mr. Krabs and his daughter, Pearl, along with Squidward, Plankton, Larry the Lobster, Flying Dutchman, Mermaid Man and Barnacle Boy.

Sandy can be a kind and sympathetic sort of squirrel, especially for SpongeBob, whom she rescues from feelings of loneliness and loss. However, she has the capacity to be aggressive, competitive and downright nasty. It's not often apparent why Sandy Cheeks qualifies as a squirrel, and the cartoon show demands an excessive amount of willing suspension of disbelief. The underwater squirrel does apparently hibernate like several squirrel species do, though most squirrels just sleep a lot. In "Survival of the Idiots," Sandy appears as a morbidly obese, gargantuan squirrel, emulating other animals that store vast amounts of body fat prior to going into hibernation. When SpongeBob and Patrick enter Sandy's snow-filled tree home and disturb her winter rest, she goes berserk and viciously attacks them.

Disturbing Sandy while she's in a deep sleep or in hibernation is one thing. Disturbing Sandy by dissing her Texas roots and heritage is a whole different kettle of sea creatures, starfish included. She incessantly insists that land animals like those that roam the Texas plains are far better than any sea creatures, and she will take personal risks to prove her point. She has no tolerance for insults or snarky observations about her home state and her Texas accent. When SpongeBob and Patrick make fun of her sensitivity about her state of origin, she chases after them and attacks Patrick with an unprecedented show of rage. Any mockery of her beloved Texas is off-limits. Sandy Cheeks continuously crows and croons about Texas, whether anyone is listening or not.

Among the *SpongeBob SquarePants* episodes that show just how far she will go to pay homage to her Lone Star State is the musical treat in which she sings her "Texas Song." This song is the plaintive cry of a homesick squirrel yearning for the good life she left behind on dry land. She mourns that the ocean is no place for a squirrel and that she'll always be a Texas girl. When she sings about missing the open skies and the Texas barbecues, images of squirrel buckaroos start to fill her head. When she begins a good loud round of Texas yodeling, the other sea creatures are so moved that they begin to fill the sea with tears. Even SpongeBob and Patrick begin blubbering as her Texas landlubber tune plays in the background.

Sandy Cheeks may grow soft and teary-eyed when she thinks of Texas, but in most other instances, she is a very tough, tomboy kind of squirrel. This is never so apparent as in the episodes that display her prowess with karate moves. She and SpongeBob share an interest in karate and fight each other for grins. The karate they perform primarily involves chops and kicks. Sandy almost always is game for extreme sports and lifts weights with Larry the Lobster and other muscular fish. In the episode "MuscleBob BuffPants," Sandy shows SpongeBob her bulging biceps and her grueling daily exercise routine. In other episodes such as "Karate Kid," "Whelk Attack," and "Christmas Who?" she exhibits her finely tuned squirrel form and muscle structure. Although she is by no means a showboat, Sandy does find opportunities to prominently display her muscular body for SpongeBob.

Some observers of SpongeBob have speculated that he is gay, perhaps in the same tradition of speculation about the sexual orientation of the British Teletubbies. They point out that all of the main characters on *SpongeBob SquarePants* are males with the exception of the squirrel, Sandy Cheeks. However, there is plenty of evidence in the cartoon series that Sandy and Sponge-Bob are sweet on each other. There is no question that SpongeBob takes notice whenever the squirrel girl sports her hot purple clothing, such as the purple bikini top and purple and green bottom. It's hard for any sea creature not to take notice in an episode like "Someone's in the Kitchen with Sandy," when her squirrel fur pelt is off and she's wearing a purple bra and purple panties.

The underwater squirrel named Sandy Cheeks is a major force in the multi-billion-dollar phenomenon that is *SpongeBob SquarePants*. Much of the credit for the squirrel's popularity has to be given to Carolyn Lawrence, whose voice provides all the Texas twang and titter for the cowgirl squirrel. In a new century of cartooning, *SpongeBob SquarePants* has consistently ranked among the top cartoon shows of all time, although some fundamentalist Christian leaders have criticized the show for supposedly promoting homosexuality and a liberal agenda.[15] The question of whether SpongeBob is gay should probably be left for the squirrel girl to answer—and an immersion in all the episodes involving Sandy Cheeks would probably put the controversy to rest.

Squirrels Hamming It Up

Plenty of cartoon characters and comic strip celebrities have found their way to the big screen and, in recent times, to the video game circuit. A list of all those who've matriculated from black ink and white paper to color screens would require many pages. One squirrel that has jumped from ink-on-pulp glory to electrified imagery is a fellow named Hammy, who has thrived as a character in a United Media comic strip titled "Hammy Over the Hedge." This syndicated comic strip, which first appeared in 1995, was a modern fable of a squirrel, a raccoon, a turtle and their other animal friends that were forced to come to terms with the encroachment of suburbia.[16] Their woodland paradise was being invaded by humans, with their sprawling

Hammy, a hyperactive red squirrel in the 2006 film, *Over the Hedge*, finds a lot to like in the world of humans. Hammy is not above trying to abscond with some prized Girl Scout cookies for his dietary requirements. He proved to be a kiddie-pleasing movie star as well as box office gold.

homes, autos, electronics and assorted gadgetry. In the comic strip, the animals despise the loss of their land but are attracted to some of the fine possessions (especially the edibles) of the neighboring humans.

The 2006 film *Over the Hedge* is a computer-animated tale that plays off some of the same themes as in the original comic strip. The movie also capitalizes on the quirks and quandaries of two of the primary comic strip characters: RJ, a conniving raccoon, and Hammy, a hyperactive red squirrel. RJ sees himself as a brainy schemer capable of outwitting humans and manipulating his naïve and childish squirrel friend. For squirrel partisans, this movie characterization begs the question of whether raccoons are really smarter than squirrels. In fact, many scientists who study mammals rank squirrels slightly ahead of raccoons in their cunning, their adaptability and their nature smarts. Squirrels also are said to have exceptional memories that allow every situation they encounter to be a learning experience.

All debate over squirrel versus raccoon intelligence aside, in *Over the Hedge*, RJ comes off as an enterprising raccoon intent on raiding a vending machine for snacks. Unable to make a successful heist, RJ attempts to steal the stored bounty of a hibernating bear named Vincent. When RJ accidentally wakes up Vincent, the angry bear gives RJ until the next full moon to replace the goods. When RJ stumbles upon Hammy and the squirrel's woodland friends, he attempts to dazzle them by talking about the wonders of the new human community in their midst—and he also convinces them that it's easy to gather and steal food from the humans. Of course, the humans aren't so easily fooled. RJ gets them all in trouble with his schemes, including one that has Hammy posing as a rabid squirrel to steal cookies from Girl Scouts, and another that fills Hammy with energy drinks so he can become double trouble for the humans.

Suffice it to say that all of the wily raccoon's schemes end up bombing. In the end, he apologizes to all of the animals for his deceit and entangling them in the troubles he made for himself by stealing from Vincent. The box turtle named Verne tells RJ that if he had been honest about his plight in the first place, they probably would have helped him because they are all an extended family. RJ becomes overwhelmed with emotion and gives Hammy a tearful hug because he now feels that he is a part of the animal family. Hammy comes off as the really smart animal after all in this story, because, in his hyper state of activity, he has been storing nuts in a giant log through thick and thin. Hammy is one heroic squirrel, because he's accumulated enough nuts to feed the entire animal family for a year.

Many critics have damned *Over the Hedge* with faint praise, describing it as "cute" but not in the same league as animation classics like *Bambi*, *Toy Story*, *Shrek*, and *Finding Nemo*.[17] There is unanimous agreement that the movie has a wholesome theme for young children about the importance of family (in this case, a family of rather weird animals). It's also agreed that the characters are not at all creepy, and the voices that give them life are a distinct treat for children and adults. Steve Carell gets plaudits for giving credibility to the squirrel character with a perfect voice for young Hammy. Bruce Willis earns honors as the voice of RJ, the sneaky raccoon. Nick Nolte comes through with the grouchiest of voices for the rudely awakened bear, Vincent. Wanda Sykes likewise gets the job done with her articulation for a sassy, ill-tempered skunk named Stella. Finally, Gary Shandling gives earnest voice to the continual frustration of the box turtle, Verne, who frequently loses his shell and constantly has to point out that he is a reptile, not an amphibian.

A particularly memorable scene for Hammy, RJ and Verne occurs when Hammy is convinced by RJ to act like a rabid squirrel. RJ covers the squirrel's lips with whipped cream, so that he appears to be frothing at the mouth, and then sends him to scare two Girl Scouts out of their cookies. However, the girls don't surrender their cookies so easily and soon go on the attack against the cookie-crazed (but hardly rabid) squirrel. Verne expresses his disgust with RJ for getting his friend into such a mess and then goes to the rescue. Verne succeeds in saving Hammy, but only after he is knocked silly (as well as out of his turtle shell).

Hammy's humorous scenes and the familiar voices of the creatures in *Over the Hedge* are a big part of what makes this movie work for audiences and for critics. There is enough humor and entertaining banter to make up for the weak storyline in what is essentially a children's film. James Berardinelli of *Reelviews* declared the movie to consist of not much more than a cute, enjoyable diversion. "There are cute CGI animals, clever dialogue, a satirical look at suburban America, and a preachy moral, but it doesn't amount to much," Berardinelli observed.[18] Reviewer Manohla Dargis of the *New York Times* was harsher, dismissing the "glop about family" and demanding more message: "There is no poetry here and little thought. That's particularly too bad since the recent alligator attacks in Florida prove that the story of human encroachment on animal turf is topical and rich in thematic possibility."[19]

Ken Fox of the online *TV Guide* offered a more positive spin on *Over the Hedge*, calling it "a sly satire of American 'enough is never enough' consumerism and blind progress at the expense of the environment." He went on to say, "It's also very funny, and the little woodland critters that make up the cast are a kiddie-pleasing bunch."[20] This favorable assessment was backed up by the box office returns. Only Tom Hanks could best the raccoon and the squirrel with his work in *The Da Vinci Code* on *Over the Hedge*'s opening weekend. The film closed 112 days after its spring 2006 release with a gross of $155,019,340 in the United States and Canada. Its overseas take was $180,983,656 for a global total of $336,002,996. The film with the crazy squirrel was produced on an $80 million budget, so it was easily assessed as a commercial success.

Et Tu, Nut Job Squirrels?

Animated squirrels in the movies have proven that they can be boffo at the box office, raking in millions of dollars over production costs. Two animated movies that prove this profit point are *The Nut Job* in 2014 and *The Nut Job 2* in 2017. Both films managed to make millions of dollars even after press reviews that were sometimes less than complimentary—even harsh. In the case of 2014's original squirrel movie caper, *The Nut Job*, critics consistently derided the plot as thin, superficial, stale and beyond redemption. The main character, a purple squirrel named Surly, was described as unlikable, detestable, crude, off-putting and lacking in any charm. The jokes and gags in the movie were dismissed as shameless, sophomoric and unsavory. According to reviewer Miriam Bale of the *New York Times*, the movie is an undistinguished failure hampered by "muddy-colored and often ugly animation, a plot that feels too stretched out and loaded with details to hold the attention of most children, and more flatulence jokes than anyone deserves."[21]

Despite the alleged lackluster characters, the charges of overusing "nuts" puns, and complaints about trite and excessive gas and burp jokes, *The Nut Job* had the biggest opening weekend ever for an indie animated feature film. The purple squirrel movie grossed $64,251,541 in North America and $56,633,986 in other countries, for a grand total of $120,885,527.[22] And despite the snarky reviews, the film won the Audience Award for Best Children's Animation at "Anima 2015," the Brussels Animation Film Festival.[23] Perhaps the film overcame the many shortcomings pointed out by critics, because it did excel with so many star-studded voiceovers for the major animal characters. Among the notables enlisted for the 2014 movie were the voices of Will Arnett, Brendan Fraser, Gabriel Iglesias, Jeff Dunham, Liam Neeson and Katherine Heigl.

The Nut Job is all about the buffoonery of Surly, an obnoxious purple squirrel in the fictional town of Oakton. Surly's irresponsible behavior results in the destruction of the winter food supply stashed away by his buddies in Liberty Park. This unspeakable offense leads to his banishment to the mean streets of Oakton. While on those streets, Surly happens upon Maury's Nut Shop, and he devises a plan to replenish the food cache for his unhappy friends that involves a grand heist of the nut shop's goodies. What Surly fails to realize is that the nut shop is a front for dangerous mobsters, who have their own plan to rob the bank next door. Surly's scheme to crack into the store's nut bonanza goes off the rails when the mobsters start executing their own bank robbery plan. After the mayhem of evil-eyed street rats doing their thing, a noisy chase sequence, police barricades, explosions and gunfire, Surly barely escapes with his life and becomes an unlikely hero by movie's end. And by that point, Surly has learned that life is not just there for the taking. "The truth is life's really there for the sharing. Once you realize that, you might discover there's a little hero in all of us. After all, we're all a little nuts," Surly concludes.

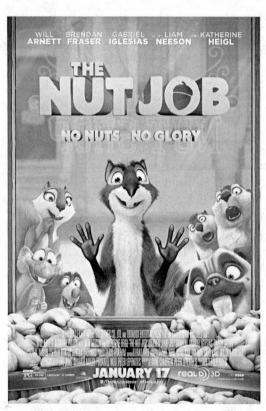

A purple squirrel named Surly is the main character in *The Nut Job*, an animated film from 2014. Surly and his unique animal friends benefited from the vocal talents of Will Arnett, Brendan Fraser, Gabriel Iglesias and Liam Neeson. Surly's movie success later helped him to find a career in video games, including *Surly's Coaster Chase*.

Of course, Surly and his first big movie, *The Nut Job*, do not really conclude anything, because a sequel, *The Nut Job 2: Nutty by Nature*, followed quickly on the heels of the original. The second round for Surly and his friends fared no better with movie critics than the first effort. Once again, the plot was found to be inane, the jokes were labeled as crass and the animation was dismissed as anemic. Reviewer Monica Castillo of the *New York Times* dissed the plot as a series of set pieces haphazardly strung together and added, "You don't need to see the first 'Nut Job' movie to follow the sequel's nonsensical plot and the script's preference for bottom-shelf puns. The film's mean-spirited tone picks on both creatures and humans, like construction workers for being illiterate, animals almost too dumb to survive and the wicked rich."[24]

Not all reviewers were so dour. Others found some good, old-fashioned wisdom woven into the squirrel tale. Among the sagacious nuggets is that there are no shortcuts in life; a successful life involves hard work. The plot picks up where the first movie left off: Surly and his friends are feeling fat and happy because they have a huge food supply in the abandoned nut shop. A cautious squirrel named Andie warns Surly and company about their complacency and determines to teach her own children how to forage for food in Liberty Park. Her wise approach to life is vindicated when a boiler room blows up at the old nut shop, destroying all the easy food pickings. Soon, Surly and his gang are back hunting for food in the park, but then Oakton's mayor decides that Liberty Park could be a profit center for the city as a money-making amusement park called Libertyland. Surly and his friends harass the construction crews, so the animal exterminators are called out and the battle begins. It's a David and Goliath struggle, but it wouldn't be a tale for children if the animals didn't triumph after lots of chaos. Some animal angst, cartoonish violence and entertaining action scenes ensue. Surly and his friends win the fight, and the park is restored to its former glory.

A pivotal moment in the film comes when the cocky squirrel Surly mistakes the groundbreaking shovel for the unwanted amusement park as a rather smallish implement that the humans will use to transform their paradise. He's not impressed, but then a giant earthmover with giant tank tracks arrives on the scene. The purple squirrel jumps into the vehicle's undercarriage and bites into its wiring, electrifying himself while catapulting the giant earthmover into the air before it crashes. The singed and tattered squirrel knows he has won a skirmish, but the war has only just begun. "If we want to beat these guys, it's going to take all of us," Surly declares in the effort to enlist and rally his furry friends.

The Nut Job 2: Nutty by Nature did not rally youngsters and their parents to head to the movie houses in numbers comparable to Surly's original incarnation. However, the energized purple squirrel did bring in millions of dollars over the sequel's production costs. Surly proved once again that plenty of humans have a soft spot for animated squirrels. So often, these critters are just like the real thing—furry, flippant and decidedly flawed, but also agile, amusing and downright astonishing.

7

Comics and Video
Game Squirrels

Comic book superheroes are no longer the province of oddball collectors and geeky adolescents wishing they had powers beyond those of mortal men. Comic book superheroes have gone mainstream, and they are powerful. How powerful? These mighty superheroes, past and present, have soared off the paper pages of comic books to mesmerize millions—and they're making astounding amounts of money for movie moguls, and even more dollars for creators of video game fantasies. The superheroes now constitute our very own mythology, according to Laurence Maslon, the coauthor of *Superheroes! Capes, Cowls, and the Creation of Comic Book Culture.*[1] Maslon argues that these towering hulks and caped crusaders are our current era's version of Greek deities. And who are these godlike figures in the mythology of our time? These supernatural beings come with descriptive names like Superman, Batman, Spider-Man, Captain Marvel, Wonder Woman ... and Squirrel Girl.

Squirrel Girl? Squirrel Girl happens to be much younger than the most other superheroes. She first appeared in 1991 in a *Marvel Super-Heroes Winter Special* edition.[2] Her squirrel attributes and unique ability to communicate with squirrels give her an unexpected advantage in defeating villains. Her real name is Doreen Green, the progeny of fictional parents Dorian and Maureen Green of Los Angeles, California. At ten years old, the youngster's abilities to communicate with squirrels became manifest. Though she was not revealed as a mutant, there did seem to be a modification in her genetic makeup that allowed her to acquire some useful capabilities common to squirrels. Of course, the acquisition of a lengthy squirrel tail, which alarmed her parents, was a dead giveaway that this was a different breed of young lady.

Squirrel Girl took an early interest in using her abilities to fight crime and all nefarious perpetrators of evil. She tried to find her place in the world of comic superheroes by ambushing Iron Man in a forest with the intention of impressing him so that he would consider making her his sidekick. On her shoulder she carried an actual pet squirrel named Monkey Joe, who just happened to be her own sidekick. Iron Man was a bit mystified, but when she rescued him from Doctor Doom by enlisting the help of a swarm of squirrels, Iron Man took a second look. He suggested that while she was still too young to be a superhero crime fighter, he would recommend her for the heroic Avengers team when she grew a bit older. When that time arrived, this favored female would make her mark on the world of superhero comics.

Squirrel Girl is one of those comic book characters who become protean and also multi-platform from the standpoint of media exposure. She has found a place in the comic book world challenging Iron Man, battling bad guys as a member of the Great Lakes Avengers, and eventually revving up a time machine that takes her to the year 2099 and back. As she grows older—without the help of a time machine—she becomes the Unbeatable Squirrel Girl, with a new sidekick squirrel named Tippy-Toe. They do battle with many more scoundrels, including Galactus, a space creature that is coming to Earth with the intention of totally devouring the human-inhabited planet. A superhero with the cunning and capabilities of Squirrel Girl could never be confined to the pages of mere comic books. Today, Squirrel Girl can be found on several video games in which she is a playable character of some popularity.

Squirrel Girl also has made television appearances in episodes of several cartoon shows, joined by her squirrel sidekicks, Monkey Joe and Tippy-Toe. Additionally, the female squirrel superhero has made her mark on the literary world. Several volumes of Unbeatable Squirrel Girl paperbacks and Kindle editions are now available, including *I Kissed a Squirrel and I Liked It*. The teaser for this book notes that she has decided to take charge of her love life and start dating. There is an obvious quandary: "But just who will kiss a squirrel and like it? Surely not … Mole Man? When the subterranean super villain mole falls deep in love, he's willing to hold the world hostage to get Doreen's attention. Can she save everything without becoming Mrs. Mole Man?" The Unbeatable Squirrel Girl books cover a lot of ground, which might be expected from a glamorous lady rodent who has already established a superhero track record in the pages of comic books.

Long before this girl squirrel broke the glass ceiling of comic books, there were male squirrels appearing in the panels of cartoon strips. A few squirrels showed up in the work of cartoon genius Gene Ahern. Though Ahern was best known for his character of Major Hoople in "Our Boarding House," most of his comic strips were about squirrelly people. Those strips bore such names as "Squirrel Food," "The Nut Bros: Ches and Wal" and "The

Squirrel Cage." The use of nuts and squirrels in the titles of these comic strips about nincompoops and nonsensical characters indicate that Ahern held the furry animals in some contempt (or, at least, low esteem). His strip titled "The Squirrel Cage," which ran from 1936 to 1953, covered the travails of the Little Hitchhiker, a bearded character who spouted nonsense and became an inspiration for counterculture artist Robert Crumb.[3] The rebellious Crumb, of the psychedelic 1960s, came up with such squirrelly strips as "Fritz the Cat" and "Keep on Truckin."

Nutsy Squirrel debuted shortly after World War II and became a top animal celebrity in a DC Comics offering known as *Funny Folks* and *Comic Cavalcade*. As the name implies, Nutsy was not an entirely rational creature. He gained some favor in the comic world after the popularity of superheroes from the

Nutsy Squirrel paved the way for many squirrel comic book characters of the future. Nutsy was not the smartest squirrel in the neighborhood tree branches, but smarter squirrels followed in his paw steps, including Squirrel Girl and a brash squirrel named Foamy in the *Neurotically Yours* comic series. The angry squirrels in the *Squarriors* comic books engage in bloody combat as the human race fades into extinction (photograph by Ursula Ruhl).

World War II era (such as Superman) began to wane. Nutsy has become a popular moniker for anyone deemed irrational or excessively silly. Nutsy is not to be confused with Nutzy the Flying Squirrel of Richmond, Virginia. Nutzy is the mascot of Richmond's minor league baseball team. He has a girlfriend (another squirrel) named Nutasha who sometimes joins Nutzy in cheering on the Flying Squirrels franchise.[4] However, neither of these contemporary Virginia squirrels bear any resemblance or relation to Nutsy Squirrel, a creature of the 1940s and 1950s comic books.

In stark contrast to the dimwit squirrel known as Nutsy, Foamy the Squirrel is an urbane, intellectual and sarcastic comic book squirrel for a new century. Foamy has roots in Goth culture and appears in a comic book and webtoon known as *Neurotically Yours*. Foamy is the pet squirrel of a Goth girl named Germaine who showed up on the radar of an eclectic group of comic book followers sometime after the 9/11 tragedy in New York. The original comic book series gave the most attention to Germaine, but by 2003 the neurotic squirrel was given a soapbox to deliver dark and provocative rants on a variety of current topics. Both Foamy and Germaine have generated a following by speaking out against the folly, absurdity and imbecility often found in the course of normal life. Several other squirrels of note have joined Foamy in virtually foaming at the mouth over injustice and stupidity.

Warrior Squirrels, better known as Squarriors, are post-apocalypse squirrels who are bloody and brutish. The backstory for the Squarriors is that humanity went extinct and the world has finally voided itself of the Anthropocene. The comic book series focuses on what's left, which is basically several clans of animals engaged in mortal combat. According to writer Ash Maczko and illustrator Ashley Witter, what we are left with is animal life that has become intelligent: "The spark of rational thought creates an internal struggle for these creatures; instinct versus reason. And the clashing of these ideas erupts into the ultra-violent wars across the planet."[5] The covers of this comic series are scary enough, but a short trip inside the books to see what the Squarriors are up to—now that humans have disappeared from the planet—can be downright traumatic.

As mentioned in the previous chapter, Secret Squirrel is an animated squirrel who performed in a popular television cartoon show not long after Rocky Squirrel and Bullwinkle Moose left the airwaves in the 1960s. However, "secret squirrel" is also a nickname used in the military for spies or operatives on highly classified missions. Actual secret squirrels in the military go on sensitive, covert operations and are forbidden to disclose their status, their service and their mission. These individuals could be from any of the branches of intelligence work or from the Central Intelligence Agency, or they might serve with Special Operations Forces.[6] In 2017, DC Comics publisher Dan DiDio posted his own squirrel on Facebook that was, in fact, a Secret Squirrel with a finger raised to its mouth indicating hush-hush. This action led to speculation on the *Fanboy Planet* blog that a Secret Squirrel comic book series might soon be in the offing, but only the Secret Squirrel drawn by Howard Porter seemed to know for sure—and he wasn't talking.[7]

Until Secret Squirrel joins the comic book squirrel cavalcade, it's best to concentrate on established comic book Sciuridae, such as Nutsy, Squirrel Girl, Foamy and the Squarriors. A closer look at these amazing squirrel characters reveals the diversity of thought and the range of imagination that go into the creation of comic book squirrels.

Nutsy Squirrel: Fit to Be Tied

What can you say about an anthropomorphic comic squirrel in short pants and a flowing necktie? Nutsy Squirrel's signature, red-and-white striped necktie extended from a neck supporting his giant head to the ground on which he marched forward. Nutsy was introduced to the comic world in 1946, but he started off as a secondary character who was overshadowed by other stars, such as an elephant and mouse who answered to the names of Pinky and Winky. However, Nutsy gained notoriety for his silly, almost irrational behavior, and he consequently moved to the top of the comic character heap thanks to an ability to garner laughs. Nutsy prospered during the post–World War II interlude when comic lovers took an overdue breather from the standard superhero fare as embodied in the characters of Green Lantern or the Flash.

From the beginning, Nutsy Squirrel had to live up to the slang word "nutsy" that implied the squirrel was imbecilic, abnormal, deranged, intellectually challenged, frivolous and goofy. Nutsy was assisted in that challenge by his co-creators at DC Comics: Woody Gelman and Irving Dressler. Their creation, Nutsy, was masterful in his obvious talent to exhibit more than a mere inclination to the irrational. Nutsy was initially partnered with the confounded character of Robert Rabbit, who was a just a hair smarter than Nutsy but still frustrated and surprised by Nutsy's seemingly insufficient brain power. The character of the Professor eventually replaced Robert Rabbit. The Professor, a bona fide academic, was presumably introduced to make Nutsy's shortcomings even more apparent. Though the Professor's cap and gown might be expected to indicate a high level of intellectual endowment, Nutsy's new human sidekick actually proved to be only a few notches brighter than the centerpiece squirrel.

A cursory glance at some of the classic Nutsy Squirrel comic book covers can reveal the full extent of this hopeless squirrel's state of mindlessness. For example, Nutsy totally flabbergasts Robert Rabbit with his exclamation, "I've got all my nuts saved up for this winter!" However, the nuts he has gathered are the metallic kind available in any hardware store. Nutsy bewilders Robert once again when he complains that the spot remover sold to him by the rabbit has had no effect in dissolving the spots on his pet leopard. "I want my money back!" the squirrel remarks angrily. Robert is likewise flummoxed when Nutsy takes a big bite out of a peppermint stick barber pole and reports his disappointment that it tastes just like wood. Sometimes the rabbit suffers from more than exasperation with Nutsy. When Nutsy becomes a super vacuum cleaner salesman, he wonders why the rabbit has disappeared on his sales call. Alas, Robert's ears are visible behind Nutsy. Most of the rabbit has been sucked into the vacuum cleaner's dust bag, so that his bunny ears are all that remains.

Despite his many failings, Nutsy Squirrel's media reach expanded in the new decade of the 1950s. In 1950, DC Comics determined that its stable of funny animals would gain more traction with appearances in some movie cartoons. The familiar *Funny Folks* title and logo for the squirrel's comic books was changed to *Hollywood Funny Folks* later that same year. A more dramatic change for the challenged squirrel came in 1954, when his name

Before achieving animated movie fame, the squirrel named Hammy was a character in the United Media comic strip titled "Hammy Over the Hedge." The comic strip, which appeared in 1995, was a fable that included a squirrel, a turtle and a raccoon. Together these animal characters tried to cope with the humans (and their suburban developments) encroaching on their own woodland paradise.

was officially changed from Nutsy to Nutsy Squirrel, as he is most commonly known today.[8] The name change did not, however, stave off the continual upheaval within the comic book industry. The funny comic book animals, and the fortunes of DC's Nutsy Squirrel, began to slip in the later 1950s. By 1957, the Nutsy Squirrel franchise had run out of steam, and the squirrel saw his last comic issue. Nutsy Squirrel may have slipped out of sight, but today he is hardly out of mind. He paved the way for future comic book squirrels and, frankly, squirrels that deserved and demanded more respect than was accorded the pathetic comic squirrel named Nutsy in the post–World War II era.

Squirrel Girl: Furry and Female

About four decades after Nutsy faded from the comic book scene, Squirrel Girl came along. In contrast to the male squirrels that preceded her in the comic book world, Squirrel Girl cannot be dismissed as "nutsy." She is not trapped in a squirrel cage. She is not some critter running aimlessly on a squirrel wheel. She is the real thing—a superhero. Besides her ability to communicate with squirrels, and to mobilize them to fight on her behalf, she has some squirrel equipment that can prove quite useful for a warrior. Her four-foot tail gives her a balancing tool to keep her from falling from high perches. She also has the strength to jump between tall trees and buildings like Superman or Spider-Man. She possesses retractable knuckle spikes for battle, in addition to sharp claws on her fingers, which assist her in climbing. In spite of all her armaments, however, Squirrel Girl is not normally very threatening. She is generally amusing until she mobilizes to take on a dangerous adversary or devious crime figures interested in inflicting evil upon the world.

Squirrel Girl's comic book victories are many, and they include triumphs over Deadpool, MODOK and Wolverine. Though she is not always as strong or as powerful as the villains whom she must face, Squirrel Girl answers the challenge by using her wits and brain power to outmaneuver her foes. She takes advantage of her opponents' overconfidence or their weakness from the rigors of earlier fights. An amusing example of her use of thoughtful strategy can be found in her defeat of the Bi-Beast in New York's Central Park. She discovers Bi-Beast fighting the Thing, and she figures out a way to favor the Thing and not get her own claws bloodied in defeating Bi-Beast. She instructs her many squirrel friends to gather the smelliest city garbage that can be found. Her squirrels then place it around the combatants, who must now hold their noses. At this point, Bi-Beast is in trouble, because he has two heads and two noses, but only two hands. He must use both hands to hold his noses, which leaves him utterly defenseless. The Thing then easily knocks him out.

Squirrels, girls and all furry creatures can find no better champion in the comic book world than the unlikely heroine of Squirrel Girl. She is a friend of all good squirrels and has impressed all fans of squirrels by her insistence on always having one or more squirrel companions. She brought Monkey Joe to prominence when she adopted him as her best fighting friend. He was allowed to show off just how brilliant squirrels can be, as he was able to use computers in his work with Squirrel Girl. When brave Monkey Joe was relegated to the afterlife at the hands of vicious Leather Boy, Squirrel Girl found a new companion in the amazing pink-bowed Tippy-Toe. Female Tippy-Toe gives Squirrel Girl an assist in defeating Thanos and MODOK, whose face she vigorously and victoriously scratches. However, Tippy-Toe is not perfect. At one point, Mr. Immortal lodges complaints with Squirrel Girl about her sidekick, as Tippy-Toe is constantly whipping up acorn smoothies that mess up his blender.

Foamy's Squirrelly Fulminations

Foamy the Squirrel is one strange cyber-rodent. The cartoon featuring Foamy has roots in Goth culture that can be traced, in part, to the post-punk subculture of 1980s England, which continues to manifest itself in America in the iconic dark music, dark literature, dark film, black dress—and sometimes even darker attitudes toward traditional lifestyles.[9] Foamy is the neurotic pet squirrel of a confused Goth girl named Germaine Endez who has developed a controversial presence in a comic book and webtoon known as *Neurotically Yours*. The original comic book series focused on Germaine and her travails in coping with modern living, but by 2003 the squirrel was given a megaphone to blast all that is plastic, superficial and phony in American life. Both Foamy and Germaine have struck a responsive chord with those who are admittedly mired in alienation and ennui. With Foamy, cartoon squirrels have come a long way since the more mundane days of the moronic squirrel named Nutsy from half a century ago.

As *Neurotically Yours* has evolved, Foamy has become something of a cult figure, with a growing following for his angry rants. In many episodes, he upstages the ostensible main character of Germaine. It's hard to describe the cartoon as having any kind of running plot. However, Germaine is consistently entertaining as a frustrated poet who lives much of her life in her own head (a noggin that is extremely cluttered). Germaine distorts reality with her paranoid musings that the pizza deliveryman might be a stalker, or that the neighbor and his canine may be outside trying to find a mythical squirrel that just happens to be her pet. In some instances, Germaine busily composes serious nonsense on her laptop computer while Foamy is bouncing around in the background spouting his many grievances with the world. In other episodes, she is hard at work creating poetry that will never be published, because it always gets rejected.

The comic strips on the *Neurotically Yours* website consist primarily of balloon banter between Foamy and Germaine. The squirrel annoys Germaine endlessly with his quips about her hypocrisy, and she invariably flips him the bird and tells him to shut his trap. For example, when Germaine is using her cell phone camera to capture her own bikini-clad image, the squirrel observes, "I like how you can complain about being objectified while displaying a bikini selfie in the same post." In another vignette, Germaine crosses her arms over her cleavage and laments, "I wish guys weren't such liars." Foamy retorts, "Said the girl with dyed hair, push-up bra and six layers of makeup." In an obvious swipe at those people who find images of Jesus in their pizza slices or jelly-covered bread, Germaine looks at her piece of toast and declares, "No, it doesn't look like a squirrel. It's just randomly burnt toast." To which the quick-witted squirrel responds, "How dare you mock the holy toast."

The *Neurotically Yours* comic strips are relatively tame compared to the YouTube cartoon series of Foamy rants. The squirrel's voice sounds like a 33-rpm record of Alvin the singing chipmunk played at 45 rpm. Throughout his rants, Foamy jumps around incessantly (as you might expect a squirrel to do). When he launches his angry fusillades from outside a New York apartment building, there are sometimes obscene acts going on in the apartment windows behind him. The scenes of debauchery are totally unrelated to the subject at hand; instead, they appear to emphasize the random chaos and overall grossness of modern living. The squirrel's tirades are often quite explicit and definitely not for the refined or the faint of heart.

In an early cyber rant from 2009 titled "Foamy Calls Tech Support," the squirrel is on the phone seeking technical help to get his laptop computer operating after a crash. Music native to India plays in the background during the service phone call, as Foamy endures the classic techie questions: Is the computer plugged in? Is the monitor for the computer switched to the "on" position? In short order, the squirrel begins unleashing the expletives many of us would like to use in these situations but are too polite to employ. Finally, the tech guru in Mumbai issues the curative instructions: "Hold down the following keys: W, F, the number 2, the spacebar, while typing out 'Ganesha is great' and tapping on the escape key for twenty minutes." Foamy finally rebels and asks, "Why am I talking to someone in India about my computer, that was made in Japan, and bought in America? Why am I paying for first-rate tech support from a Third World Country?"

Foamy uses his cyber soapbox to pontificate on many current issues, and he has been rewarded with many reader posts on his site reflecting positive feedback. The squirrel tackles political correctness, bullies, religious opposition to gay marriage and the constant drumbeat of blaming video games for violence in society. Foamy disputes the influence of games and notes that his early years of playing *Super Mario Brothers* never brainwashed him into becoming a plumber, nor "did I ever get stuck in a drainpipe looking for a princess." Foamy also denounces parents for buying violent games too early for their youngsters and never taking the time to understand and use the Entertainment Software Rating Board (ESRB) rating system, which assigns age and content ratings for video games to help parents and consumers make intelligent decisions on game purchases.[10]

Foamy gets especially worked up over the issue of Christian opposition to gay marriage, a stance that he finds sanctimonious and morally repugnant, contrary to the U.S. Constitution, and a generally irritating waste of time. He insists that you've got to be pretty egotistical to claim to know God's will about these things. "What if God changed his mind? Huh?" asks Foamy. "He didn't send you a memo? Deal with it!" Foamy thinks the institution of marriage is overrated in any case, so why make a big deal about it? "Let them get married and figure out it's a hollow institution just like the rest of us have," the snarky squirrel advises. "And seriously, guys, how many of you, right now, hope a hot lesbian couple moves right next door?"

Foamy is one of four squirrels that inhabit the world of *Neurotically Yours*, although he gets the most visibility. The other squirrels are named the Hatta, Begley and Pilz-E. The Hatta is the poster child for reverse racism and believes that all white people are out to get him. He pulls the race card frequently and insists that his misfortunes are the result of a "white conspiracy." He is an ardent supporter of legalizing marijuana. Begley is a British squirrel with a purple Mohawk haircut; he was accidentally transported to New York City in a suitcase, where he met up with Germaine and fellow mischief-maker Foamy. The squirrel Pilz-E is aptly named because he overuses medicines for psychosomatic illnesses. He is variously described as susceptible to hallucinations, slurred speech and bouts of insanity. In addition to the squirrels, there are a wide assortment of humans, a dog by the name of Roswell and a cat named Puff in *Neurotically Yours*.

Foamy, Germaine and their friends are the creation of Jonathan Ian Mathers at Ill Will Press. Mathers and Dawn Bennett provide voices for the characters. The webtoons debuted in 2003, and the comic strip format, primarily in single panels, began appearing in 2009. The *Neurotically Yours* website offers Foamy Cult Cards as well as books, T-shirts, CDs, DVDs and books.[11]

Squarriors: Red in Tooth and Claw

Warrior Squirrels (better known as Squarriors) are post-apocalyptic comic squirrels who are beastly, bloody and brutish. They may be exactly what the Victorian writer Alfred Lord Tennyson had in mind when he expounded on the state of nature, so red in tooth and claw. Tennyson's popular elegy (from which the phrase "nature, red in tooth and claw" is derived) is an appropriate reference when examining the Squarriors.[12] Tennyson lamented that it is one thing for insensate animal species to go extinct but quite another thing for mankind to go extinct, because humans are aware of what it is to live and die, and people have tried their best to honor and placate God by praying to him and building churches and temples. So how could a just and attentive deity permit humanity to die off?

In fact, mankind's imminent demise is exactly what is happening in the hellhole world of the Squarriors. Here, humanity is very near extinction. The comic book series is all about what's left behind. With humans out of the picture, the remaining animal life has acquired unaccustomed powers of reasoning. However, their rational thought is obscured by age-old instinctual impulses and a predisposition toward bloody violence. The Squarriors comic details the battles of the warring animals in the new world bereft of humans. The tribe of Tin Kin, a band of warrior squirrels, do their best to protect each other and to build a sustainable life amid hostiles, such as the neighboring Maw tribe.

Squarrior characters seem to live in constant fear for their lives, and the comic books, while beautifully and colorfully illustrated, are exceedingly dark. The illustrations show plenty of images of bared teeth, bloodied faces and overall chaos on the depopulated plains of Illinois. The second issue of the series begins with a few remaining humans in a farmhouse discussing the losses among friends and family as the end of their world draws nigh. They are replaced by warrior squirrels standing sentry in the trees and doing their best to stay undetected by both their predators and their prey. Their survival depends on their solidarity with each other and their surveillance of all that might be lurking out on the dreary and bleak landscapes of a dangerous planet that they seem to have inherited.

In a review of issue #4 of the initial four-part comic series, Nick Nafpliotis reveals that the squirrels betray each other more than the cast of *House of Cards*. However, even though the squirrels and other assorted wildlife once again "beat the hell out of each other," a crucial moment in the tribal history of Tin Kin versus Maw is uncovered in this issue. The still panels featuring landscapes are frame-worthy pieces of art, according to Nafpliotis. "And to be honest, the action scenes could be, too, as long as you don't mind gruesome and awesome-looking squirrel-on-squirrel violence adorning your walls," he adds.[13] Nafpliotis thanks the team of writer Ash Maczko and illustrator Ashley Witter at Devil's Due Entertainment for making the trials and tribulations of the lowly creatures running through his backyard into something gorgeous, compelling and fun.

The Squarriors comic book series flies in the face of all the human-authored scholarship lamenting the loss of various animal species due to humankind's degradation of land, water and air. Studies show that humans aren't going extinct, but they are on a rampage, destroying flora and fauna at unprecedented rates. One in three animal species is threatened or endangered. Animal farming by humans is contributing heavily to greenhouse gases and consuming more and more land. Scholars such as Elizabeth Kolbert, the researcher and writer for *Field Notes from a Catastrophe: Man, Nature, and Climate Change*, speculate that the current Anthropogenic era may be ushering in the next mass extinction.[14] We are overfishing the oceans, overhunting the wild, and eating ourselves off the planet. Every day humans kill twenty-seven million animals for food (not including sea life).

Despite the overwhelming evidence that humans have dominion over the sea, the heavens, and the earth (not to mention all of the animals that inhabit these realms), could it be that the Squarriors will actually be the creatures to inherit the Earth? Consider that during 3,400 years of "civilized existence," humans have been at war for 3,132 years, with just 268 years of tranquility on the globe.[15] Consider that the human species is estimated to have been in existence for a maximum of 350,000 years. By comparison, fossils for a squirrel-like species are reported to be more than two hundred million years old. The smart money has to be on squirrels in confronting the question of who will inherit the Earth—perhaps the survivors will be the Squarriors.

McLuhan: Comics, Games and Squirrels

Before moving on from comic book squirrels to video game squirrels, it might be useful to take a brief pause to consider what Marshall McLuhan had to say about both comics and games. From his vantage point in the 1960s, McLuhan saw the story panels of comic books as a clue to understanding the new medium of television, with its unfolding images.[16] It's certainly no coincidence that comic book animal characters came to dominate Saturday morning television for kids. As the new medium scrambled to find content to fill its many hours of broadcasting in the 1950s, comics came to the rescue to fill the void for children's TV fare. For youngsters already attuned to and comfortable with the comic book medium, it was not much of a stretch for them to sit on the family room floor, reach for the television dials, and tune in to see their favorite cat, dog or rabbit characters from the comics.

It's true youngsters in the early age of television did not find many squirrels on the initial TV programs tailored for their tastes. That's probably due to the fact that squirrels are not domesticated animals and thus can be a little scary. Squirrels may be best suited for more mature audiences. They will never replace man's best friend or compete favorably with kittens, cats or even rabbits. However, even though squirrels may not have been the darlings of the new television age, they were not total no-shows. And squirrels have found more screen time in recent years at movie theaters, on the monitors of laptop computers and on the display devices used by video games. Squirrels are naturals for games, because they are playful creatures that are all about finding, hoarding and protecting their valuable food quarry.

In his study, *Understanding Media: The Extensions of Man*, McLuhan had a lot to say about games. In an overbearing corporate world, McLuhan argued that games are crucial for a healthy, functioning society. Games are not just a diversion but an essential part of the mass media mix. McLuhan went out of his way to answer those who scoffed at the idea of games as mass media. To the question of whether games constitute mass media, he answered with a resounding "Yes." In making that point, McLuhan emphasized that games are situations contrived to permit the simultaneous participation of many people in roles beyond their everyday life. He added, "That games are extensions, not of our private but of our social selves, and that they are media of communications, should now be plain."[17]

The media guru of the 1960s foreshadowed today's video game producers, designers and avid players in pronouncing on what games are all about. McLuhan said that games fulfill a number of functions: Games provide an escape and a release valve from the anxiety and tensions that build up in a population enmeshed in a highly organized society. They enable individuals to stand aside from the pressure of daily routines and conventions and allow them to observe and question the social construction of reality. Games also help restore a sense of self. According to McLuhan, "A man or society without games is one sunk in the zombie trance of automation."[18]

McLuhan's views may sound pretty serious when considering the simplicity of the early video games such as *Home Pong*, *Pac-Man* or *Donkey Kong*. McLuhan may also sound a bit too earnest if one subscribes to the stereotype of the video game player as an introverted adolescent male with an acne problem. However, studies now show that video games are played by almost half of the American population, with the average age of a game player being thirty-nine. Additionally, the percentage of players who are women has surpassed 40 percent. With more than 130 million American video game players, and with advertising agencies increasingly placing their messages within the games, the video game scene is definitely part of the schemata of mass media.[19]

Although McLuhan believed that games are a critical component in the makeup and functioning of a healthy modern society, he did not view games in themselves as totally serious affairs. In fact, McLuhan remarked on the important role of laughter in modern society and the humor within the game paradigm that generates laughter. McLuhan quotes Wyndham Lewis, who said that "laughter is the mind sneezing" as a result of the contradictions that the intellect grapples with when confronting modern life. Games can provide the tickling feather that leads to the laughter of the mind sneezing. "We think of humor as a mark of sanity for good reason," McLuhan observed. "In fun and play we recover the integral person, who in the workday world and professional life can use only a small sector of this."[20]

Fun, play and fantasy are inherent in almost all video games, and the games that feature squirrels certainly are no exception. Ray the Flying Squirrel is a video game character familiar to fans of the *Sonic the Hedgehog* series. Ray is capable of extreme speeds in flight (and equally capable of inspiring a few laughs). Conker the Squirrel is a bad boy game character, who in his early *Diddy Kong Racing* days was reasonably well behaved and perfect for youngsters. Somewhere along the way, however, this squirrel took a very bad turn and became one of the top anti-heroes for mature audiences. By contrast, Squirrel Girl has become the Wonder Woman of fur partisans. *Slate's* culture blog has described Squirrel Girl as "not the hero we deserved [but] the one we needed."[21] Then there is the mischievous squirrel, Ratatoskr, a popular squirrel of ancient times traced to Pagan religions and Norse mythology. Ratatoskr appears as a notorious melee character in the video game *Smite*.

As described above, squirrels found a place in comic books from the early days of that medium, and it should be no surprise that they quickly adapted to the video game platform when that medium began to evolve into storytelling modes.

Squirrels have found video game fame in a variety of formats and settings. Ray the Flying Squirrel found notoriety on Eggman Island along with his friends Mighty the Armadillo and Sonic the Hedgehog. Game reviewers described the flying squirrel and his video game friends as amusing, if not downright hilarious.

Ray the Flying Squirrel

Before there was a squirrel named Ray, there was a hedgehog named Sonic. Video game designer Manabu Kusunoki saw that the hedgehog in the original 1993 *Sega-Sonic the Hedgehog* was an odd, solitary fellow and very lonely. To remedy this situation, he created the new game characters of Mighty the Armadillo and Ray the Flying Squirrel.[22] They collaborated in trying to escape an island after they were kidnapped and stranded there together by the evil Doctor Eggman. Video game players were instructed to use a trackball to move the three characters. In order to escape the island, the hedgehog, armadillo and flying squirrel had to dodge formidable obstacles and collect valuable rings. Also, Ray the Flying Squirrel could not get his pretty white gloves dirty.

Like so many mass-mediated squirrels, Ray the Flying Squirrel of the 1984 video game remake wears some quality white gloves. Of course, the most famous rodent sporting fancy white gloves is the Disney superstar known as Mickey Mouse. A number of explanations have been floated as to why Mickey Mouse, Ray the Flying Squirrel and so many other famous rodents wear gloves. One rationale holds that these rodents are all stage stars of sorts, and, like vaudeville entertainers of yore, they must don white gloves as a part of the act. Another theory is that the gloves are a tradition from the days of black-and-white films, when dressing the hands in white helped them to stand out visually for the cameras.

The most likely explanation for the white gloves is very simple: Squirrel "hands" are pretty darned ugly—with furry backsides, pink palms and terrible claws. In order to transform a common squirrel into a people-friendly, anthropomorphic delight, a good pair of white gloves serves to hide the frightful rodent features. However, gloves are not all that is needed to camouflage loathsome rodent attributes. Among other things, Ray the Flying Squirrel sports large cuffs to go with his gloves and other finery.

In his early years, Ray was known for his memorable and colorful sneakers: red with a white buckle strap and white sock-like tops. Over time, Ray traded in his red sneakers for blue ones with white soles that sported white dots on each side of the heel, which helped to further distinguish the squirrel from his hedgehog and armadillo compatriots.

Flashy dress serves to distract from natural squirrel endowments (beyond the claws) that may not be so attractive. In the case of Ray the Flying Squirrel, those endowments include a bulbous and shiny black nose as well as a long, club-shaped tail. On either side of the nose are smallish, triangular ears. A furry skin membrane connects his waist to his lower arms—all the better for flying above trouble when necessary. Ray has dark brown skin on his muzzle and on all parts not covered in golden fur, as well as black eyes and a tapered hair tuft growing out of the back of his head. When Ray is in flight, he almost looks like a buzzing honeybee that has lost all the normal black stripes of a bee's back end. These peculiar endowments serve to make him a comic-relief kind of character.

Ray the Flying Squirrel isn't just about being airborne. He has a number of marvelous advantageous beyond flight. Ray can burst and burrow through just about any material obstacle—that is, if he is able to work up enough speed before making contact. He has the ability to become a bull in a china shop when he performs his best spin jump, a maneuver in which he curls into a ball or cutting disk and aims himself at adversaries to throw them totally off guard. Like his counterpart hedgehog, he can also accelerate to high speeds when his video game master requires that of him.

The game story behind Ray the Flying Squirrel involves his abduction and transportation to Eggman Island. Ray was to be executed there along with his friends, Mighty the Armadillo and Sonic the Hedgehog. Together, the three conspire to escape imprisonment, only to be blown to the other side of the island. It's then a matter of negotiating hazards and traps to get to Eggman Tower. At the tower, Dr. Robotnik triggers a self-destruction sequence, but the squirrel, armadillo and hedgehog make a break for it and escape the island before it explodes. The game of getting off the island takes place on several levels and must be completed as quickly as possible. If a character's health bar is fully depleted, it is fatal (meaning game over). Restoration of a character's health index can be accomplished by capturing rings and bonus rings in enemy confrontations. *SegaSonic the Hedgehog* is modeled after the old arcade game design in an effort to harken back to the earlier Sega Genesis games.

The video game squirrel, armadillo and hedgehog received good reviews in gaming magazines. The characters were described as amusing, if not hilarious. The game likewise collected superlatives in the areas of animation, background music and cinematic appeal. *Electronic Gaming Monthly* tagged the game with a perfect score and remarked that it "shatters your perception of what a good game should be."[23] It's hard to go wrong with a well-dressed flying squirrel, who gets more than a little help from his armadillo and hedgehog friends.

Game Bad Boy: Conker the Squirrel

At one time, he was a very good boy. Conker the Squirrel was a friendly young chap in a blue vest and yellow cape. It was just the right get-up for entertaining the younger set in 1997 as a friendly character in Nintendo's *Diddy Kong* series. Conker was notable for his large Converse All Star shoes and his even larger tail. As a well-behaved anthropomorphic video game squirrel, his wise parents taught him early in life to be polite, to never be greedy or aggressive and to never drink or relieve himself in public. Although he was not perfect, he was a role model of sorts. The young squirrel behaved himself quite well in the game *Conker's Quest* by Rareware for enthusiastic younger audiences.

And then Conker the Squirrel got older, just like his audience, many of whom were boys on their way to the trials of adolescence and manhood. Conker dropped the kid look and became scruffier and stubbier; his blue hoodie outfit took on patches and many zippers—perhaps for contraband, as his lifestyle took on a dramatically different demeanor. When backs were turned, this well-bred squirrel took up bad habits. He began swilling alcohol and spewing obscene utterances (and occasionally the contents of an abused stomach). Meet the new Conker the Squirrel, exclusively released for the Xbox in June 2005. Gamers began to know the transformed creature from *Conker's Bad Fur Day* and, later, *Conker: Live & Reloaded* and *Project Spark*.[24]

Conker the Squirrel was a good kid in his early video game days, but as he got older, he took to heavy drinking, spewing outrageous obscenities, and finding love with a chipmunk porn star. Gamers came to know the transformed video game character through such offerings as *Conker's Bad Fur Day* and *Conker: Live & Reloaded*.

Prior to 2005, Conker made some family-friendly appearances with *Diddy Kong Racing* before achieving the stature of an independent game character. Perhaps it was inevitable that as Conker grew up in an ever-changing world of mass media and popular culture, he was going to evolve. He was simply not going to remain as some choir boy squirrel. What is surprising is that little Conker grew up to become a big drinker and a hangover-prone squirrel wondering just what happened the night before. Also surprising is the consistent popularity of the boozy squirrel, as he became known for puking over his shoulder and hurling lewd comments. What may not be so surprising is Conker's listing in *Game Daily's* "Top 25 Anti Heroes."[25] It also may not be surprising that Conker found love with a wayward chipmunk with a bad reputation as a buxom porn star.

Berri, the porn star chipmunk, wasn't always a red-light district kind of rodent. Originally, she was a cute, brownish, acorn gatherer with an eye for Conker. However, just as Conker's admirable image went south over time, so did Berri's reputation. She developed into a lanky and curvaceous chipmunk who started hanging out with Conker—and a bad crowd. After a number of close calls with unsavory characters, Conker's chipmunk girlfriend is finally rubbed out by a weasel mafia boss known as Don Weaso. At this point, the light of Conker's chaotic life is extinguished. The death of Berri is, indeed, an extremely bad fur day for the squirrel as he realizes that without her, life is probably not worth living.

Gamers who have chosen to get mixed up in the tumultuous life and times of Conker and Berri have found game action involving battles with dastardly enemies and harrowing races with adversaries. Game action also involves solving mysteries and competing for cash necessary to gain admittance to different sectors or game levels. Conker the Squirrel has a wide range of weapons and physical abilities that can be utilized by a player controlling his actions. Among the weapons that Conker uses are such basic items as a slingshot, a frying pan, a spiked baseball bat, throwing knives and urine. On the more serious side, Conker can also use a bazooka, a pair of machine guns, a flamethrower and a chainsaw. As far as his own physical prowess is concerned, Conker can run, jump, climb ladders and ropes, push heavy items and swim underwater when necessary.

Despite Conker's access to an assortment of weaponry and his amazing abilities to run, jump and swim, the squirrel obviously has lifestyle issues. His abuse of alcohol often leaves him seriously incapacitated, and gamers must come to the rescue. They can do this by utilizing "context sensitive" pads and pressing buttons that permit the squirrel to recover from his various maladies. For example, if one makes the right moves and pushes the right buttons, Conker can drink some Alka-Seltzer to knock out his hangovers. The game can then proceed. Any health problems arising from Conker's poor lifestyle choices can also be addressed by prompting the squirrel to eat "antigravity" chocolate morsels. These sweet pieces can be found at various game levels and will provide the squirrel with the needed sustenance to continue the action.

Conker the Squirrel had various incarnations and reincarnations throughout his history in video games. Starting with his original innocent appearance in *Diddy Kong Racing* in 1997, Conker went on to *Conker's Bad Fur Day* in 2001 and *Conker Live & Reloaded* in 2005. As Conker became edgier through his use of obscenities and consumption of alcohol, the squirrel was marketed for more mature audiences. Advertisements for the rollout of *Conker's Bad Fur Day* appeared in more adult-oriented media venues, including *Playboy*. The game had obviously become a little too violent and too controversial for reviewers looking in the rearview mirror for the more family-friendly squirrel. However, Conker did receive a positive reception from those who understood that the character had moved on from being just another critter in a kid's game.

The game *Conker's Bad Fur Day* benefited from industry reviews that looked very favorably on the squirrel's evolution. Praise was granted for innovations in game lighting, shadowing, texture and the portrayal of the squirrel himself. Matt Casamassina of IGN (formerly the Imagine Games Network) noted that the jokes were clever and occasionally over-the-top funny. He was especially impressed with the technological effects on the squirrel. Casamassina declared, "Conker himself is equipped with an in-game facial animation system that realistically portrays his different moods as he travels the lands. When he's scared, he looks it, and when he's pissed off, players will be able to see his teeth showing in a frown."[26]

Squirrel Girl: Video Game On

Given the popularity of Squirrel Girl in comics, books, trading cards and toy collectibles—along with several notable television appearances—it should be no surprise that this most versatile of superheroines has found her way onto the video game circuit. However, it wasn't necessarily an easy climb to get there. The standout squirrel starlet created in 1992 had to vanquish many powerful villains before becoming an electronic action figure ready to do vigorous battle via video game consoles and online sites. Her superhuman strength, signature squirrel tail, and close friendship with literally thousands of smaller squirrel allies helped propel her to ultimate game fame. And, of course, she got a little help from some very close furry friends—her sidekick squirrels, Monkey Joe and Tippy-Toe.

Squirrel Girl is a playable character in *Marvel Super Hero Squad: Comic Combat*, a video game based on characters from the Marvel comic books. The comic combat game involves the infamous Doctor Doom, and all of his minions are present to scheme and to find a way to become actors in the real world, so as to subdue and conquer the comic book universe. Game players may choose from ten so-called Squaddies based on characters from classic comic books: Iron Man, Thor, Captain America, Wolverine, Falcon, Scarlet Witch, Invisible Woman, Reptil, Hulk and (last but not least) the unbeatable Squirrel Girl. The game benefits from a total of six comic book–designed stages of video play. Additionally, players can excel by winning "hero points," which can then be employed to upgrade all the impressive Squaddies, including Squirrel Girl.[27]

Squirrel Girl also finds a place in Lego video games such as *Lego Marvel Super Heroes* and *Lego Marvel's Avengers*. The amazing use of the multicolored plastic blocks in a spate of movies and video games has revived interest in these miniature building materials, which were once considered merely a kid's toy. These days, Legos are not just a box of plastic bricks to snap and pile together to build inanimate objects. In the hands of video game designers, Legos become the building blocks for telling very good stories. The Lego incarnation of Squirrel Girl becomes an artful anthropomorphic animal capable of putting evil conspirators in their place.

As a creature born of Legos, Squirrel Girl takes on a flesh-toned head with reddish-brown hair, light olive-green arms, flesh-toned hands and a mostly brown torso. She also sports brown hips and light olive-green legs. Her torso and legs benefit from printing that aids in portraying her brown costume, feminine curves, and brown boots. Obviously, a Lego-created Squirrel Girl cannot possess the large bushy tail found in her comic or book iterations. However, her tail in video games still manages to sway and mesmerize. Her face is printed to depict black eyes with white pupils, accented by black squirrel-styled markings and a rather petite feminine mouth.

The Lego Squirrel Girl finds success thanks to some talented voiceovers by well-known female talents. In *Lego Marvel Super Heroes*, the voice is that of Tara Strong, who has been the voice of numerous animated characters, from those found in television's *Rugrats* to *Family Guy*. She wows admirers with her attendance at Comic-Con Conventions. Strong has won many voice acting awards and was selected as Voice Actress of the Year for 2013.[28] Squirrel Girl also gets a nice assist in the voice department from Misty Lee. In *Lego Marvel's Avengers*, Lee performs the magic required to give the squirrel a memorable audio component. In fact, Lee is a celebrated magician who began performing magic tricks in her teens. At Comic-Con International in 2015, Lee designed and tutored celebrities in custom effects for the "Magic of Comics" themed awards show. In addition to her magic talents, Lee is a recognized voice actor, bringing life to Squirrel Girl and appearing in award-winning video games such as *The Last of Us*, *Grand Theft Auto* and the *Fire Emblem* series.[29]

Additional video games in which Squirrel Girl appears are *Marvel Future Flight*, *Pinball FX 2* and *Marvel Puzzle Quest*. In *Marvel Future Flight*, Squirrel Girl takes on one of her more seductive looks, which is a disappointment to some female fans who have praised comic and game artists for not over-sexualizing the character. In her books, Squirrel Girl comes off as wholesome, upbeat and high powered, but not hostile. In *Marvel Future Flight*, Squirrel Girl looks far more imposing with more of a Wonder Woman vibe. Her black gloved fists are clenched on each side of her hips, as if to challenge all comers to just try to mess with her.

Squirrel Girl sports high, red, lace-up boots and sleek silver tights in *Marvel Future Flight*, as well as a red one-piece suit that makes her look quite chesty (especially compared to her earlier versions). A tight black leather jacket serves to frame the bosomy squirrel's upper torso. In addition to the apparel makeover, the Squirrel Girl in *Marvel Future Flight* is much more human in form. She has more attractive facial features and dangling bangs that seem to curl down from more of a pageboy-type haircut. Squirrel Girl also seems to have become a strawberry blonde for this game and has ditched the coarse, brown squirrel hair so typical of her look in other venues. Her bobbing tail moves up and down behind her when she is not in combat mode.

As a battler in *Marvel Future Flight*, Squirrel Girl gets mixed reviews. She is said to be well designed and is credited with being able to handily lock down her opponents to render them powerless. Reviewers give her the highest marks for her eye framing, her use of squirrel bombs, her scurry roll and her tail whip for exacting great physical damage.[30] If her assets are used properly, she has deceptive skills that make her especially formidable to anyone who underestimates her. And then there is her sidekick, Tippy-Toe, who seems to grow taller and even more tenacious than Squirrel Girl in the heat of battle. The electrified Squirrel Girl of video gaming seems to be more and more unchained and unshackled, so there is some anticipation in the video game world as to her next evolution.

Smite: *Battle of the Gods*

The ancient mythological squirrel Ratatoskr was selected in the second decade of the new millennium as the 66th godly figure to join various other deities that do battle in the video game *Smite*.[31] Ratatoskr constitutes the tenth god from the Norse pantheon of mythological figures. He also has been numbered as the thirteenth assassin added to *Smite*. The idea of a squirrel playing an assassin only makes sense in the context of the character's mythological origins and in the context of the cutthroat video game developed by Hi-Rez Studios for Microsoft Windows with a release in 2014. (*Smite* was later released for Xbox One, PlayStation 4 and for macOS.)

Under the rules of *Smite*, players control a goddess, god or other mythological figure such as Ratatoskr and compete in team-based combat using skills and tactics that are logically associated with their characters. These skills and strategies are employed against other player-controlled gods and non-player-controlled minions. The game has become popular on the e-sports scene and has been featured in a host of tournaments, including the annual Smite World Championship.[32] However, the game is not so popular with a number of religious groups that have objected to their deities becoming warriors in a video game. Fortunately, there are few Vikings left in the modern world to object to the appropriation of their mythological squirrel, Ratatoskr, for use in *Smite*.

The name *Smite* is derived from the Old Testament; it is a biblical term denoting the actions of an angry god intent on injuring or destroying enemies of his chosen people. The word "smite" is used in the first book of the Bible, Genesis, and many more times in the Book of Exodus. In Exodus, the God of the Old Testament vows to smite the borders of Egypt with frogs, to smite its people with a pestilence, to smite the firstborn of both man and beast, and to smite the dust of the land with lice.[33] There is a considerable amount of smiting done in the books of Deuteronomy and Numbers as well. Obviously, when it came to picking a name for a video game about killing and conquest, *Smite* was a well-chosen moniker from world's top-selling "Good Book." And Ratatoskr is a well-chosen squirrel to be incorporated into the game play of *Smite*, despite the fact that he does not have origins in Old Testament tradition.

Artists and designers for *Smite* have made Ratatoskr into a startlingly strange variation on a red squirrel. His ears are extremely long and pointed, so that when he is at rest, they have the look of a rabbit; however, when he is airborne, his ears appear to blow back in the breeze like the wings of Zephyr. His eyes are very large, glassy almonds without pupils. The eyes are inscrutable, whether they are exhibiting a glassy, deep blue or a purple glare. His tail is long and fluffy (in later incarnations, the tail sports iridescent turquoise stripes). When bared, his two long, front teeth are tightly spaced (true to his ancient nickname of "Drill Tooth"). Ratatoskr's two upper paws stand out from his sides as if he is about to draw some holstered weapons for a duel, although the armaments he is most likely to clutch are special demolition acorns.

According to Norse legend, the original Ratatoskr was a troublemaker, a busybody, and an undesirable meddler. He also was a gossip, a backbiter and a treacherous purveyor of the most malicious hearsay. Ratatoskr used all these reprehensible traits to inflame tensions and aggravate the relationship between an eagle and a monstrous serpentine dragon. The eagle found a home at the top of the tree of life, while the dragon resided in the tree's gnarly roots—and Ratatoskr ran up and down the tree delivering messages between the two of them. However, the mischievous Ratatoskr poisoned these messages with spite and horrible deceits that angered the eagle and the dragon, to the point that their fury threatened to destabilize and destroy the great tree of life.

The developers and animators of *Smite* were attracted to the Norse lore about the impish squirrel named Ratatoskr, a small furball who could cause so much trouble scurrying up and down a giant tree. The enigmatic and magical squirrel has presented a mystery to more than just game designers. Psychoanalysts and folklore historians have offered various explanations about Ratatoskr's meaning—some of which are complex and even flattering to the otherwise disparaged squirrel. One interpretation draws on Sigmund Freud, positing that the dragon represents the id and the eagle represents the superego, while the squirrel runs interference between the two of them and actually represents the psychological balancing act (and mediation) performed by intelligence.[34] A less complicated account of the Ratatoskr myth holds that ancient Vikings simply took great offense to aggressive squirrels chattering and barking at them from the treetops in their native lands. In response, the Norsemen concocted stories around the campfire to express the depths of their contempt for the loud but nimble inhabitants of the trees of Northern Europe.

In some fashion, the troublemaking Ratatoskr can be construed as a symbol of the unhappiness that the video game *Smite* has caused a number of religious groups. Hindu leaders issued a statement in 2012 urging the removal of such deities as Kali, Agni and Vamana from the game.[35] Their inclusion purportedly trivialized the Hindu faith, and the notion of *Smite* players directing Hindu deities with video game controllers was offensive.

However, the game developers and Hi-Rez Studios were unimpressed by these arguments. They were intent on expanding the pantheons of gods and mythic figures included in the game, from Greek, Chinese, Egyptian, Hindu and Norse sources.

Although the game caused discomfort among some religious devotees, *Smite* proved to be a hit among gamers. Hi-Rez Studios organized competition in 2014 in which players could join *Smite* leagues in teams of five. Players progressed through online contests, and then they moved to offline battles. Top team finalists were invited to play in a Smite World Championship in 2015, and teams from North America, South America, Europe, and China traveled to Atlanta for the big tournament. Hundreds of thousands of dollars were at stake in prize pool money in tournament play. In 2015, prize winnings were the third highest in e-sports, even outranking the League of Legends World Championship.[36] At the time of this writing, *Smite* world competitions are still going strong.

8

Legendary
American Squirrels

Most Americans know about the Pilgrims and Thanksgiving, the Boston Tea Party, Paul Revere's famous ride, and George Washington crossing the Delaware. Far fewer Americans know that squirrels were present for the first Thanksgiving. Most Americans also are probably unaware that squirrels played a role in winning the Revolutionary War, much less about the role that squirrels played in the pioneers' subsequent taming and settlement of the American continent. Squirrels provided essential sustenance in early America and deserve much credit for keeping colonial settlements nourished. They certainly merit more accolades as early American culinary offerings than turkeys, which have received undue attention thanks to the mythology that surrounds the first Thanksgiving dinner of the Pilgrims. Squirrel meat was, in fact, the real meal deal in North America both before and after independence was declared in 1776.

After America achieved its independence and began acquiring new lands in the west, there was considerable curiosity about what kinds of animals might be found in these untamed wildernesses and unexplored expanses. The Lewis and Clark expedition traveled up the Missouri River and cataloged the flora and fauna encountered on the long route to the Pacific Ocean. Captain Meriwether Lewis wrote a number of detailed accounts, including an interesting dispatch about the small gray squirrel, which he declared extraordinarily common in all corners of the Rocky Mountain timberlands. Squirrels were everywhere.

Lewis wrote about the gray squirrels when the expedition was well under way. However, months before that, he had recorded observations about squirrels on his way to the St. Louis area, where the trip to explore the west was to begin. In September 1803, while crossing a wide stretch of the Ohio River, he was shocked to see a mass migration of squirrels, with many of the animals swimming across the river. He noted in his journal that the squirrels were

This celebrated bronze statue in St. Charles, Missouri, features Captain Meriwether Lewis putting a reassuring hand on the shoulder of fellow frontiersman Captain William Clark as Lewis' intrepid dog, Seaman, looks forward to more adventure. During his travels, Lewis was surprised to find migrating squirrels swimming across wide expanses of water to get to their own unknown destinations (photograph by Holly Shanks).

surprisingly able swimmers and kept up a very good speed. He described them as appearing "black, [and] they swim very light on the water."[1] Not one to miss out on an easy meal, Lewis set his faithful dog loose upon the squirrels. His campfire probably crackled with the fat of the roasted black squirrels as he prepared several portions of the wilderness delicacy on his trip to Missouri.

The common wisdom of the Revolutionary War period was that if you were an able shooter of small squirrels, you were bound to be an effective marksman when it came to taking down the Redcoats. Many regiments of the British army wore the familiar red uniform in their confrontations with the colonial army. If a colonial recruit could prove his mettle against a red squirrel (or a brown or a gray squirrel), he would likely have success when targeting a Redcoat. Squirrel hunters found considerable favor with the officers of the armed colonial units, just as they later found favor with officers of the Union army in the war against the Confederates almost a century later.

Squirrel hunters of Ohio found fame in the Civil War when Confederate forces began moving through Kentucky on their way to attack the important Union outpost of Cincinnati. The men who became known as the "Squirrel Hunters" joined militia groups to aid the Union forces aligned to repulse Confederates in any potential assault. One local legend maintains that the volunteers acquired their fame as the Squirrel Hunters for their proven shooting abilities.[2] These men were credited with being able to shoot the little varmints out of the trees on the Kentucky banks of the Ohio River, firing their rifles from the Ohio side of the river. The legacy of these men lives on—even as a great number of squirrels continue to live on—on either side of the Ohio River.

More than two centuries after hostilities ceased between Great Britain and the fledgling United States of America, a new war has broken out between the Brits and the Yanks. In Britain, the native red squirrels are under siege by the uppity, imported North American gray squirrels. Some British partisans speak of the unwanted invasion of the gray squirrels as a form of Yankee revenge for the time when the British marched upon the colonial turf and attacked American settlements. Loyal Englishmen's attempt to rid their turf of the American squirrels is described as a hopeless exercise by expert observers. No Winston Churchill showed up in the nick of time to rally his countrymen for a campaign against the gray squirrels, and so the window of opportunity against the gray squirrels slammed shut. Yankee squirrels now number in the millions and have subdued much of southern England. The red squirrels have dwindled to less than 150,000 and have been chased north to the British Midlands and up to Scotland.[3]

Gray squirrels are not just overrunning England. Squirrels have also been multiplying in America because of the decline in natural predators and human hunters. The only major threat to squirrels now comes on four wheels, but even the ubiquitous American automobile is not up to the task of keeping squirrel numbers under control. As mentioned in chapter 2, some American communities have been experimenting with squirrel birth control and other extreme measures. Officials with hunting organizations have launched campaigns to classify squirrels as legitimate game, but they admit that they are hampered by a number of misconceptions and fabrications about the efficacy of squirrel hunting. Among the myths that they are trying to shoot down:

154

Squirrels aren't glamorous. Squirrels aren't challenging. Squirrels have no place in a modern hunter's world. Real men don't hunt squirrels.

The case can be made that real men certainly do hunt squirrels. The Revolutionary War's musket carriers, who gained their skills through shooting at squirrels, were certainly real men. The popular Squirrel Hunters, ready to face down Johnny Reb on the banks of the Ohio River in the Civil War, were real men. And today there is one real man ready to give the sport of squirrel hunting a shot in the arm. No one has tried more to bring back the once-popular sport of hunting squirrels than the controversial rock star Ted Nugent. Nugent has bagged squirrels with firearms and hunting bows. He also won the National Squirrel Shooting Archery Contest by successfully picking off unsuspecting rodents from a distance of 150 yards. Nugent has advocated for squirrel hunting as a patriotic American exercise on MTV and in the pages of *Rolling Stone*. Nugent has even tried to bring back the guts and glory of eating squirrel with his recipes for squirrel casseroles in his popular *Kill It & Grill It: A Guide to Preparing and Cooking Wild Game and Fish*.[4]

Squirrels: Unsung Colonial Heroes

A major part of the mythology of early America involves a fantasy of golden brown, succulent turkey appearing at the Pilgrims' first Thanksgiving feast at Plymouth. However, historians have produced research in recent years that serves to dissolve those tantalizing images of turkey, dressing, sweet potatoes, cranberry sauce and pumpkin pie. Much of what is now traditional Thanksgiving fare simply was not available for the rough-hewn table set some 400 years ago. Historians tell us that the feast more likely included local fish—lobster, bass, bluefish and cod. The meat was probably duck, geese and unlimited portions of venison from the deer inhabiting the area. There is no mention of squirrel, although squirrel meat may have been an ingredient in some of the stews and meat pies of that time.

Squirrels may not have had a prominent place at the autumn harvest celebration, but squirrels' preferred foods were very likely on the first Thanksgiving table in the form of side dishes. Those much-coveted morsels would have included chestnuts, pine nuts and walnuts. The close availability of these food items was a guarantee that squirrels were thriving in the vicinity of the Pilgrims' encampments. So, even if plates piled high with fried or grilled squirrel were not shared among the Pilgrims and the Wampanoag tribesmen on that first Thanksgiving, it's a sure bet that squirrels were in the neighborhood in some quantity. They would have been making their presence known by running across the roofs of the colonists' shelters and enjoying their own fall bounty of nuts from the nearby trees.

Despite the absence of turkey and squirrel at the first Thanksgiving, squirrels did constitute a primary food source for Native Americans. The newly arrived Europeans also ate squirrels, as they were plentiful and readily available as targets for the colonists' muskets. Squirrel meat could be quickly prepared and cooked in a variety of ways. However, as the settlers became farmers, squirrels came to be viewed much more as pests and less as a ready food source. Squirrels grew to be such a nuisance for pioneer farmers that the colonial authorities began accepting squirrel scalps for payment of taxes. Plagues of the rodents in the farmers' fields prompted Pennsylvania authorities to offer hunters three pence for each squirrel that they put out of its misery, thus reducing the misery of the early farmers.[5]

Colonists honed their shooting skills through taking down squirrels with their long-barreled rifles. Those skills are often credited with giving them an edge over the British in the battle for independence. Given their sacrifice, squirrels should probably have a special place in today's Fourth of July celebrations. Legends of the Revolutionary War hold that the colonists' encounters with squirrels gave them an eye for very small targets—an advantage that later became crucial for shooting the soldiers of King George at great distance and driving them from the new continent.[6]

July Fourth celebrations may seem like the natural time to acknowledge the role of the squirrels in the War of Independence, but the Thanksgiving holiday would actually be more appropriate. Squirrels could be prepared for Thanksgiving tables in homes across America. Of course, squirrels will never replace the turkey that has become the focal point of the annual great American get-together. However, a healthy helping of squirrel stew could potentially accompany the presentation of the bird and become a welcome addition to the table.

For a major part of American history, squirrels have been a popular dining tradition in many parts of the country. In the northern states and Alaska, squirrels have found their way to the American table in a stew called booyah. In southern states, squirrels have long been a tasty treat in the popular Brunswick stew. In the Midwest, the squirrels have found their way into the supper pot in stews called burgoos.

Squirrel booyah is a strange gumbo of thick broth, softened vegetables and shredded squirrel meat. Squirrels are harvested for booyah with a light shotgun or .22-gauge rifle. (Larger armaments will blow the animals to pieces and make the meat difficult to salvage.) Vegetables accompanying the meat may include corn, tomatoes, cabbage, potatoes, onions, lentils and whatever else is available. Booyah is simmered for hours, to the point of becoming a virtual mush surrounded by the occasional rivulet of juicy broth. *Booyah* is considered a contrived word derived from *bouillon* or from *bouillir* (the French word for "boil").[7]

Squirrel burgoo has sometimes been compared to an Irish stew and has many of the same vegetables as booyah, with the addition of okra, lima beans and other local favorites depending on where it is put together. As with booyah, it is slowly cooked and thickened to the point at which the ingredients seem to meld. A good burgoo is reportedly so thick that a kitchen utensil will stand upright when half submerged in the concoction. Burgoo has sometimes been referred to as "roadkill-and-veggie ragout." Burgoo often is served with biscuits, corn muffins or cornbread. Burgoo community cooking festivals were once common harvest season events in Kentucky, southern Illinois and southern Indiana. Today these social events are sometimes used as fundraisers. Several cities in Illinois have claimed the title of "burgoo capital of the world," as has the town of Owensboro, Kentucky.[8]

Brunswick stew is a dish of the American South, with three states (Virginia, Georgia and North Carolina) laying claim to having originated the popular dish. Of these three states, Georgia may have the strongest argument as the Brunswick stew capital. Brunswick, Georgia, keeps an original stew pot on its Farmers Market pavilion. Mounted near the old, iron pot is a plaque maintaining that the first stew was made in the Georgia town on July 2, 1898. However, the county of Brunswick, Virginia, has different ideas, and the Virginia state legislature claims that one of its earliest members was involved in the invention of the recipe for Brunswick stew on a hunting expedition in 1828.[9]

There are so many concoctions of booyah, burgoo and Brunswick stew that it would be hard to argue that there is an official recipe for any of the three. Brunswick stew often has a smoky flavor that is absent from booyah and burgoo, although even that claim is subject to dispute. *American Cookery*, the James Beard recipe book originally published in 1972, offered directions for Brunswick stew that included three squirrels, veal stock, a half cup of Madeira, corn, lima beans, tomatoes and okra. Beard insisted that squirrels have long been associated with elegant dining, even while being the simple food of the trapper and the explorer.[10] Indeed, high-class restaurants in sophisticated American big cities once had squirrel on the menu. Chicago's Everett House Hotel had a Thanksgiving menu featuring three kinds of squirrel, black bear and buffalo after the Civil War and into the 1970s.[11]

Booyah, burgoo and Brunswick stew all saw an unfortunate change in their makeup after World War II, when squirrel meat was increasingly replaced by pieces of chicken, pork, venison or beef. The reasons for the decline in the use of squirrel in the stews are many: Hunters started acquiring more firepower and turned to bigger game, such as turkeys and deer. Busy people had little time to simmer stews for hours, especially when frozen foods came along with quick preparation directions. Also, the humble squirrel was labeled a rudimentary dish for backwoods hicks. Finally, a health scare emerged in the 1990s when doctors in the neurological department at the University of Kentucky warned that squirrels might carry a variant of mad cow disease that could be transmitted to humans. Doctors noted that several victims of spongiform encephalopathies were all "squirrel-brain eaters."[12] Further medical analyses discounted the scare over squirrels as a dish for dinner, but the damage was done.

Today, calls for bringing squirrels back to the supper table are growing louder. It's all part of the growing sustainability movement in America. Squirrels are a local source of meat that's high in protein, with a savory, nutty flavor due to the animal's own lifetime of gorging on nuts. Project Squirrel at the University of Illinois at Chicago notes that squirrels are so prolific that 80 percent of the population could be harvested annually without putting a dent in their numbers.[13] The environmental impact of turning to squirrels for sustenance is nonexistent compared to what the beef industry is doing around the world to give us hamburgers. Squirrel meat advocates argue that it's time to plan for a crockpot full of squirrels for next Thanksgiving—time to replace that dry and unhealthy turkey stuffing with a serving of squirrel-laden Brunswick stew. It's time to acknowledge the importance of the American squirrel and do what is sustainable, environmentally sound, and patriotic on the holiday established by President Abraham Lincoln in 1863.

Squirrels: Louisiana Purchase Bonus

When President Thomas Jefferson displayed his talent for a good deal with the French in finalizing the Louisiana Purchase in 1803, he did not have a clue as to how many squirrels he was buying with that $15 million. However,

Jefferson must have gotten an inkling of the incredible size of his squirrel acquisition when Meriwether Lewis and William Clark returned from their exploration of the new lands in the west. The Lewis and Clark Expedition (also known as the Corps of Discovery Expedition) departed from a point close to St. Louis in May 1804 and returned in September 1806. In that time, the explorers traveled up the Missouri River and drew crude maps and took note of geographical features in the new territory, in addition to cataloging the flora and fauna along the route.

Lewis wrote about many new species that the Corps of Discovery encountered on their travels, making observations about bighorn sheep, mountain beavers, white weasels and various species of squirrel, rabbit, fox and wolf. Lewis sent five live animals to President Jefferson in 1805, including a "barking squirrel" that lived out the rest of its days at the White House.[14] (This "squirrel" later was identified as a black-tailed prairie dog.) Lewis wrote a brief dispatch about a small gray squirrel, which he said was common in all areas of the Rocky Mountain timberlands. He described the squirrel as extremely nimble and active. Lewis noted "its back neck, sides, head, tail and outer sides of the legs are of a brown lead coloured grey; the tail has a slight touch of the fox color near the extremity of some of the hairs. The throat, breast, belly, and inner parts of the leg are the colour of tanner's ooze."[15]

Lewis may have taken a special interest in all the details of the squirrels discovered on the expedition because of his fondness for squirrel meat. Several times in his travel journals he remarked upon the agreeable taste of squirrel. And, as stated at the beginning of this chapter, he was already writing about squirrels in September 1803, months before the expedition began. While crossing a wide stretch of the Ohio River, he was surprised to see so many squirrels swimming from one shore of the river to the other. "I made my dog take as many each day as I had occation for, they were fat and I thought them when fryed a pleasant food," Lewis wrote on September 11.[16]

Lewis came to realize that he was observing a mass migration of squirrels. At first, he speculated that there must be a greater abundance of acorns and nuts on one shore of the Ohio River that was attracting the squirrels. Upon observing that the quantity of food for the squirrels was roughly the same on each shore, he suggested that changes in the climate must be the reason for the squirrels' unusual actions. Lewis was giving an account of one of the first recorded squirrel migrations in American history. These migrations fascinated his fellow and future countrymen as, like him, they marveled at the mass movement of squirrels. At the same time, however, they were befuddled by what prompts this remarkable squirrel behavior.

Less than a decade after Lewis made his observations on the migrating squirrels, historian Charles Joseph Labrobe wrote about an extraordinary mass squirrel movement that seemed to happen without rhyme or reason. He described the 1811 migration event in *The Rambler in North America* and noted that a strange spirit of change and restlessness pervaded the furry forest inhabitants: "A countless multitude of squirrels, obeying some great and universal impulse, which none can know but the Spirit that gave them being, left their reckless and gamboling life, and their ancient places of retreat in the north, and were seen pressing forward by the tens of thousands in a deep and sober phalanx to the south."[17]

More squirrel migrations were reported in 1842, 1847, 1857, 1881, 1885 and 1887. A mass migration in the northwest is described in the 1846 book, *Viviparous Quadrupeds of North America*, authored by John Audubon and John Bachman.[18] They were convinced that the squirrels on the move were a separate species from gray squirrels. Bachman wrote that the squirrels "congregate in different districts of the far Northwest, and in irregular troops bend their way instinctively in an eastern direction. Mountains, cleared fields, the narrow bays of our lakes, or our broad rivers, present no unconquerable impediments. Onward they come, devouring on their way everything that is suited to their taste, laying waste the corn and wheat fields of the farmer." A mass movement in 1857 through Texas came after an unusual spring cold snap. A dispatch from Henry Garrison Askew reported that his horse and carriage were almost toppled near Dallas, as the horses were spooked by the chaos going on in the tall prairie grass. He watched in horror with his family as thousands of squirrels crossed the road in an army that took an hour to pass.[19] In 1881, another large migration occurred near Tennessee's Reelfoot Lake: squirrels crossed the Mississippi River and entered cornfields, destroying everything as they went. In 1885, Arkansas newspapers reported that millions of squirrels were traveling through the state, leaving residents wondering what part of America could ever produce so many.[20]

Among the great squirrel migrations of recent times is the 1968 mass movement in the eastern United States from Maine to Maryland to the Carolinas. Tens of thousands of squirrels were reported traveling en masse out of woods, across rivers, up and down mountains, and through woods. An enormous number of them became roadkill on the nation's thoroughfares. Hotspots of squirrel activity were reported up and down the East Coast. In

North Carolina, the *Asheville Citizen Tribune* ran a September 17 article headlined "Starvation, Cars, Killing Squirrels by the Thousands."[21] The Asheville paper and several others reported on a wildlife resources commission meeting in which regional managers from across the state described a dire situation. One manager, stationed near Waynesville, described squirrels "pouring" out of the Smokies and swimming across the Fontana and Cheoah lakes. Another claimed to have counted forty dead squirrels on a roughly 20-mile stretch of road near Asheville. The story, "Squirrels Starving in Smokies' Area," was reported by the *New York Times* on September 22, 1968.[22]

All these accounts of mass squirrel migrations suggest that squirrels can be long-distance travelers when the mood strikes them. Scientists are not always sure what puts them in the mood, but it can be quite startling for humans who are used to squirrels staying put in the same backyards, the same parks, the same neck of the woods. Great squirrel migrations, from the 1803 event observed by Meriwether Lewis to the 1968 event described by newspapers of the Carolinas, are all now part of the lore of natural America. Some of that lore is legendary, as illustrated in the account by John Bakeless in his book, *America as Seen by Its First Explorers*.[23]

Bakeless described the 1803 event in the Ohio River area and noted that for hunters it was like shooting fish in a barrel. Squirrels were everywhere, and a hunting party could bring literally hundreds, even thousands, home from an outing. For farmers, however, the scourge of so many hungry squirrels in their fields was like a biblical pestilence. In addition, according to Bakeless, "Boatmen near Marietta found the river completely overrun with immense quantities of black and gray squirrels. They climbed fearlessly up the oars to rest on the boats, which sometimes had five or six of them aboard at once. Since about a third of the little animals drowned before they reached the other bank, travel was sometimes unpleasant because of thousands of dead squirrels putrefying on its surface and its shores."[24]

Are there more great squirrel migrations in America's future? Some scientists suggest not. Too much of the natural landscape has disappeared. Forests have been cleared, and wooded swamplands have been drained. Unnatural barriers to movement have been erected, from cities of concrete and steel to interstate ribbons of asphalt. Nevertheless, climate change has already prodded some animals more common to the southern United States to move north. If large parties of clunky armadillos can risk it all and abandon the Texas heat for the uncertain winters of Missouri, can a mass of messy migrating gray and brown squirrels be far behind?

Squirrel Hunters Fight a Civil War

As stated earlier, one legend of the Revolutionary War was that if you were an able shooter of small squirrels, you were bound to be an effective marksman against the much larger British Redcoats. When the Civil War commenced in 1861, this story was sure to see a new chapter in some shape and form. That addition concerned fighters who were called the "Squirrel Hunters." One legend of the Civil War holds that these recruits were able to knock squirrels out of the trees with their rifles from a distance as wide as the Ohio River.

The Confederate attack on Union forces at Fort Sumter in South Carolina launched a conflict that would eventually claim an estimated seven hundred thousand lives. The Union and Confederacy quickly put together volunteer and conscription armies that fought primarily in the South for more than four years. The Union finally triumphed when General Robert E. Lee surrendered to General Ulysses S. Grant at the Appomattox Court House in 1865, followed by more surrenders by other officers throughout the southern states. There is some debate as to whether squirrel hunters made the difference in the victory of the North over the South. However, Union partisans have declared that squirrel hunters made a crucial difference in protecting one very large Union state (namely, Ohio) against the encroaching forces of the Confederacy.

In 1862, Cincinnati was an American boomtown as large as many coastal cities and relatively insulated from the destruction that was taking place in the Civil War. The busy port city was prospering thanks to its new role of supplying Union troops. That all seemed about to change in August 1862, when Confederate forces routed Union forces at Lexington, Kentucky. With their success in Kentucky (including plans to install a pro–Confederate governor there), the enemy forces were getting too close for comfort to the Buckeye State. Confederate General Kirby Smith dispatched a detachment under Brigadier General Henry Heth to capture Covington, Kentucky, and then to move on the giant prize of Cincinnati. Union military leaders were in shock and quickly came to the realization that an invasion of Ohio could be in the making.

Ohio's governor, David Tod, in Columbus issued a warning to all citizens that an incursion on their southern border was imminent. His proclamation recommended that "all your loyal men of your counties at once form themselves into military companies and regiments to beat back the enemy at any and all points he may attempt to invade our State. Gather up all arms in the country and furnish yourselves with ammunition for the same. The service will be but a few days. The soil of Ohio must not be invaded by the enemies of our glorious government."[25] The Ohio citizenry heeded the call, and in no time sixteen thousand irregulars poured into Cincinnati from the backwoods, all ready to repulse the rebel invasion.

The "minuteman" force was a ragtag mob sporting every manner of weaponry and wearing plenty of buckskin accompanied by coonskin caps. Though poorly equipped and lacking any training, they were welcomed by the good people of Cincinnati with baskets of food and pots of coffee. City residents and merchants were grateful to learn that farmers had deserted their plows and picked up their rifles in defense of the "Queen City" of Ohio. Union army paymaster Malcolm McDowell dubbed the colorful influx of volunteers the "Squirrel Hunters."[26] The description was appropriate on many counts and soon became a popular assignation. Governor Tod took to referring to these fighters as the Squirrel Hunters in official dispatches to Washington, D.C., and to War Secretary Edwin Stanton of President Abraham Lincoln's administration.

Not everyone was excited about the outpouring of pugilistic enthusiasm displayed by the Squirrel Hunters. Some military leaders were wary of the sort of rabble that had entered Cincinnati and the party-like atmosphere that they brought with them. Green and untried, their actual abilities to wage war were in question. At Oberlin College, some 200 miles to the northwest of Cincinnati, President Charles Grandison Finney delivered a sermon predicting inevitable ruin. The problem was not just the underprepared volunteer Squirrel Hunters but also the sin of slavery that Abraham Lincoln would have to summon the will to denounce in no uncertain terms. However, back on the ground in Cincinnati, the locals were more confident and praised demonstrations of the Squirrel Hunters' sharp-shooting abilities.

In the end, the sheer number of assembled Squirrel Hunters gave the Confederate forces great pause. Confederate scouts for Brigadier General Heth were alarmed by the Yankee military operations in Cincinnati and the thousands of men occupying the hills across from Cincinnati in northern Kentucky. The scouts reported that many among the Union forces were called "squirrel shooters," and they were crack-shot farmboys who never had to take a second shot at any squirrel they had in their sights. Less than three weeks after Governor Tod sounded the alarm, the Confederates were in retreat. They were not interested in taking on the overwhelming force assembled in and around Cincinnati. A Union general subsequently remarked that with the Confederates in full retreat, "Cannot I get rid of the Squirrel Hunters?"[27]

The Cincinnati Civil War Roundtable's David E. Roth notes that the volunteers, so renowned for their squirrel hunting, did not immediately disperse even as the fever of war subsided: "Many lingered on, taking advantage of the government's meal ticket and the fine fare doled out by the ladies of the area. No final date of the disbandment is known. It is safe to assume that some of the hunters, inspired by their brief stint in the 'Siege of Cincinnati,' joined the incomplete regiments Governor Tod had forwarded posthaste to the scene of impending danger. But for the most of them, they simply disappeared back into the woods from whence they came, or back to the untended plow left in a hurry when panic reigned along the Ohio."[28]

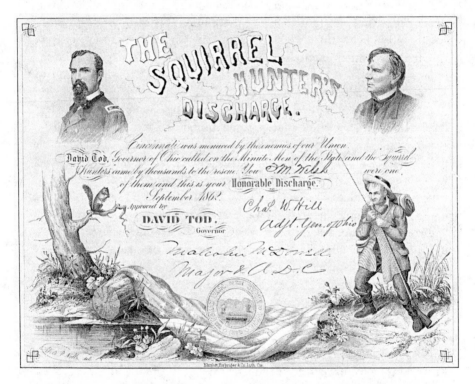

Squirrel hunters volunteered for armed service on the Union side in the Civil War and are credited with dissuading Confederate forces from attacking Cincinnati, Ohio. More than 15,000 volunteered to fight. They were later acknowledged by the governor and state legislature of Ohio with dismissal papers noting their official designation as the "Squirrel Hunters" (courtesy Ohio History Connection).

The federal government did not recognize the great contribution of the Squirrel Hunters in frightening the Confederates into retreat, even after a request for such recognition came from Governor Tod. The state legislature of Ohio did, however, officially thank the patriotic volunteers with the following resolution: "Resolved by the Senate and the House of Representatives of the State of Ohio, that the Governor is hereby authorized and directed to appropriate out of his contingent fund, a sufficient sum to pay for printing and lithographing discharges to the patriotic men of the State, who responded to the call of the Governor, and went to the southern border to repel the invader, and who will be known in history as the SQUIRREL HUNTERS."[29]

Records of the Ohio Historical Society indicate that 15,766 volunteers were issued official discharge certificates. Several versions of these documents exist, but the most amusing depict a hunter holding his rifle on one side of the certificate and a squirrel perched on a tree limb and looking a little uncomfortable on the other side. In 1908, the Ohio General Assembly passed a resolution to pay each Squirrel Hunter a sum of $13, equal to one month's pay for an Ohio militiaman in 1862.[30] With all due respect to the Ohio volunteers, however, the role of the squirrels in this Civil War legend should be acknowledged, just at the squirrels' role should be acknowledged in the resolution of the Revolutionary War.

Squirrel Revenge upon the Redcoats

By the end of the Revolutionary War in 1783, it was crystal clear that the British soldiers were no match for the guerrilla warfare tactics employed by the Continental Army's militia units. Many of the American patriots who employed such strategies were immortalized and romanticized as time passed. Although guerrilla warfare was useful for harassing the British and avoiding heavy casualties in pitched battles, Americans also fought in conventional linear formations against the British. During these engagements, the British were surprised by the Yankee upstarts' marksmanship abilities—which had been honed through hunting for squirrels in the backwoods. Squirrel hunters found favor with the officers of the armed colonial units, just as they later found favor with officers of the Union army in the long and bloody war against the Confederates.

The British suffered an ignominious defeat in October 1781, and the war came to a virtual end when General Cornwallis was forced to surrender at Yorktown, Virginia. Two years later, the Treaty of Paris made it official: America was independent, and the British were gone. No doubt, the exhausted British had to feel some relief at being done with the American guerrilla fighters, done with the sharp-shooting squirrel hunters, and done with the ubiquitous gray squirrels that had indirectly assisted in their defeat on the North American continent. The British were safely back home, but the hostilities were far from over. There were American insurrectionists on their shores, in their midst, ready to do them harm. The worst of it was that the British brought the catastrophe upon themselves by inviting these interlopers onto their island. They brought home to Britannia the dreaded American gray squirrel.

The gray squirrels first came to Great Britain to be pets for the upper classes, who found their playfulness amusing. Thomas Brocklehurst, a banker residing in Cheshire, was among England's world travelers who happily brought the gray squirrels back from visits to America. Interestingly enough, Brocklehurst's gray squirrels escaped from their cages in 1876, the 100th anniversary of America's Declaration of Independence. From this point on, the gray squirrels began to wreak havoc on Britain. Brocklehurst's squirrels were joined by many other gray squirrels who were purposely let loose upon the island nation. Ironically, Herbrand Russell, the president of the Zoological Society of London and a well-known supporter of animal conservation, let some of his gray squirrels loose in London's Kew Gardens and Regents Park. Russell, along with other well-meaning Brits who gave gray squirrels their freedom, had no idea that as these squirrels began to propagate, their country's native red squirrels would suffer and decline.[31]

The North American gray squirrel has tremendous advantages over the native red squirrels of Britain. First, the grays are hardier and larger than their red cousins. Second, the grays can reduce red squirrel food supplies with their ability to digest the unripe seeds of broadleaf trees. Third, the grays eat much more than the reds and will raid the hidden stashes of seeds and nuts collected by the red squirrels. Fourth, the grays thrive in higher population densities, while red squirrels do not fare well in a crowd. Fifth, even though gray squirrel males cannot mate with red squirrel females, they will feign interest and scare the smaller red squirrel males away. Sixth, gray squirrels carry a disease known as squirrel poxvirus, which has little effect on them but is deadly for the red squirrels. Seventh, the gray squirrels are known to be explorers and are always looking for new territories to inhabit, while the meeker red squirrels get pushed aside.[32]

The gray squirrels have so many advantages over the weaker British red squirrels that they have been labeled an invasive species. Fifty years after being released in Britain, the nation's forestry commission sounded the alarm in response to the declining red squirrel population. The commission urged a campaign against the growing number of grays. Some American partisans of gray squirrels were offended by this action. The *New York Times* published a story of indignation with this headline: "American Squirrel on Trial for His Life in England." Unfortunately, British laws and bounties levied against the gray squirrel intruders proved ineffective. Estimates of the gray squirrels now residing in the United Kingdom exceed five million, but the dwindling red squirrel population is pegged at perhaps less than one hundred forty thousand.[33] Today more and more British organizations are mobilizing on behalf of their native squirrels. The Red Squirrel Survival Trust (an organization intent on bringing the red squirrels back into abundance) has argued that the red squirrels could completely disappear in fifteen years and urged more active steps to protect the species.

Prince Charles, heir apparent to the British throne and a member of the Red Squirrel Survival Trust, has promoted the "Squirrel Accord," an agreement hammered out at Dumfries House, his stately home in Scotland. This agreement between the government and forestry officials promotes measures to actively diminish the gray squirrel population in England. Some of the steps that have already been taken against the gray squirrels involve traps, poison and culling. In Cornwall, landowners put down poison bait in areas heavily inhabited by the gray squirrels in an attempt to create "gray-free exclusion zones."[34] In Aberdeen, traps have been set along transit routes for migrating grays. Traps also have been put out in the rural regions of Northumberland. Once trapped, there is no quarter and no fair trial for the gray squirrels—just certain death.

Animal Aid, a British animal rights organization that promotes cruelty-free lifestyles, has condemned many of the tactics advocated by the Red Squirrel Survival Trust. Animal Aid contends that "the poisoning, shooting or bludgeoning grays to death in a sack is irrational, inhumane and doomed to fail."[35] The charity denounces what it terms the propaganda foisted upon the public using the "emotive anthropomorphism" of children's author Beatrix Potter, who obviously favored red squirrels like the famous Squirrel Nutkin, while showing contempt in her story about the gray squirrel, Timmy Tiptoes. Thanks to Potter, the rascally little red squirrel, Nutkin, became the United Kingdom's best-known and most popular squirrel, while the unsavory and oafish gray squirrel called Timmy Tiptoes was doomed to secondary status.

The gray squirrels have literally been under siege in Britain for several decades. Despite plenty of evidence to the contrary, Prince Charles insists the gray squirrels are being trapped humanely and compassionately disposed of in an appropriate fashion. Environmentalists, ecologists and animal rights groups take a dim view of his attempts to reduce the number of gray squirrels in Britain. They suggest that gray squirrels are wildlife that has adapted to the new territory and should no longer be mistreated as alien creatures. They argue that any real opportunity to eradicate the gray squirrels vanished decades ago; there are just too many of them at this point. They are permanently established in the British Isles. The Redcoats have been beaten again.

Squirrels: Lost Legends Found

On July 4, 1776, the Declaration of Independence for the new United States of America was approved. However, something else transpired on that momentous day in Congress, which is encapsulated in this proclamation: "Resolved, That Dr. Franklin, Mr. J Adams and Mr. Jefferson, be a committee, to bring in a device for a seal for the United States of America."[36] As it happened, this instruction to devise a great seal was not so easy to carry out. The first committee included some of the most distinguished founders of the country, but it took several years and several more committees to finalize the great seal. In June 1782, all the committees' concepts merged to create a new design, which is still used as the Great Seal of the United States today. The core element is the bald eagle, supporting thirteen stripes representing the original thirteen states, clutching a bundle of arrows and an olive branch in its claws.

Ben Franklin was not pleased with the eagle as a national symbol for the new country. Franklin expressed his great displeasure about the choice of the eagle in a famous letter to his daughter dating from 1784. He argued that the eagle is a bird of bad moral character that steals from other birds, such as the fishing hawk, to support himself and his family. Franklin declared that the eagle is like those "among Men who live by Sharping and Robbing he is generally poor and often very lousy. Besides he is a rank Coward: The little King Bird not bigger than a Sparrow attacks him boldly and drives him out of the District."[37] Franklin said a proper emblem should represent the brave and honest Americans who drove the kings out of the colonies. Conceding that hindsight is always better than foresight, there are those who now argue that the American squirrel would have made an appropriate national symbol.

According to popular historical legend, the redoubtable American squirrel has played a role in both the founding and the preservation of the United States. As described earlier, the squirrel contributed in its own small way to the survival of the colonies and the success of the revolution. As an abundant game animal, it provided much-needed food. The marksmanship necessary to successfully hunt such an elusive animal was an important exercise for the citizen soldiers who fought in the American Revolution, in the War of 1812 and on the Union side in the American Civil War. Additionally, as an import to the country where King George once dictated policy to the American colonies, the gray squirrel today serves as a reminder for the royal authorities of the grit and tenacity of their former subjects across the Atlantic.

Several American states have chosen the squirrel as an appropriate representation for their pursuits and purposes. The gray squirrel was named and designated as the official Kentucky Wild Animal Game Species in 1968 by the state legislature of Kentucky.[38] This designation recognized that the gray squirrel feels most at home in an "untouched wilderness" environment, but many of the squirrels are not averse to living and playing in city parks and suburbs. A year later, the North Carolina General Assembly chose the squirrel as its official state mammal, noting that the species, *Sciurus carolinensis*, is commonly recognized for its courage and thriftiness.[39] These designations by states such as Kentucky, North Carolina and others are the best indication that proposing the squirrel as a national symbol is not so far-fetched.

Two diverse national constituencies, which share few common interests but would be natural allies in giving the squirrel more visibility as an American symbol, are the centuries-old hunting community and the enclaves formed in support of New Age Shamanism. The teachers within the different incarnations of the New Age movement will sometimes cite the benefits of adopting totems or power animals for spiritual guidance, and they single out the squirrel as exemplary. The tree squirrel's inspirational gifts include agility, resourcefulness, foresight, discovery and the flexibility to change in order to avoid danger. For the squirrel, there is no obstacle that can't be overcome. The New Age mantra holds that the squirrel is an inspirational power animal to rely on when adverse situations call for perseverance and a readiness to try different routes to success.[40] The squirrel also is admired for achieving a balance between work and play, frenetic activity and restful contemplation, spirited debate and quiet harmony. The New Age teachers maintain that there is a reason why the squirrel has been revered as sacred for centuries by different Native American tribes.

Some voices in America's hunting community are every bit as dedicated to giving the squirrel more serious attention and visibility. The hunting community's reverence for the squirrel, however, is less ethereal and more grounded in reality. These squirrel partisans can be traced to the animal's legacy in the founding and preservation of America. Many advocates within the hunting community are desperate to restore the tradition of chasing bushy tails and bringing them back as a staple of the American dinner table. Their arguments for the return of this tradition require wholesale destruction of the myths that have led to the decline in American squirrel hunters, whose numbers were once legion. Among the myths that they are trying to shoot down: Squirrels aren't glamorous. Squirrels aren't challenging. Squirrels have no place in a modern hunter's world—real men don't hunt squirrels.

Perhaps the most insidious of these fabrications is the notion that squirrel hunting is not a manly sport. Ask General George Washington of the Revolutionary War whether the squirrel hunter is manly. Ask Ohio Governor David Tod, who called upon the Squirrel Hunters to defend Cincinnati in the Civil War. Ask M.D. Johnson, who writes for *Field & Stream* and the Realtree website. Johnson is a sportsman who has done yeoman work in puncturing the myth that squirrel hunting is not for the modern hunter. Johnson writes, "Without exception, the best all-round multi-species hunters—no, the best all-round woodsmen—I've known in my 50 years were, and still are, first and foremost squirrel hunters. As squirrel hunters, these men were shown and learned everything they needed to know in order to become skilled hunters of larger game—patience, persistence, self-discipline, camouflage and stealth. They learned how to move without being seen, and when the opportunity presented itself, they hit with a single shot what they were aiming at. They could tell you not only which trees were which, but which trees produced the best mast. And when. [They could tell you all about] mushrooms, plants, wild berries, tracks, Eastern box turtles; they know it all. Many could tell you what bird that is simply by the song. To the squirrel hunter, nothing is more important than time—and they enjoy every single moment of it. You'll never see a squirrel hunter sitting under a one-hundred-year-old oak texting his buddies. 'Nough said.'"[41]

Well into the twentieth century, America's appetite for squirrel seemed innate and unlikely to fade. But a combination of dining developments after World War II, including frozen food and fast food, eventually led to a precipitous decline in squirrel consumption. By the end of the twentieth century, squirrels had to a great extent shaken off their number one adversary: human

In the 2010 film *Winter's Bone*, Jennifer Lawrence plays a teenage girl in the Missouri Ozarks who instructs her young siblings on how to shoot, skin and eat squirrel. Although most Americans seem to lack an appetite for squirrel meat, rock star Ted Nugent has taken up the cause of promoting squirrel dishes with his book, *Kill It & Grill It: A Guide to Preparing and Cooking Wild Game and Fish*.

beings. However, in recent times, high-profile hunters such as Ted Nugent have tried to restore the celebrated stalking of squirrel meat for supper. Nugent refers to bushy tail cuisine as the ultimate, hard-earned white meat. In his view, hunting down squirrels is something of a patriotic duty, and he has promoted the culinary cause with a celebrated squirrel recipe book.[42] Anyone for New England Squirrel Pie? Louisiana Creole Squirrel? White Trash Broiled Squirrel? Nugent's mission is to make squirrel popular in our culture, popular for our dinner plate, popular for our palates—and revered in our hard-earned history.

9

Squirrels in Myth
and Folklore

Long before there were books, newspapers, television or movies, humans got their information through talking and listening to each other. Ears and mouths were the primary instruments of communication, as there were no microphones or speakers. There were no televisions or computer screens, no movie houses or video game arcades—not even an old print shop with a flatbed printing press. Children's books were not around to introduce young-sters to the small, furry animals living just beyond their sleeping quarters. Newspapers were not around to warn unsuspecting humans about disease-carrying rodents with bushy tails. Television news was not promoting feature stories about squirrels on bicycles or water skis. There were no movies or animated cartoons about silly squirrels acting like crack private investigators or high-flying, stunt-plane daredevils. The mechanical and electrical devices for communication via the mass media simply did not exist.

It can be argued that mass media did not even arrive for human com-munication until newspapers could be printed by the tens of thousands on roll-fed printing presses in the 1800s. However, books and single-sheet news-papers did become possible earlier with the invention of the flatbed press by Johannes Gutenberg in Germany in the 1440s. Both printing press inventions are part of the age of literacy, which runs roughly from the beginning of writ-ing (about five thousand years ago) to the start of the electronic communi-cation era with the invention of the telegraph in 1844. Marshall McLuhan divides man's communication modes into three eras, with the first era con-sisting of the oral tradition, the second era consisting of the age of literacy and the third era consisting of electronic communication characterized by constant innovation in mass media technology.[1]

Before the age of literacy and the eventual arrival of mass media, there was a long period of what McLuhan referred to as the evolving oral tradition, when information was spread by word of mouth. Some of that information was conveyed through storytelling around outdoor campfires or in caves. Some of those ancient stories were inevitably about squirrels and were told over and over again. They achieved familiarity and longevity through being repeated by mouth from one generation to the next. They morphed into folk tales, sacred legends and useful mythology—all shared orally. Stories and mythology about squirrels acquired a new kind of permanency with the age of literacy and written communication. Then, when the age of electronic communication came along, some portions of those transcribed squirrel tales were adapted as content for movies, video games and more.

Modern, mass-mediated humans have found enjoyment and enlightenment from the ancient stories originating in the oral traditions of their ancient tribal ancestors. Among these stories are myths about evil, noisy, trouble-making squirrels, which have been traced to the Vikings. It may be hard to imagine that Vikings were bothered much by a bunch of chattering squirrels. After all, Vikings are most often described as brutes, pillagers, rapists and ruthless colonizers. The Viking warriors known as "Berserkers" were infamous for employing their own weird kind of spiritual magic to induce trance-like frenzies that made them impervious to injury in battle.[2] Squirrels might be expected to go a little berserk and run the other way when these Vikings set foot in their neck of the woods. Nevertheless, squirrels did apparently stick around to aggravate the Norsemen. These Vikings were sufficiently irritated by the neighborhood squirrels to create unflattering stories and mythology about the unruly behavior of the rodents in their woods.

A number of Native American tribes, located on the other side of the Atlantic from the Vikings, also had a few bones to pick with the squirrels in their woodland habitats. The Wabanaki peoples, whose ancestral homeland stretched from New Hampshire to Newfoundland, Canada, are responsible for the popular legend of a squirrel called Meeko. The tales of Meeko, exchanged verbally centuries ago among the Wabanaki, have today inspired a number of children's stories. The Wabanaki described Meeko as a ravenous, red wretch with a nasty temper and demeanor more appropriate to an animal many times his size. Meeko was noted for a brand of squirrel talk that included jeering, barking and scolding, in addition to the usual chattering.

The insights and advice of the Wabanaki people, based on their oral tales of Meeko, are abundantly clear: Don't trust the squirrels. This same message rings loud and clear in the squirrel stories handed down from the Choctaw tribes of North America. The Choctaw peoples originally inhabited much of the Southeastern United States, where they lived in the wooded valleys of Mississippi River tributaries. Their lands were prime squirrel territory before European settlers came to clear the land and remove the Choctaw to Oklahoma. The Choctaw tribes blamed black squirrels for such evils as stealing the sun during the phenomena of solar eclipses. The Choctaw concluded that humans should eliminate the squirrels if they wanted to stay warm and have light from the sky. The European settlers followed the Choctaw's advice and proceeded to have hunts and mass roundups of squirrels for the slaughter (in part for culinary reasons).

Marshall McLuhan took a special interest in the plight of Native Americans with the evolution of communication and the impact of new technologies. In McLuhan's time, indigenous peoples were still tribal and continued to communicate through the oral tradition long after Europeans had "detribalized" and learned to cope with a new world of literacy and advanced communication devices. Ironically, just as Native Americans have been in the midst of abandoning the oral tradition and adjusting to new ways, the majority culture is "retribalizing" with the wave of new technological advances. A new connectivity in sight and sound in McLuhan's "global village" is encouraging the majority culture to return to more tribal ways and the storytelling of the oral tradition.[3]

As a sense of place and commonly held values are obliterated by omnipresent and instantaneous communication, the majority culture increasingly fragments in the quest for some sort of identity. Ironically, segments of the dominant culture have begun to go tribal to replace identities lost in a world of communication overload. One example of this new compulsion to find identity in the tribe is the rise of the so-called New Age movement. As an innovative strain of Western esotericism, the New Age identity rejects common religious traditions and white Western worldviews. The New Age tribe favors alternative spiritual paths and notions of achieving divine essence through altered states of mind and enhanced intuition, which can mean adopting the philosophies and practices of indigenous peoples. Perhaps not surprisingly, some Native American tribal leaders have spoken out against the New Age movement. They decry the Westernized shamans or spiritual leaders and the misappropriation of age-old practices and sacred ceremonies from tribes such as the Lakota, Navajo, Shawnee, Creek or Choctaw.[4]

This study is not the place to debate whether indigenous leaders are right or wrong in viewing the New Age identity as a sham that has little to do with authentic shamanism or ancient Native American spirituality. The point is that some members of the majority culture have literally attempted to turn tribal in their quest for identity. They have made an unconscious decision to be "retribalized" (as McLuhan might term their movement). What makes all these developments relevant for this study is that part of the New Age spirituality involves practicing the art of envisioning or calling out one's "power animal." The power animal is a shamanic belief that an animal spirit can be implored or inspired to guide, to aid, or to protect individuals who believe in their otherworldly power to influence both individual and communal reality.

New Age practitioners, who advise others on how to establish a spiritual relationship with a power animal, argue that they are part of the tradition of shamans in indigenous cultures around the world. These shamans have taught their acolytes and followers about the venues available to reach out to animal guides, animal helpers, spirit animals or power animals. The original shamans have been providing this knowledge for many thousands of years. New Age practitioners (sometimes referred to as neo-shamans or modern-day shamans) suggest that the process of achieving a spiritual relationship with a power animal is a two-way street: An acolyte or follower can choose a power animal, but the power animal also has autonomy and choice as to whether a relationship will be established. In fact, the power animal may have already done the choosing with a determination to be made on when and where to reveal a developing relationship with a human counterpart.

New Age practitioners have cataloged the powers or attributes of particular animals in the spirit world. For example, the spirit of the antelope promotes finely honed survival skills, keen acuity abilities, mental alertness and sensitivity to danger. The spirit of the bear promotes watchfulness, innate courage and strength for the requirements of self-preservation and protection of its young. The spirit of the goat promotes stubborn independence, an agility accented by sure-footed confidence and an inspiring virility. And the spirit of the squirrel promotes constant awareness, pleasure-seeking sociability and endless energy devoted to both purposeful planning and playfulness.[5]

Norse Wisdom: Why Ancients Feared Squirrels

Scandinavians of yore knew better than today's humans: squirrels are not for dressing up in top hats or for teaching how to steer small Viking ships on inland seas. The Viking antipathy for the squirrels of their day was manifest in the mythology of "Drill Tooth," otherwise known as Ratatoskr. According to an assortment of Nordic myths, Ratatoskr loved to sow discord and spread malevolent gossip wherever he scampered or climbed. As discussed in chapter 7, he was famous for running up and down the tree of life, instigating fights between an eagle living atop the tree and a gnarly dragon in the tree's roots. The Vikings knew squirrel chatter is not innocent or innocuous, but rather a noisome messaging that can mean only one thing: trouble.

Before plowing too deeply into the Norse myth of Ratatoskr, it is useful to dissect this squirrel's peculiar name. *Ratatoskr* is a combination of "rat" and "tooth" and implicitly acknowledges a dining dilemma facing all rodents. Squirrels may love eating berries, tomatoes and flower seeds, but if they don't find hard foods, their front teeth can literally grow through their heads. Squirrels have four chisel-like teeth up front that grow continuously. Gnawing on hard foods, like nuts and other woody items, serves to keep those teeth filed down. A squirrel that fails to keep its incisors under control can die of

In Norse mythology, a squirrel named Ratatoskr runs up and down the tree of life carrying messages between the eagle atop the tree and a dragon that dwells in the tree's roots. The squirrel (also known as "Drill Tooth") is up to no good because he spreads rumors that aggravate other creatures. Ratatoskr's slanderous gossip threatens the stability of the tree of life (courtesy the Missouri Department of Conservation).

starvation, because the teeth can attain a length that makes chewing impossible. Thus Ratatoskr had good reason to keep those teeth boring and drilling into hard foods.

However, the Norse tale about Ratatoskr has less to do with eating and drilling and much more to do with climbing and gossiping. The Norsemen obviously noticed that a squirrel is one heck of a climber. It can move quickly all around a tree and can back up head first and tail first. The squirrel has double-jointed ankles, so it can turn completely around and hold on to trees with sharp claws and move in any direction. In addition to climbing skills, the Norsemen could not fail to notice the constant squirrel chatter that was probably more annoying than soothing for fellows camping in the woods when not bludgeoning enemies or sailing the seas.

The ancient squirrel Ratatoskr took up quarters in the tree of life, dubbed Yggdrasil, a world-class tree that provided home for an eagle at its crown and a basement headquarters for a troll-like dragon in the knotted root system. Ratatoskr had a habit of running back and forth, up and down, delivering rancorous gossip to the high-flying eagle and the low-life dragon. The squirrel was a first-class troublemaker, intent on creating hatred and strife between the two inhabitants, one residing close to heaven and the other close to hell. He would tell the dragon that the eagle above would like to see his ultimate demise, and none too soon. He likewise told the eagle that the dragon would like to fell the tree and bring evil and destruction upon the magnificent bird.[6]

Interpretations of the tale of Ratatoskr disagree regarding what the squirrel has in mind as he traverses up and down the tree delivering hateful messages. Is Ratatoskr hoping that his spiteful gossip will bring about Armageddon, a great apocalyptic war between the forces of heaven and hell? Is Ratatoskr hoping to bring down the tree of life by instigating a battle between the eagle and the dragon? Some literary analyses suggest that the squirrel is jealous of the power of both the magnificent eagle and the devilish monster, and, as a puny squirrel, the best that he can do is use his clever words of hoax and hooey to precipitate the destruction of the two superior creatures. In any case, Ratatoskr relishes the opportunity to rile up the two tree creatures by carrying fabricated insults back and forth between them. Ratatoskr may be the original messenger of fake news.

Unfortunately, the Vikings did not leave Cliff Notes to help sort out the meaning of their myth about the giant tree, the proud eagle, the nasty dragon, and the pesky squirrel. Modern Scandinavians are similarly mum about the moral lesson of the tale of Yggdrasil, the tree of life. However, one fact stands out quite clearly: Ratatoskr is not simply a malicious rodent; he's a troublemaker with a bushy tail. He is a sly, noisy, aggressive and ill-intentioned squirrel. In a scholarly essay titled "Ratatosk: The Role of the Perverted Intellect," the psychoanalyst Lilla Veszy-Wagner contends that Ratatoskr misuses his creative intellect to perpetuate unnecessary conflict. She maintains that the kind of intelligence available to Ratatoskr often results in a classic Freudian battle between the demands of the id and the superego, as symbolized by the sage eagle above and the rapacious monster below.[7]

Meeko: One Nasty Little Squirrel

Meeko, the mythical squirrel of the Wabanaki tribe of North America, has a lot in common with Ratatoskr, the mythical squirrel of the Vikings. Both groups seem to have had a similar take on squirrels. At some point in human history, did the Wabanaki tribesmen swap squirrel stories around the fire with visiting Viking seafarers from Scandinavia? Further investigation might confirm that Leif Erikson and his Vikings actually did make it to North America many years before Christopher Columbus landed in 1492. Of course, this kind of speculation can only kindle more hard feelings between the Italians, who champion their explorer Columbus, and the descendants of the Norsemen, who revel in the exploits of Leif Erikson. Hard feelings? Troublemaker Ratatoskr would be proud. However, it is time to put this kind of argument aside and focus on another mischief maker by the name of Meeko.

The mythology of the Wabanaki holds that the squirrel named Meeko was originally a great beast, an actual monster of giant proportions. The outrageous size and ill temper of this dangerous squirrel gave the gods pause. Finally, a divine entity known as Glooskap confronted Meeko and asked him what he might do if he met a man in the forest. Meeko responded that he would use his claws to scratch down the trees upon any man he might encounter in the forest. Glooskap furrowed his brow and frowned, but he took the squirrel into his arms and stroked his furry back. With each reassuring stroke, Meeko became smaller and smaller until he was finally the size of squirrels we see today. After he became so small, Glooskap again confronted Meeko and asked him what he might do if he met a man in the forest. Meeko was suddenly weak, and a little timid, and he confessed that he would run up a tree to get away from a man.[8]

The original Meeko was a mistake of creation. He was as large as a bear. He also had the horrible demeanor and ferocity of a weasel, which is known to kill for the fun of it and will latch on to the neck of larger prey to drain all the blood from the jugular vein. Fortunately for humankind, Meeko was downsized from the bulk of a bear to a physical stature equal to that of a small pup. However, as the Wabanaki tribal elders point out, the gods did not do a complete job of humbling Meeko. They neglected to downsize his disposition, so that Meeko maintained his notorious temper and tendency to gripe, grouse, scold, screech and chatter.

Meeko and his progeny jump from perch to perch, where they can bark and bluster and aggravate others from a safe distance. Even now, humans are subjected to the "cut-a-chuck, cut-a-chuck, cut-a-chuck" chatter of squirrels that have no use for people getting too close to territory that they have staked out as their own. Even worse, squirrels will invade spaces where they don't belong. Squirrels will tear up and destroy the property of others to meet their own needs. They will steal provisions and carry away the foodstuffs generously left out for other inhabitants of the natural world. When challenged for their indiscretions, squirrels will jeer and chuckle loudly with their own rebuke of "cut-a-chuck, cut-a-chuck, cut-a-chuck, woooohhh."

Meeko and his brethren are disturbers of the peace. Meeko definitely seems to be a cousin of Ratatoskr, the rogue squirrel of Norse mythology. Unable to subdue or intimidate the other residents of his great tree of life, Ratatoskr decided to taunt them and to spread disinformation with claims that one or the other was engaging in vicious rumors, insults and innuendo. So, too, does Meeko scurry around the woods making mischief wherever he goes. No longer as big and bad as he was in former times, he jumps about with his small body and super-sized temper and begins to bellow, yelp, howl and quarrel. He is forever angry that he has been downsized, depreciated and diminished.

In fact, Meeko should be appreciative of a gift given to him for survival that he lacked as a hulking squirrel of bearish proportions. With his smaller size, flexible body and sail-like tail, Meeko can now jump from enormous heights—an impossible feat before his transformation by the wise god Glooskap. He can also flatten his light body and spread his bushy tail to literally fly from one tree top to another tree. However, far from being grateful for his godly gift of flight, Meeko has used this divine attribute for devilish deeds. William J. Long, an outdoor writer who has expanded and elaborated upon the Wabanaki squirrel myth, makes the following observation: "When you have listened to Meeko's scolding for a season, and have seen him going from nest to nest after innocent fledglings; or creeping into the den of his big cousin, the beautiful gray squirrel, to kill the young; or driving away his little cousin, the chipmunk, to steal his hoarded nuts; or watching every fight that goes on in the woods, jeering and chuckling above it, then you begin to understand the Indian legend."[9]

Long has spent enough time in the woods to have the Wabanaki's wisdom about Meeko confirmed. Wherever you go in the wilderness, Long observes, Meeko is way ahead of you, and all the best campgrounds are pre-empted by him. Even on the islands in the stream or the peninsulas jutting into lakes, Meeko has already claimed the prettiest spots. And when you stumble upon these Arcadian wonders, Meeko is on hand to dispute mightily your right to stay there.

Meeko's protests are not entirely without cause. After all, he and his kind can be traced back to two hundred million years ago. By comparison, the ancestors of humans have been around for about six million years. The modern form of humans only came into existence about 200,000 years ago.[10]

Choctaw: Beware Sun-Swallowing Squirrels

Solar eclipses were never too popular among the ancients. First of all, the sun's disappearance agitated the animals and set dogs to barking loudly and relentlessly. Second, there was the question of whether the sun, once eaten by a mythical animal or the gods, would ever be regurgitated. It might not come back! The Choctaw were sure that a monstrous squirrel—with equally monstrous incisors—was responsible for gobbling up the sun. Not surprisingly, the Choctaw Nation never found squirrels cute or entertaining; they were animals that merited only contempt and distrust (and perhaps a hot fire to roast upon). Squirrels had good reason to be wary around the Choctaw. However, the Choctaw peoples, with their sun myths, also had some very good reasons to be distrustful of the squirrels.

Early humans and indigenous peoples (and especially their leaders and wise men) had to have some explanation for the disappearing sun. Science eventually explained the orbits of the planets and the moon and how the sun and the moon could be eclipsed. Before science, however, humans came up with their own interpretations of heavenly events. These were myths that aligned with native cultural and religious beliefs. The legends and superstitions inevitably contained some element of violence, because the loss of the sun in daytime always was a huge disruption of the established order.

The mythology of the Inuit of northern Canada and Alaska involves a fight between the moon god Anningan and his sister, the goddess Malina. He chases Malina, but Anningan grows tired and forgets to eat. He then grows smaller, like a waning moon. When he catches Malina on one of these chases, everything goes dark, causing a solar eclipse. By contrast, the Kwakiutl tribe on the west coast of Canada believed the heavens were in disarray and the mouth of heaven had consumed the sun, or the moon, or both. The Tewa tribe of New Mexico also believed that the disappearance of celestial bodies meant the gods were angry. At these times, the sun became so upset that it would decide to leave the skies for the underworld, though prayers and exhortations could persuade it to return. The Pomo, an indigenous people from the northwest United States, believed a heavenly bear fought with the sun and took a bite out of it every so often. All of these eclipse myths mirror the ravenous black squirrel myth and folklore of the Choctaw.[11]

When North Americans experienced a solar eclipse in August 2017, more than 200 million residents of the United States viewed some portion of the celestial event. The eclipse generated reports of abnormal behavior in both plant and animal life. Farm animals, including domestic chickens, came out from under their coops and began their evening ritual of grooming as the sky darkened. Horses became nervous and, along with increased whinnying, began running and jumping after the eclipse. Humans did some strange things as well. Weddings were officiated and marriage proposals were made. In Illinois, a rock festival called Moonstock was well attended and headlined by Ozzy Osbourne, who played throughout the eclipse. In Tennessee, a rock music event featured the Pink Floyd Appreciation Society, a band that performed Pink Floyd's "The Dark Side of the Moon" just prior to the total eclipse of the sun.[12]

The Choctaw tribes of North America did not hold rock concerts in the Mississippi River Delta or conduct marriages as the shadows of the eclipse rolled across the southeastern portion of the continent. A solar eclipse was serious business and an omen of potential catastrophe, if not a calamity in itself. However, as the land darkened and a larger slice was taken out of the sun, the Choctaw people were not totally helpless. The Choctaws believed a giant black squirrel was the culprit for the loss of light and heat as an eclipse grew to totality. The black squirrel was hungry and eating the orange ball in the sky. It had to be driven off if the Choctaw were to survive and their way of life saved.

Choctaws were convinced that the ravenous squirrel could be chased away from his meal of the sun. Part of the required action was to take up the chant: "Black squirrel is eating the sun! Black squirrel is eating the sun!" Or, as chanted in the vernacular of the time, "Funi lusa hushi umpa! Funi lusa hushi umpa!" If the black squirrel was made aware that the tribal peoples knew what he was up to in nibbling on their sacred luminary, he might be discouraged from finishing his meal and inspired to leave the celestial diner. However, there was much more to do—and much more noise to be made with yelps and beating on pots and pans—to scare away the black squirrel and stop him from completing his evil deed of devouring the sun.[13]

According to the website First People—Native American Legends, "Then the women shrieked and redoubled their efforts upon the tin pans, which, under the desperate blows, strained every vocal organ to its utmost and whole duty in loud response, while the excited children screamed and beat their cups, and the sympathetic dogs ... barked and howled—all seemingly determined not to fall behind the other in their duty since the occasion demanded it; while the warriors still stood in profound and meditative silence, but firm and undaunted ... then, as the moon's shadow began to move from the disk of the sun, the joyful shout was heard above the mighty din: 'Funi-lusa-osh mahlatah!' The black squirrel is frightened!"[14]

The Choctaw beliefs may seem like primitive superstitions now, but it should be noted that the pots and pans came out in many locales in the United States during the August 2017 solar eclipse. There was noise making and shrieks, whooping and hollering, and vigorous hand clapping—most often to celebrate the sun's return after several minutes of darkness. So what did the squirrels of North America think about all this racket on an August afternoon in 2017? Was it similar to the noise made by the indigenous peoples at the height of the great Choctaw Nation? Will the great noise to scare away the sun-eating black squirrel return to North America for the next solar eclipse on April 8, 2024?

Cinderella: Glass or Squirrel Slippers?

Plenty of little girls, and their fawning parents, think they know the Cinderella story. They've seen the Disney movies—a wondrous animated tale from 1950, and another with big-name actors made in 2015. The story of Cinderella is a magical tale about a kingdom that existed many years ago in a faraway place. Here Cinderella lives comfortably with her mother and father until her mother dies. Her father remarries a cruel creep of a woman with two daughters of her own. Later Cinderella's father dies, and the wicked stepmother turns the poor young girl, who has lost her protective parents, into a servile peasant in her own house.

Cinderella's only chance to escape her misery comes when the local king decides that his son, as a prince, must find a bride and provide him with grandchildren. The king invites every eligible maiden to a splendid ball, where his son will be able to choose a suitable bride. Cinderella cries as the one dress that she has for the ball is torn apart by her evil stepsisters. That's when Cinderella's fairy godmother steps in and provides a pumpkin carriage, a lovely white gown, and some enchanting glass slippers. However, her fairy godmother warns her that all these accoutrements will only last until the final stroke of midnight.

Cinderella goes to the ball, and this is when things get very interesting. The ball just bores the prince—that is, until Cinderella makes her entrance. They dance a waltz and things go swimmingly until the clock strikes midnight. Cinderella bolts from the palace but loses a glass slipper on the steps as she flees. Later, the prince yearns to find his dream girl who disappeared so suddenly. The glass slipper is the only clue. The king assigns the duke the task of trying the slipper on every girl in the kingdom, and Cinderella's stepmother and stepsisters do everything in their power to thwart the discovery of the right maiden. To make a long fairy tale short—and skipping over some great scenes—the duke eventually locates the right foot: Cinderella's. The glass slipper fits perfectly, and just about everybody lives happily ever after.

Yes, moms and dads and little girls all know the Cinderella story—except maybe they don't. After all, there are several hundred versions of the much-loved fairy tale. Mythical stories about the young heroine come from countries all over the world and from many centuries ago. An ancient Greek myth involves a maid whose sandal is snatched by an eagle that later drops the beautiful footwear in the lap of a startled king. The curious king immediately sends scouts to find out what kind of a lady can possess such taste in casual foot apparel. Naturally, once the right woman is found, he falls in love with her and marries her.[15]

Stories from China and Vietnam dispense with the eagle, and the magic happens for an oppressed damsel all because of a strange fish. In the Chinese version, "Xe Xian," a peasant girl makes friends with a fish that turns out to be the reincarnation of her deceased mother. Her evil stepmother and jealous sister kill the fish, but Xe Xian retrieves the magic fish bones, which give her tips on how to dress fashionably for the New Year's festival. Her wicked family members spy her at the dance, and Xe Xian loses a slipper as she rushes to get away from them. The king retrieves the slipper, figures out that Xe Xian is the owner, and rescues her from the harsh stepmother, after which they marry.[16]

One of the darker versions of the Cinderella tale comes from the home of dark bock beers. The German brothers Jacob and Wilhelm Grimm are credited with composing the rather grim tale of "Aschenputtel."[17] There is no magic fish or fairy godmother to rescue the damsel in distress in this take on the Cinderella myth. Instead, there is a wishing tree that the heroine plants on the grave of her beloved mother. When the persecuted Aschenputtel's plans to go to a festival are hijacked by her mean and thieving stepsisters, the distraught girl returns to her mother's grave, where a flock of doves rains down just the right clothes for an evening festival: a gold and silver gown as well as some adorable silk shoes.

Aschenputtel captivates the prince at the festival, but, like most Cinderella types, she loses a shoe very early in the budding courtship and the prince loses track of her. He does find one of Aschenputtel's silk shoes and declares that he will hook up with the maiden whose foot finds a good fit in the fanciful shoe. What makes the story of Aschenputtel particularly dark is the ill-advised shortcuts her stepsisters take to try to ensure that their feet are a match for the tight shoe in possession of the prince. One stepsister hacks off her toes in the interest of getting a comfortable fit. The other stepsister finds a way to carve off her heel to keep the shoe from being too snug. Needless to say, the prince is only temporarily fooled by the treachery afoot with the two stepsisters. He ultimately finds the right fit with Aschenputtel, the girl he danced with at the festival. As for the deceitful stepsisters, the doves appear again to pluck out their eyes and leave them blind for the rest of their lives.[18]

Little wonder that Walt Disney Studios did not choose to base their upbeat Cinderella productions on the infamous fable of Aschenputtel. The romantic Disney films are said to be derived from the French version of the Cinderella story published by Charles Perrault in 1697. The French version is a joy for animal lovers, as there are no dead fish involved (as with the Asian variations on the Cinderella story). Cinderella finds help in preparing for the big dance not through the magic of fish bones but through the powers of her fairy godmother. The fairy godmother turns a pumpkin into a carriage, some mice into carriage horses, a rat into a coachman, and a few lizards into footmen. There's a lot of fun in all that, even if it is only temporary.

The Disney people loved everything that Cinderella's godmother was up to with the pumpkin carriage, the magnificent gown and those wonderful glass slippers that she procured for her goddaughter. However, the costumes for Disney's 2015 *Cinderella* movie proved to be a significant challenge. Cinderella's gown required more than 270 yards of fabric and ten thousand crystals after nine versions of concepts for the ball gown were studied. More than five hundred hours were required to make the gown (and that was with the work of eighteen tailors). Award-winning costume designer Sandy Powell, who directed costuming for the film, worked on costume concept designs for almost two years before filming began in 2013.[19]

Then there was the small matter of the glass slippers. Glass was not deemed satisfactory because it did not sparkle. Powell decided crystals would be required for aesthetic reasons. Numerous pairs of crystal shoes were designed for *Cinderella*, though none of them proved wearable. Some critics argue that Cinderella did not belong in glass slippers in the first place. Glass slippers were bound to be uncomfortable and downright dangerous. Cinderella's original slippers were supposedly made of squirrel fur, as confirmed by authors of *The Book of General Ignorance*.[20]

Critics contend that Charles Perrault intended to tell a tale featuring squirrel fur slippers, not impractical footwear made of unforgiving glass. In his version of the story, Perrault was not using the word *verre* (glass) but *vair*, which refers to a type of rare fur from squirrels worn by royalty and the nobility in the Middle Ages. Somehow a serious translation mistake or spelling error put Cinderella in foot apparel that would make today's high heels feel like a pair of comfortable walking shoes or some wool lounge loafers.

On the downside, squirrel fur booties are not the kind of footwear to be ordered up by a fairy godmother, and they may seem a bit lacking when it comes to adorning the feet of a potential bride-to-be for a prince. Squirrel fur also is not likely to fit into the costuming plans for a $90 million Disney production. Some argue that the idea of glass slippers may simply have been a stroke of genius on the part of Perrault. Perhaps he came up with the idea of glass slippers as perfect for a fairy tale and to capture the public imagination. In the context of the present-day, Westernized version of the Cinderella story, glass slippers may represent every starry-eyed woman's dream shoe. Glass slippers also are going to require an exact fit, unlike squirrel fur slippers, which would have a lot more flexibility.

Still, it's hard to give up on squirrel fur as perfectly suitable for a peasant girl of more than three centuries ago—a modest girl looking to go just a little bit upscale for the king's ball. Even today, the best-designed glass slippers leave a lot to be desired. In order to not be a health hazard for Cinderella, the shoes would have to be made from thermal-toughened safety glass.[21] However, the aesthetic value of such a shoe would diminish as the required reinforcement and hardening come into play. Even with added safety features, Cinderella would still be taking a great risk of shattering her shoes, whether as a result of toe strikes during a royal waltz or landing on her heels in a last-minute attempt to flee the ball before the last strike of midnight. Certainly a fairy godmother would put a premium on safety for a goddaughter. A good fairy godmother also would want to spare her goddaughter the humiliation of shoe failure in the elegant setting of a royal ball. The smart money has to be on squirrel fur slippers. Both common and uncommon sense dictate: Go with the squirrel fur, Cindy!

Choosing a Power Animal: Squirrel?

When the Age of Aquarius dawned in the late 1960s, many Americans began expressing doubt about the accepted norms of social life, traditional religious practices, customary political affiliations and popular conventions for literature, film, music and dress. Young people in particular were expressing their dissent and unhappiness with the status quo. Theodore Roszak, who wrote *The Making of a Counter Culture*, said that out of this rebellion grew an ambitious agenda for reappraising cultural values and society's rules.[22] Everything was called into question: family, work, education, success, child rearing, male-female relations, sexuality, urbanism, science, technology and progress. Also under scrutiny were the meaning of wealth, the meaning of love, and the meaning of life.

The 1960s rebellion led to a quest for something fulfilling to replace failed belief systems, dissolving creeds and disappearing doctrines. A major response to the search for an alternative worldview was the New Age movement of the 1970s. The movement peaked during the 1980s but has never completely gone away. The New Age brought experimentation with sex, drugs, musical theater and the arts. It also brought alternative medicine and holistic healing, as well as repudiation of a stilted social and political life in favor of wholesale lifestyle changes. New Age adherents employed eclectic practices drawn from cosmology, astrology, channeling, esoteric religions and past cultures. Some of those past cultural practices were adopted from Native American tribal customs and beliefs.

The New Age movement demanded an authentic and energized respect for the sanctity of creation, the primacy of protecting the environment, and reverence for the natural world. The natural world includes the earth that we walk upon and the air that we breathe. It also includes all the flora and fauna. "Fauna" refers to the entire collection of animals on Earth, which can assume a totemic sacred value, according to the spiritual customs and beliefs of many Native American peoples. Some tribal traditions provided that each person can be connected with different animals that will accompany the individual through life, acting as helpful guides. Although people may identify with different animal guides throughout their lifetimes, there should be one primary animal spirit, animal guide or power animal that watches over a human life as an appropriate guardian spirit. How about a squirrel?

The shamans or teachers of the New Age often offer instruction on how to find the right spirit or power animal. Among their recommendations: Get out and observe nature, and consider keeping a diary of what is being experienced. Be open and attentive to animals in the vicinity, from the largest to the very smallest. Take note of repetitive encounters, because repeated apparitions can constitute an important signal from beyond. Meditate and channel to a specific animal, especially an animal that keeps coming around as a physical or mental presence. Be attentive to dreams, because dreams constitute the actions of the subconscious mind in processing and ordering experiences and complex emotions.

The shamans of the New Age also urge that considerable research be undertaken. This can include viewing nature films and video programs on animals, as well as reading serious literature about animals. Study can help the students of New Age thought to discover the animal that addresses their mental or physical weaknesses and to learn what complements certain emotional and spiritual strengths that are already present. The gurus of the New Age argue for bio-mimicry practices, which can point followers or neophytes to psychic areas where they can find solutions to human problems.[23] Some remedies or needed improvement can come through emulating certain patterns or strategies already existing in nature.

For example, if a person works as a police officer or a firefighter, bio-mimicry would suggest that the individual engaged in such physically taxing professions consider studying (and perhaps identifying with) the cheetah as a spirit or power animal. After all, a person who must move stealthily through dangerous and potentially lethal situations must learn decisive and lightning fast movements. A cheetah as a totemic animal is characterized by a thin and light body that makes it well suited to short, explosive bursts of speed, rapid acceleration, and executing sharp changes in direction while moving incredibly fast. The cheetah shows little aggression toward human beings, and it can even be tamed. This may well indicate that the cheetah in spirit form is ready and receptive to the kind of human connection expounded upon by New Age gurus.

To give another example, if a person works in intellectually demanding professions, such as a philosophy professor or a state or federal judge, bio-mimicry would suggest that the individual consider studying (and perhaps identifying with) the owl as a spirit or power animal. A person who must read voraciously and quietly examine documents with laser-like focus on details must have excellent vision and the intuition to determine what is relevant and what is not. An owl as a totemic animal is characterized by an upright stance, a large broad head with binocular vision. A solitary animal, the owl is known for its disproportionally large eyes and the ability to swivel its head by as much as 270 degrees to view its surroundings. The owl makes an excellent spirit or power animal for those in professions demanding concentration and circumspection.

And then there is the squirrel. The squirrel as a totemic animal can be classified as sociable, playful and resourceful, but it also has more serious characteristics typical of a planner, a gatherer and an explorer. However, Native American mythology is not at all kind with its descriptions of the squirrel: Meeko is noisy, anxious and full of mischief, and other squirrels are said to cause eclipses by eating the sun. So, who would seek out the squirrel to be their spirit or power animal? Perhaps someone engaged in fields involving communication, someone with a nimble wit and an aversion to the sedentary life—think standup comedian, editorial cartoonist, columnist or humorous feature writer as potential candidates who would be logically attracted to squirrels for emotional support and spiritual strength. However, the blog *Nordic Wiccan* offers caution about adopting the squirrel as a power animal: "Ask yourself are you too active, not active enough, afraid of enough, hung up on accumulating and collecting. Squirrel people tend to be a little erratic—trying to do many things at once. Take the time to stop and listen to your inner self—and don't forget to play!"[24]

The New Age movement has certainly performed a valuable service in opening up the American mind to new ideas, while also bringing to light the spiritual paths and mythology of past tribal cultures. It has popularized ancient rituals and belief systems. However, the movement is not without its critics. Scientists warn that many practices, whether relying on magic crystals for good fortune or channeling spirit animals, represent descents into irrational behavior. Christian evangelicals are especially harsh critics of some New Age practices, which they feel reject monotheism in favor of Pagan or pantheistic approaches to the conceptions of the divine. Pagans themselves have criticized the New Age movement as materialistic and an attempt to cash in on beliefs that their religions have espoused for centuries. Native Americans also have taken aim at New Age adherents, targeting their leaders as "plastic shamans," thus echoing the critique of Pagans who charge that these new spiritual guides are simply trying to cash in on beliefs and practices that have been around for a very long time.[25]

Squirrels have been the subject of myth and folklore from the time of the Norsemen and even before the great Age of the Vikings. Human fascination with squirrels continues, as evidenced by this impressive monument to the black squirrels of Marysville, Kansas. Marysville celebrates the unique creatures as important to the town's identity and for tourism (photograph by Fernando Ugarte, MD, courtesy the Office of Marysville Convention and Tourism).

Despite all the clamor against the New Age movement, squirrels have generally prospered within the New Age system and achieved a kind of visibility not generally granted by other religious or neo-religious denominations. This development has been duly noted by the blog *Nordic Pagan*, which adds, "Whether Urban or Country Pagan, most people have seen or heard a squirrel, or a member of the squirrel family, throughout the world. They are playful, curious and quick climbers. The gathering power of a squirrel is a great gift. It teaches us balance within the circle of gathering and giving out. They remind us that in our quest for our goals, it is vital to make time for play and socializing. Squirrels teach us to conserve our energy for times of need."[26]

Postscript:
Squirrels Unlimited

America is a polarized country—distressingly so—on a wide range of social, political and economic issues. Red state partisans are in a panic over religious liberty, a loss of national sovereignty to globalism, and expansion of the welfare state. Blue state partisans fret over the triumph of plutocracy over democracy, a loss of freedom to make individual health care choices, and the fraying of the social contract to care for indigent humans. If there is one sector of life where agreement might be found, one small portion of common ground, it ought to be this very simple premise: When it comes to squirrels, there's no need to panic. These creatures are harmless, amusing, and common. As a longtime newspaper journalist, however, I know better. There is no compromise, no agreement, and no final word on the ostensibly simple subject of squirrels.

Squirrels are one of the most benign and least dangerous species on the planet. "No, they're not!" comes the irate response. They are vectors of disease and can carry rabies and even bubonic plague in some cases. Yes, but squirrels are one of the least destructive and most entertaining animals on the planet. "No, they're not!" comes the irate response. They ravage gardens, chew their way through soffits, invade attic spaces and then proceed to destroy homes. As a newspaper journalist, I have witnessed readers criticize and pillory each other over the subject of squirrels in numerous exchanges of letters to the editor. For every person who advocates poison peanuts and drowning caged squirrels in tubs of water to rid the Earth of the miscreants, there are many more readers with this harsh retort: "Why don't you move to a barren desert where you won't have to deal with the squirrels? I am glad you are not my neighbor, as I think you are exceedingly cruel and you should be checked into a facility!"

The very idea of this book on squirrels has been the subject of disagreement among my friends in the journalism field and among my academic col-

190

leagues. A clear majority argued that the topic of squirrels in media and popular culture is simply not broad enough to sustain a full-length book. My rejoinder was that, as the definitive work on mass-mediated squirrels, there would be plenty of bushy-tailed grist for the mill. An exhaustive treatment on the world of squirrels could certainly make for a good book. Alas, there is nothing exhaustive, definitive or final about this volume. The subject is too big. The pages are too few. Squirrels are not ready for the last word. Very early in this project, it became apparent that this work could only be a sampler at best.

Squirrels are ubiquitous and present in all seasons. These are some of the characteristics that attract New Age followers to adopt the squirrel as their so-called power animal. The squirrel can be a totemic inspiration, because it is sociable, playful and resourceful, but it also has a more serious side as a planner, gatherer and expert explorer (courtesy the Missouri Department of Conservation).

Yes, this book does give Rocky the Flying Squirrel, Secret Squirrel, Conker, Ray the Flying Squirrel, Squirrel Girl and many more furry characters their due. But where is Scrat—the acorn-obsessed saber-toothed squirrel of the Earth's ice age period? Where is Princess Sally Acorn—the daughter of King Nigel Acorn and leader of the Knothole Freedom Fighters in the ongoing battle against the Empire of Eggman? Where is Amy the Squirrel—the playful and mischievous mascot of the animated Amiga community? Where is the infamous Rodney J. Squirrel—an anthropomorphic American red squirrel in love with a yellow female squirrel named Darlene and the main character in something called *Squirrel Boy*? Where is Squeaks the Squirrel—a friend of Bugs Bunny with a slim body and enormous bushy tail? Where is Darly Pants—a squirrel wearing a polka dot ribbon on her yellow fur head, a head that is full of paranoia about bumper cars due to a traumatic vehicular encounter?

And so I conclude this postscript with a proviso: The woods are so lovely, dark and deep—and full of so many squirrels—that I have promises to keep. It's a promise to research and to compose more on the subject of squirrels.

There is so much to explore. My appetite has been whetted but hardly satiated. There is more to taste and savor when it comes to squirrels. How might the taste buds react to squirrel on thin crust pizza, squirrel and mushroom gravy, chicken fried squirrel, crockpot roasted squirrel, sloppy squirrel sandwiches, Grandpa's squirrel stew, mesquite squirrel or a simple squirrel cacciatore?

Finally, there are so many weighty questions to be answered about squirrels. As we look to a future full of uncertainty and anxiety, is the shaky coexistence between squirrels and humans in jeopardy? How will squirrels adapt to increasing climate change as the Earth's average temperatures continue to hike skyward? As the environmental costs of factory farms and giant cattle operations become more apparent, will we humans come to appreciate a few helpings of squirrel and noodles upon our dinner plates? As the most disruptive, sensational, and controversial media platforms take up a disproportionate amount of our attention, will we humans lose sight of what a real, live squirrel actually looks like? Will real squirrels give way to cyborg squirrels as we approach the twenty-second century? Let us hope this will not be the case.

As Marshall McLuhan was wont to say, "There are no passengers on spaceship earth. We are all crew." Be mindful that an essential member of your spaceship earth crew in the not-so-distant future may turn out to be the squirrel. Not a virtual squirrel wearing a diving helmet and living under the sea with a weird creature named SpongeBob, but a real squirrel in a squirrel meat gravy heaped upon your plate—a reliable source of protein in an age when sustainability is no longer a trend but a key to survival.

Chapter Notes

Preface

1. Douglas Coupland, *Marshall McLuhan: You Know Nothing of My Work!* (New York: Atlas & Company, 2010).
2. Marshall McLuhan, *The Gutenberg Galaxy* (New York: Routledge & Kegan, 1962).
3. Marshall McLuhan, *Understanding Media: The Extensions of Man* (New York: McGraw-Hill, 1966).
4. McLuhan, *Understanding Media*, 206.
5. Richard Kostelanetz, "Understanding McLuhan (In Part)," *New York Times*, January 29, 1967, http://www.nytimes.com/books/97/11/02/home/mcluhan-magazine.html

Introduction

1. Richard Kostelanetz, "Understanding McLuhan (In Part)," *New York Times*, January 29, 1967, http://www.nytimes.com/books/97/11/02/home/mcluhan-magazine.html
2. Mike Johnston, "And Then Advertising Got Weird: What Is Oddvertising?" *ThinkGrowth.org* (blog), October 28, 2016, https://thinkgrowth.org/and-then-advertising-got-weird-what-is-oddvertising-f595a8741f59
3. Marshall McLuhan, *Understanding Media: The Extensions of Man* (New York: McGraw-Hill, 1966).
4. "Ratatoskr and Meeko: Spiteful Squirrels of Norse and Wabanaki Mythology," *EsoterX* (blog), July 6, 2013, http://esoterx.com/2013/07/06/ratatoskr-and-meeko-spiteful-squirrels-of-norse-and-wabanaki-mythology/
5. "Eclipse of the Sun Blamed on Black Squirrel: A Choctaw Legend," First People—Native American Legends, accessed June 7, 2017, http://www.firstpeople.us/FP-Html-Legends/EclipseOfTheSunBlamedOnBlackSquirrel-Choctaw.html

Chapter 1

1. Beatrix Potter, *The Tale of Peter Rabbit* (London: Frederick Wayne & Co., 1902).
2. Beatrix Potter, *The Tale of Squirrel Nutkin* (London: Frederick Wayne & Co., 1903).
3. Josephine Gardiner, "Squirrel Nutkin: Anarchy for Under Fives," *Channel Light Vessel* (blog), May 11, 2015, http://emeraldlamp.blogspot.com/search?q=squirrel+Nutkin
4. Beatrix Potter, *The Tale of Timmy Tiptoes* (London: Frederick Wayne & Co., 1911).
5. Daphne M. Kutzer, *Beatrix Potter: Writing in Code* (New York and London: Routledge Press, 2003), 130–131.
6. Melanie Watts, *Scaredy Squirrel at Night* (New York: Kids Can Press, 2009).
7. Richard Fowler, *A Squirrel's Tale* (Tulsa, OK: EDC Publishing, 1983).
8. Adam Rubin, *Those Darn Squirrels!* (New York: Houghton Mifflin Harcourt, 2008).
9. J. Hamilton Ray, *Squirrels on Skis* (New York: Random House, 2013).
10. Nancy Tarfuri, *The Busy Little Squirrel* (New York: Simon & Schuster, 2007).
11. Belle Yang, *Squirrel Round and Round* (Somerville, MA: Candlewick Press, 2015).
12. Nancy Rose, *The Secret Life of Squirrels* (New York: Little, Brown, 2014).
13. Jo Wright, *Cyril the Squirrel* (Grendon Warks, UK: Lemon Press, 2010).
14. Don Freeman, *Earl the Squirrel* (New York: Puffin Books, 2005).
15. Richard W. Thorington, Jr., and Katie Ferrell, *Squirrels: The Animal Answer Guide* (Baltimore: John Hopkins University Press, 2006).
16. Kim Long, *Squirrels: A Wildlife Handbook* (Boulder, CO: Johnson Books, 1995).
17. Bill Adler, Jr., *Outwitting Squirrels: 101 Cunning Stratagems to Reduce Dramatically the Egregious Misappropriation of Seed from Your*

Birdfeeder by Squirrels (Chicago: Chicago Review Press, 2014).

18. Adler, *Outwitting Squirrels*, 214–215.

19. Grace Marmour Spruch, *Squirrels at My Window: Life with a Remarkable Gang of Urban Squirrels* (Boulder, CO: Johnson Books, 2000).

Chapter 2

1. Margaret Matray, "Contractor Sues Virginia Couple for $90K over Squirrel Attack," *Style Weekly*, January 3, 2017, https://www.styleweekly.com/richmond/contractor-sues-virginia-couple-for-90k-over-squirrel-attack/content?oid=2386837

2. "Crazy Squirrel Is Executed by Police Officer," *The Dispatch* (Moline, Illinois), April 3, 1929, https://www.newspapers.com/image/338598190/

3. Leonard Downie, *The New Muckrakers* (New York: Mentor Books, 1976), 19–20.

4. J.R. Minkel, "The 2003 Northeast Blackout—Five Years Later," *Scientific American*, August 13, 2008, https://www.scientificamerican.com/article/2003-blackout-five-years-later/

5. Jon Mooallem, "Squirrel Power," *New York Times*, August 31, 2013, https://www.nytimes.com/2013/09/01/opinion/sunday/squirrel-power.html

6. Mooallem, "Squirrel Power."

7. Ryan Wilusz, "Squirrel Causes Fire That Destroys Home," *The News Herald* (Morganton, NC), March 26, 2018, http://www.morganton.com/news/squirrel-causes-fire-that-destroys-home/article_4827faca-3132-11e8-afed-1f52b4d8382f.html

8. Theodore J. Kury, "What Would It Take for the U.S. to Bury Its Power Lines?" *Fortune*, September 20, 2017, http://fortune.com/2017/09/19/hurricane-destruction-bury-power-lines/

9. Gilpin N. Kenneth, "Stray Squirrel Shuts Down Nasdaq System," *New York Times*, December 10, 1967, https://www.nytimes.com/1987/12/10/business/stray-squirrel-shuts-down-nasdaq-system.html

10. William Alden, "Computer Bugs and Squirrels: A History of Nasdaq's Woes," *New York Times*, August 22, 2013, https://dealbook.nytimes.com/2013/08/22/computer-bugs-and-squirrels-a-history-of-nasdaqs-woes/

11. Robert Neurith, *Shadow Cities: A Billion Squatters, a New Urban World* (New York: Routledge, 2004).

12. "Protect Your Car from Wire-Gnawing Squirrels," *The Allstate Blog*, March 17, 2014, https://blog.allstate.com/protect-your-car-squirrels-chewing-on-car-wires/

13. William Broad, "Nuclear Pulse: Awakening to the Chaos Factor," *Science*, May 29, 1981, http://science.sciencemag.org/content/212/4498/1009

14. John S. Foster, Jr., Earl Gjelde, William R. Graham, Robert J. Hermann, Henry (Hank) M. Kluepfel, Richard L. Lawson, USAF (Ret.), Gordon K. Soper, Lowell L. Wood, Jr., and Joan B. Woodard, *Report of the Commission to Assess the Threat to the United States from Electromagnetic Pulse (EMP) Attack, Volume 1. Executive Report* (2004), http://www.dtic.mil/dtic/tr/fulltext/u2/a484497.pdf

15. Jerry Schappert, "Keeping Squirrels Out of Your Car Engine," *Pest Cemetery* (blog), July 8, 2009, http://pestcemetery.com/keeping-squirrels-out-of-your-cars-engine/

16. Meghan Keneally, "How Ebola Emerged Out of the Jungle," ABC News, July 28, 2014, https://abcnews.go.com/Health/ebola-emerged-jungle-photos/story?id=24740453

17. Paul Sisson, "Plague Squirrels Found in Palomar Campground," *San Diego Union Tribune*, September 17, 2013, http://www.sandiegouniontribune.com/news/health/sdut-plague-squirrel-campground-palomar-2013sep17-story.html

18. Albert Camus, *The Plague* (New York: Vintage, 1971).

19. Esther Inglis-Arkell, "Why People in the United States Are Still Dying from the Bubonic Plague," *io9 Gizmodo*, January 25, 2013, https://io9.gizmodo.com/5978781/why-people-in-the-united-states-are-still-dying-from-the-bubonic-plague

20. "Plague," Centers for Disease Control and Prevention, last modified October 23, 2017, https://www.cdc.gov/plague/

21. Sandra Blakeslee, "Kentucky Doctors Warn Against a Regional Dish: Squirrels' Brains," *New York Times*, August 29, 1997, https://www.nytimes.com/1997/08/29/us/kentucky-doctors-warn-against-a-regional-dish-squirrels-brains.html

Chapter 3

1. Richard Kostelanetz, "Understanding McLuhan (In Part)," *New York Times*, January 29, 1967, http://www.nytimes.com/books/97/11/02/home/mcluhan-magazine.html

2. Kim Janssen, "Kamikaze Squirrel Gets Revenge on Alderman Brookins," *Chicago Tribune*, November 22, 2016, http://www.chicagotribune.com/news/chicagoinc/ct-brookins-squirrels-1122-chicago-inc-20161121-story.html

3. Robert Price, "Patriotic Squirrels Recorded Stealing Family's American Flags," FOX-TV (San Antonio), June 3, 2017, http://foxsanantonio.com/news/local/patriotic-squirrels-recorded-stealing-american-flags-from-familys-yard

4. John Kelly, "Tommy Tucker: Washington's Most Famous Squirrel," *Washington Post*, April 8, 2012, https://www.washingtonpost.com/local/tommy-tucker-washingtons-most-famous-squirrel/2012/04/08/gIQAddnZ4S_story.html?noredirect=on&utm_term=.56d72e472b18

5. Kelly, "Tommy Tucker: Washington's Most Famous Squirrel."

6. John Kelly, "Tommy Tucker: Eternity's Satin Doll of a Squirrel Is at Last Located," *Washington Post*, April 18, 2012, https://www.washingtonpost.com/local/tommy-tucker-eternitys-satin-doll-of-a-squirrel-is-at-last-located/2012/04/18/gIQAu5jeRT_story.html?utm_term=.bfd9aaeb92c1

7. Paul Greeley, "How a Local News Catch-Phrase Was Born," *TVNewsCheck*, January 6, 2014, http://www.tvnewscheck.com/article/73067/how-a-local-news-catch-phrase-was-born

8. Greeley, "How a Local News Catch-Phrase Was Born."

9. "Obsessed with My Pet Squirrel, 'Sugar Bush' | My Crazy Obsession," YouTube (video), posted by TLC, April 24, 2013, https://www.youtube.com/watch?v=NyWSEQDX-jM&t=1s

10. "Obsessed with My Pet Squirrel, 'Sugar Bush.'"

11. "Sugar Bush Squirrel—International Superstar," accessed June 2, 2017, www.sugarbushsquirrel.com/

12. John Kelly, "Experiencing World Events Through the Eyes of a Squirrel," *The Washington Post*, April 10, 2013, https://www.washingtonpost.com/local/experiencing-world-events-through-the-eyes-of-a-squirrel/2013/04/10/dee513f8-a1e5-11e2-9c03-6952ff305f35_story.html?utm_term=.654e3bf2f15e

13. Lou Harry, *The Sugar Bush Chronicles: Adventures with the World's Most Photographed Squirrel* (New York: Sterling Publishing, 2015).

14. Raisa Bruner, "Squirrel Almost Collides with Daniela Ulbing at Olympics," *Time*, February 26, 2018, http://time.com/5175480/squirrel-snowboard-olympics/

15. Ed Barkowitz, "Squirrel Driving Phillies Nuts," *Philadelphia Enquirer*, October 5, 2011, http://www.philly.com/philly/sports/phillies/Squirrel_driving_Phillies_Cardinals_nuts.html

16. Tyler Kepner, "A Gritty Bullpen of Fierce Creatures," *New York Times*, October 18, 2011, https://www.nytimes.com/2011/10/18/sports/baseball/for-st-louis-cardinals-nutty-way-to-win-dont-forget-squirrel.html?_r=1&ref=sports

17. "The Rally Squirrel Song," YouTube (video), posted by Randy Mayfield, October 7, 2011, https://www.youtube.com/watch?v=sk0vDEoTTEc

18. Heather Drennan, "Tony LaRussa: All-Star for Animals," *PETA* (blog), November 2, 2011, https://www.peta.org/blog/tony-la-russa-star-animals/

19. Kevin Eck, "Twiggy the Waterskiing Squirrel Proves Love of Sports, Pees on Reporter," *TVSpy*, January 9, 2015, http://www.adweek.com/tvspy/twiggy-the-watersking-squirrel-proves-love-of-water-sports-pees-on-reporter/138613

20. Stephen Messenger, "Hero Squirrel Pees on TV News Reporter," thedodowww, January 14, 2015, https://www.thedodo.com/squirrel-pees-on-news-reporter-931954004.html

21. Phyllis DeGioia, "Squirrels as Pets: A Really Bad Idea," *VetzInsight*, November 7, 2016, https://www.vin.com/vetzinsight/default.aspx?pid=756&id=5454945

Chapter 4

1. Katie Leach, "Kellyanne Conway Interrupts CNN Interview to Tell a Squirrel Hi," *Washington Examiner*, October 27, 2017, https://www.washingtonexaminer.com/kellyanne-conway-interrupts-cnn-interview-to-tell-a-squirrel-hi

2. "Rally Squirrel Raising Money for Charity," KMOV-TV, October 10, 2011, https://web.archive.org/web/20111012164810/http://www.kmov.com/news/local/Rally-Squirrel-raising-money-for-charity—131445878.html

3. Mike Johnston, "And Then Advertising Got Weird: What Is Oddvertising?" *ThinkGrowth.org* (blog), October 28, 2016, https://thinkgrowth.org/and-then-advertising-got-weird-what-is-oddvertising-f595a8741f59

4. Marshall McLuhan, *Understanding Media: The Extensions of Man* (New York: McGraw-Hill, 1966), 202.

5. "Bridgestone Tires Squirrel Advert," YouTube (video), posted by Will Riker, July 7, 2018, https://www.youtube.com/watch?v=_mP5

D-0fIgk (all the advertisements in this chapter can be found on YouTube, including the ad mentioned here for Bridgestone Tires).

6. John Castanga, "What Business Can Learn from a Squirrel," *QuickSilver Edge Strategic Communications*, February 6, 2015, http://quicksilver edge.com/views-from-the-edge/

7. Castanga, "What Business Can Learn from a Squirrel."

8. Castanga, "What Business Can Learn from a Squirrel."

9. "White Squirrels of Olney," *City of Olney*, accessed June 6, 2017, http://www.ci.olney.il.us/visitors/white_squirrels/index.php

10. "City of Olney Municipal Code," *City of Olney*, accessed August 26, 2017, www.ci.olney.il.us/docs/Title_6__Animals__5_16_12.pdf

11. "White Squirrel Wars," *Roadside America*, May 6, 2014, www.roadsideamerica.com/story/29067

12. "Black Squirrel Squabbles," *Roadside America*, May 6, 2018, www.roadsideamerica.com/story/29130

13. "Black Squirrel Squabbles."

14. Linda Godfrey, *Weird Michigan: Your Travel Guide to Michigan's Local Legends and Best Kept Secrets* (New York: Sterling Publishing, 2006), 81.

15. "Kent State University Celebrates Black Squirrels with Statue," *Akron Beacon Journal*, October 8, 2009, https://www.ohio.com/akron/news/kent-state-university-celebrates-black-squirrels-with-statue

16. Rebecca Satawa, "What They Probably Won't Tell You during Your Campus Tour: The Top 10 Quirks of Albion College," *Golden Opportunities* (blog), February 21, 2012, http://campus.albion.edu/students/2012/02/what-they-probably-wont-tell-you-during-your-campus-tour/

17. Allison Palm, "A Squirrelly Outcome—College Selects Black Squirrel as Mascot," *Albion Pleiad*, April 1, 2011, https://www.albionpleiad.com/2011/04/a-squirrely-outcome—college-selects-black-squirrel-as-mascot/

18. "Black Squirrel Productions | Augustana College," accessed August 10, 2017, https://www.augustana.edu/student-life/groups/black-squirrel-productions

19. Johnston, "And Then Advertising Got Weird."

20. Stanley J. Baran, *Introduction to Mass Communication* (New York: McGraw-Hill, 2014), 310–311.

21. Don Corrigan, "The Great Truck Nutz Controversy," Popular Culture Association (PCA), paper presentation, Boston, Massachusetts, April 2012.

22. Ed Young, "Squirrels Masturbate to Avoid Sexually Transmitted Infections," *Discover*, September 28, 2010, http://blogs.discovermagazine.com/notrocketscience/2010/09/28/squirrels-masturbate-to-avoid-sexually-transmitted-infections/#.WwI71EgvyUk

Chapter 5

1. Lindsay Barnett, "PETA Wants to Use Michael Jackson's Song 'Ben' to Help Lab Rats," *L.A. Unleashed*, July 7, 2009, http://latimesblogs.latimes.com/unleashed/2009/07/peta-wants-to-use-michael-jacksons-song-ben-to-help-lab-rats.html

2. Marshall McLuhan, *Understanding Media: The Extensions of Man* (New York: McGraw-Hill, 1966), 249.

3. McLuhan, *Understanding Media*, 254.

4. Manny Farber, *Farber on Film: Mugging Main Street*, edited by Robert Polito (New York: Library of America, 2009), 307–309.

5. "The Onion Looks Back at 'It's a Wonderful Life,'" YouTube (video), posted by Peter Rosenthal, *The Onion*, December 23, 2016, https://www.youtube.com/watch?v=GGko87FAMPg

6. Steven Zeitchik, "'Winter's Bone' Wins Grand Jury Prize for Drama at Sundance," *Los Angeles Times*, January 31, 2010, http://articles.latimes.com/2010/jan/31/entertainment/la-et-sundancewinners31–2010jan31

7. Ehab Zahriyeh, "'Hunger Games' Star Jennifer Lawrence on Squirrel Scene in 'Winter's Bone': 'Screw PETA,'" *New York Daily News*, April 10, 2012, http://www.nydailynews.com/entertainment/tv-movies/hunger-games-superstar-jennifer-lawrence-attacks-peta-rolling-stone-interview-article-1.1059041

8. Zahriyeh, "'Hunger Games' Star Jennifer Lawrence on Squirrel Scene in 'Winter's Bone': 'Screw PETA.'"

9. Jocelyn Vena, "Jennifer Lawrence's 'Screw PETA' Remark Peeves Animal Rights Org," *MTV News*, April 11, 2012, www.mtv.com/news/1682879/jennifer-lawrence-peta-comments/

10. Christine Haugney, "'Anchorman' Spoof of 1970s TV News Is Basis for Newseum Exhibition," *New York Times*, November 13, 2013,

https://www.nytimes.com/2013/11/14/business/media/anchorman-spoof-of-1970s-tv-news-is-basis-for-newseum-exhibition.html

11. Paul Greeley, "How a Local News Catch-Phrase Was Born," *TVNewsCheck*, January 6, 2014, http://www.tvnewscheck.com/article/73067/how-a-local-news-catch-phrase-was-born

12. Mark Harris, "It Came from Beneath! The 20 Best Giant Animal Horror Movies," *Thoughtco*, March 20, 2018, https://www.thoughtco.com/best-giant-animal-horror-movies-1873298

Chapter 6

1. "The Story of Moosylvania," *Flying Moose* (blog), accessed August 17, 2017, http://flyingmoose.org/moose/moose.htm

2. "7 Things You Might Not Know about Atom Ant," *Me TV*, March 15, 2016, https://www.metv.com/lists/7-things-you-might-not-know-about-atom-ant

3. Rich Sands, "TV Guide Magazine's 60 Greatest Cartoons of All Time," *TV Guide*, September 24, 2013, http://www.tvguide.com/news/greatest-cartoons-tv-guide-magazine-1071203/

4. Deb Sopan, "With a Singing SpongeBob, Nickelodeon Aims for a Broadway Splash," New York Times, November 27, 2017, https://www.nytimes.com/2017/11/22/theater/spongebob-squarepants-the-broadway-musical-nickelodeon.html

5. Manohla Dargis, "Woodland Creature Stumbles into Peril in 'Over the Hedge,'" *New York Times*, May 19, 2006, https://www.nytimes.com/2006/05/19/movies/woodland-creatures-stumble-into-peril-in-over-the-hedge.html

6. Monica Castillo, "Review: 'The Nut Job 2' Squirrels Away the Laughs for Itself," *New York Times*, August 11, 2017, https://www.nytimes.com/2017/08/11/movies/the-nut-job-2-nutty-by-nature-review.html

7. Richard W. Thorington, Jr., and Katie Ferrell, *Squirrels: The Animal Answer Guide* (Baltimore: John Hopkins University Press, 2006).

8. Dennis Hevesi, "Alex Anderson, Creator of Rocky and Bullwinkle, Dies at 90," *New York Times*, October 25, 2010, https://www.nytimes.com/2010/10/26/arts/television/26anderson.html

9. Ramsey Ess, "There's Never Been a Better Time to Revisit 'Rocky and Bullwinkle,'" *SPLITSIDER*, January 23, 2017, http://splitsider.com/2017/01/theres-never-been-a-better-time-to-revisit-rocky-and-bullwinkle/

10. David Kaplan, "Rocky and Bullwinkle Brave the Comeback Trail," *New York Times*, May 7, 1989, https://www.nytimes.com/1989/05/07/movies/television-rocky-and-bullwinkle-brave-the-comeback-trail.html

11. Michael Cavna, "RIP, June Foray: The 'Queen of Animation' Voiced 'Rocky and Bullwinkle' Roles," *Washington Post*, July 27, 2017, https://www.washingtonpost.com/news/comic-riffs/wp/2017/07/27/rip-june-foray-first-lady-of-animation-acting-voiced-rocky-and-bullwinkle-and-tweety-roles/?utm_term=.83c622c1ccb3

12. "7 Things You Might Not Know about Atom Ant."

13. Deirdre Sheppard, "The Secret Squirrel Show," Common Sense Media, accessed September 20, 2017, https://www.commonsensemedia.org/tv-reviews/the-secret-squirrel-show

14. Maurice LaMarche et al., *Steven Spielberg Presents Animaniacs: Volume 1. Special Features: Animaniacs Live!* (Warner Home Video, 2006), DVD.

15. Gregory Miller, "5 Times SpongeBob Caused a Controversy," *New York Post*, February 6, 2015, https://nypost.com/2015/02/06/5-times-spongebob-caused-a-controversy/

16. Roger Ebert, "Over the Hedge," rogerebertwww, May 18, 2006, https://www.rogerebert.com/reviews/over-the-hedge-2006

17. James Berardinelli, "Over the Hedge (United States, 2006)," *Reelviews Movie Reviews*, www.reelviews.net/reelviews/over-the-hedge

18. Berardinelli, "Over the Hedge (United States, 2006)."

19. Dargis, "Woodland Creature Stumbles into Peril in 'Over the Hedge.'"

20. Ken Fox, "Over the Hedge—Review," *TV Guide*, https://www.tvguide.com/movies/over-the-hedge/review/279933/

21. Miriam Bale, "These Criminals Are Throwbacks," *New York Times*, January 16, 2014, https://www.nytimes.com/2014/01/17/movies/in-the-nut-job-a-surly-squirrel-plans-a-heist.html

22. "The Nut Job (2014)," *Box Office Mojo*, January 17, 2014, http://www.boxofficemojo.com/movies/?id=nutjob.htm

23. 'The Nut Job' at the 2015 Brussels Animation Festival," Alchetron, The Free Social Encyclopedia of the World, https://alchetron.com/The-Nut-Job

24. Castillo, "Review: 'The Nut Job 2' Squirrels Away the Laughs for Itself."

Chapter 7

1. Laurence Maslon and Michael Kantor, *Superheroes! Capes, Cowls, and the Creation of Comic Book Culture* (New York: Crown Archetype Publishing, 2013).

2. Steve Ditko and Will Murray, *The Coming of … Squirrel Girl* (Marvel Super-Heroes vol. 3, #8, Marvel Super-Heroes Winter Special, 1991).

3. Paul Tumey, "Gene Ahern Covers the (Comic Book) Conventions," *The Comic Journal*, August 11, 2016, http://www.tcj.com/gene-ahern-covers-the-conventions/

4. "Meet the Flying Squirrel Mascots," Flying Squirrels Baseball, accessed August 23, 2017, http://www.milb.com/content/page.jsp?ymd=20131002&content_id=62329802&sid=t3410&vkey=team3

5. Ash Maczko and Ashley Witter, "Squarriors," Devil's Due Comics, accessed August 23, 2017, http://www.devilsdue.net/squarriors.html

6. Theo Dyssean, "How a Tongue Twister Led to Spies Being Called 'Secret Squirrels,'" *NEWSREP*, November 10, 2016, https://thenewsrep.com/66922/how-a-tongue-twister-led-to-the-phrase-secret-squirrel/

7. Derek McCaw, "Clearly, It's Secret(ly) Squirrel Day," *Fanboy Planet*, July 11, 2017, http://fanboyplanet.com/clearly-its-secretly-squirrel-day/

8. "Character: Nutsy Squirrel," *Comic Vine*, accessed August 26, 2017, https://comicvine.gamespot.com/nutsy-squirrel/4005-16839/

9. Dave Simpson, "Back in Black: Goth Has Risen from the Dead—and the 1980s Pioneers Are (Naturally) Not Happy about It," *The Guardian*, September 29, 2006, https://www.theguardian.com/music/2006/sep/29/popandrock

10. Charlie Hall, "A Brief History of the ESRB Rating System," *Polygon*, March 3, 2018, https://www.polygon.com/2018/3/3/17068788/esrb-ratings-changes-history-loot-boxes

11. "Shaky Rocket: Foamy the Squirrel," *Ill Will Press*, accessed May 2, 2018, http://illwillpress.com/EP/SHAKY.html

12. Alfred Lord Tennyson, "In Memoriam A.H.H.," Literature Network, accessed September 2, 2017, http://www.online-literature.com/tennyson/718/

13. Nick Nafpliotis, "Is It Good? Squarriors #4 Advance Review," *AIPT!* (blog), September 15, 2015, www.adventuresinpoortaste.com/2015/09/15/is-it-good-squarriors-4-advance-review/

14. Elizabeth Kolbert, *Field Notes from a Catastrophe: Man, Nature, and Climate Change* (New York: Bloomsbury, 2015).

15. Chris Hedges, "What Every Person Should Know about War," *New York Times*, July 6, 2003, https://www.nytimes.com/2003/07/06/books/chapters/what-every-person-should-know-about-war.html

16. Marshall McLuhan, *Understanding Media: The Extensions of Man* (New York: McGraw-Hill, 1966), 155–161.

17. McLuhan, *Understanding Media*, 216.

18. McLuhan, *Understanding Media*, 207–216.

19. Stanley J. Baran, *Introduction to Mass Communication* (New York: McGraw-Hill, 2014), 217–218.

20. McLuhan, *Understanding Media*, 207–216.

21. Stephen Burt, "Squirrel Girl Is Not the Hero We Deserved. She's the One We Needed," *Slate*, May 21, 2015, http://www.slate.com/blogs/browbeat/2015/05/21/squirrel_girl_why_you_should_be_reading_the_unbeatable_squirrel_girl_marvel.html

22. John Szczepaniak, *The Untold History of Japanese Game Developers: Volume 3* (SMG Szczepaniak, 2018), 309.

23. "Sonic the Hedgehog," *Electronic Gaming Monthly* 6, no. 8 (August 8, 1993), 60, 62, https://retrocdn.net/images/9/93/EGM_US_049.pdf

24. Hilary Goldstein, "Conker: Live and Reloaded," IGN, June 17, 2005, http://www.ign.com/articles/2005/06/17/conker-live-and-reloaded

25. "Gaming's Most Notorious Anti-Heroes," IGN, March 5, 2012, http://www.ign.com/articles/2012/03/05/gamings-most-notorious-anti-heroes

26. Matt Casamassina, "Conker's Bad Fur Day—Review," IGN, March 2, 2001, http://www.ign.com/articles/2001/03/03/conkers-bad-fur-day

27. Robert Workman, "Squirrel Girl Crashes THQ's 'Super Hero Squad: Comic Combat,'" *Comic Book Resources*, September 15, 2011, https://www.cbr.com/squirrel-girl-crashes-thqs-super-hero-squad-comic-combat/

28. "Shorty Award Winners Cassey Ho and Tara Strong on Fox News Live," *Shorty Awards* (blog), April 11, 2013, http://blog.shortyawards.com/post/47720027964/shorty-award-winners-cassey-ho-and-tara-strong-on

29. "Magician," Misty Lee, accessed September 12, 2017, http://mistylee.com/about/

30. "Squirrel Girl Review! Marvel Future Fight," YouTube (video), posted by CynicalAlex,

June 28, 2017, https://www.youtube.com/watch?v=VedY4pkE6oM

31. Tom Christiansen, "Smite's Newest Norse God Is a ... Squirrel?? Meet Ratatoskr!" *EPIC BREW* (blog), May 16, 2015, https://epicbrew.net/2015/05/16/smites-newest-norse-god-is-a-squirrel-meet-ratatoskr/

32. Chris Thursten, "Smite World Championship 2015: Grand Finals in Review," *PC Gamer*, January 12, 2015, https://www.pcgamer.com/smite-world-championship-2015-grand-finals-in-review/

33. "Smite in the KJV Bible," *King James Bible Online*, accessed September 15, 2017, https://www.kingjamesbibleonline.org/smite

34. P. Geller, "Ratatosk," Mythology.net, accessed September 18, 2017, https://mythology.net/norse/norse-creatures/ratatoskr/

35. William Usher, "SMITE Offends Hindus, Catholics, Jews, with Porno-Style Depiction of Kali," *CINEMABLEND*, accessed September 18, 2017, https://www.cinemablend.com/games/SMITE-Offends-Hindus-Catholics-Jews-With-Porno-Style-Depiction-of-Kali-44645.html

36. "Top 100 Largest Overall Prize Pools," *e-Sports Earnings*, accessed September 20, 2017, https://www.esportsearnings.com/tournaments

Chapter 8

1. Joseph Mussulman, "Eastern Gray Squirrel," *Discovering Lewis & Clark*, revised November 2006, http://www.lewis-clark.org/article/2173

2. David E. Roth, "III—Squirrel Hunters to the Rescue," *The Civil War, 1861–1865* (New York: Smithmark, 1992), http://www.cincinnaticwrt.org/data/ohio%20in%20the%20war/1862%20Defense%20of%20Cincinnati/iii_squirrel.pdf

3. "Red or Dead: Grey Squirrel Cull Goes On," *The Scotsman*, February 28, 2012, https://www.scotsman.com/news/environment/red-or-dead-grey-squirrel-cull-goes-on-1-2141924

4. Ted Nugent and Shemane Nugent, *Kill It & Grill It: A Guide to Preparing and Cooking Wild Game and Fish* (Washington, DC: Regnery, 2012).

5. Mike Sula, "Chicken of the Trees," *Chicago Reader*, August 16, 2012, https://www.chicagoreader.com/chicago/why-eating-squirrels-makes-sense/Content?oid=7215952

6. Rebecca Rupp, "Time to Savor the Squirrel (Again?)," *National Geographic*, June 24, 2016, https://www.nationalgeographic.com/people-and-culture/food/the-plate/2016/06/time-to-savor-the-squirrel-/

7. Paul Srubas, "Getting to the Bottom of Booyah," *Green Bay Press-Gazette*, November 19, 2015, https://www.greenbaypressgazette.com/story/news/2015/11/19/getting-bottom-booyah/75528814/

8. Hank Shaw, "Kentucky Burgoo," *Hunter Angler Gardner Cook*, accessed September 20, 2017, https://honest-food.net/kentucky-burgoo-recipe/

9. Ann Pringle-Harris, "FARE OF THE COUNTRY; Who Invented Brunswick Stew? Hush Up and Eat," *New York Times*, October 24, 1993, https://www.nytimes.com/1993/10/24/travel/fare-of-the-country-who-invented-brunswick-stew-hush-up-and-eat.html

10. Rebecca Rupp, "Time to Savor the Squirrel (Again?)."

11. Will Hansen, "Pass the Squirrel, Please: Thanksgiving in 1870," *Newberry Graff Collection*, November 24, 2014, https://www.newberry.org/pass-squirrel-please-thanksgiving-1870

12. Sandra Blakeslee, "Kentucky Doctors Warn Against a Regional Dish: Squirrels' Brains," *New York Times*, August 29, 1997, https://www.nytimes.com/1997/08/29/us/kentucky-doctors-warn-against-a-regional-dish-squirrels-brains.html

13. Rupp, "Time to Savor the Squirrel (Again?)."

14. "Lewis & Clark Expedition: Scientific Encounters," National Park Service, accessed September 21, 2017, https://www.nps.gov/nr/travel/lewisandclark/encounters.htm

15. Adrian Forsyth, *Mammals of North America: Temperate and Arctic Regions* (Buffalo, NY: Firefly Books, 1999), 102–103.

16. Mussulman, "Eastern Gray Squirrel."

17. Squirrel World, "Skwerl Migration—History of the Crisis," February 8, 2012, http://www.scarysquirrel.org/history/migration

18. John James Audubon, *Viviparous-Quadrupeds-North-America* (Memphis: General Books LLC, 2012).

19. Stanley D. Casto, "The Texas Gray Squirrel Migration of 1857," *East Texas Historical Journal* 41, issue 2 (2003): 48–49.

20. Wayne Capooth, "Massive Squirrel Migrations Recorded in North America," *Delta Farm Press*, July 21, 2006, http://www.deltafarmpress.com/massive-squirrel-migrations-recorded-north-america

21. Colleen Kimmett, "The Great Squirrel Migration of 1968," *Mental Floss*, April 8, 2017, http://mentalfloss.com/article/94069/great-squirrel-migration-1968

22. Kimmett, "The Great Squirrel Migration of 1968."

23. John Bakeless, *America as Seen by Its First Explorers: The Eyes of Discovery* (Mineola, NY: Dover, 2011).

24. Bakeless, *America as Seen by Its First Explorers*.

25. Roth, "III—Squirrel Hunters to the Rescue."

26. Roth, "III—Squirrel Hunters to the Rescue."

27. Roth, "III—Squirrel Hunters to the Rescue."

28. Roth, "III—Squirrel Hunters to the Rescue."

29. Roth, "III—Squirrel Hunters to the Rescue."

30. Roth, "III—Squirrel Hunters to the Rescue."

31. Linda Rodriguez McRobbie, "The Epic Century-Long English Battle to Rid Itself of American Squirrels," *Atlas Obscura*, April 27, 2016, https://www.atlasobscura.com/articles/the-epic-centurylong-english-battle-to-rid-itself-of-american-squirrels

32. McRobbie, "The Epic Century-Long English Battle to Rid Itself of American Squirrels."

33. Leo Hickman, "'If You Want Red Squirrels, You Have to Kill Greys,'" *The Guardian*, September 5, 2012, https://www.theguardian.com/environment/2012/sep/05/red-grey-squirrels-cornwall

34. Hickman, "'If You Want Red Squirrels, You Have to Kill Greys.'"

35. Hickman, "'If You Want Red Squirrels, You Have to Kill Greys.'"

36. John D. MacArthur, "First Great Seal Committee—July/August 1776," *Great Seal*, accessed September 22, 2017, http://greatseal.com/committees/firstcomm/

37. David Bruce Smith, "Why Didn't Benjamin Franklin Want the American Eagle to Be the National Symbol?" Grateful American Foundation, accessed September 22, 2017, http://gratefulamericanfoundation.com/facts/why-didnt-benjamin-franklin-want-the-american-eagle-to-be-the-symbol-of-america/

38. "Gray Squirrel: Kentucky State Wild Game Animal," State Symbols USA, accessed September 22, 2017, https://statesymbolsusa.org/symbol-official-item/kentucky/state-mammal/gray-squirrel

39. Steven Case, "State Mammal of North Carolina: Gray Squirrel," *NCpedia*, 2012, https://www.ncpedia.org/symbols/mammal

40. Lucy Hammer, *Discovering Your Spirit Animal* (Berkeley, CA: North Atlantic Books, 2009).

41. M.D. Johnson, "Squirrel Hunting Myths and Facts: And Why Some Yankees Don't Squirrel Hunt," Realtree, July 4, 2017, https://www.realtree.com/small-game-hunting/articles/squirrel-hunting-myths-and-facts

42. Nugent and Nugent, *Kill It & Grill It.*

Chapter 9

1. Robert K. Logan, "The 3 Eras of Communication According to McLuhan and Innis," *McLuhan Galaxy* (blog), June 9, 2015, https://mcluhangalaxy.wordpress.com/2015/06/09/the-3-eras-of-communication-according-to-mcluhan-innis/

2. Howard D. Fabing, "On Going Berserk: A Neurochemical Inquiry," *Scientific Monthly* 83, no. 5 (November 1956): 232–237.

3. Ericka Goerling, "Marshall McLuhan and the Idea of Retribalization," *McLuhan Galaxy* (blog), August 7, 2014, https://mcluhangalaxy.wordpress.com/2014/08/07/ marshall-mcluhan-and-the-idea-of-retribalization

4. Terry Macy and Daniel Hart, *White Shamans and Plastic Medicine Men* (indigenous documentary film), Native Voices Program, University of Washington, 1996.

5. "Native American Totem Animals & Their Meanings," *Legends of America*, March 18, 2018, https://www.legendsofamerica.com/na-totems/

6. Jessie Eubank Harris, *Legends and Stories of Famous Trees* (Philadelphia: Dorance, 1963).

7. Lilla Veszy-Wagner, "Ratatosk: The Role of the Perverted Intellect," *Psyche: Zeitschrift für Psychoanalyse und ihre Anwendungen* 23, no. 3 (1969): 184–195.

8. Gilbert Livingston Wilson, *Indian Hero Tales* (New York: American Book Company, 1916).

9. William J. Long, *Secrets of the Woods* (Boston: Ginn & Company, 1902), 73–74.

10. Charles Q. Choi, "Ancient Squirrel-Like Creatures Push Back Mammal Evolution," *LiveScience*, September 10, 2014, https://www.live

science.com/47774-ancient-squirrels-push-back-mammal-evolution.html

11. "Solar Eclipse Myths and Superstitions," Toledo Science Center, accessed August 25, 2017, https://www.imaginationstationtoledo.org/visit/events/solar-eclipse-celebration/solar-eclipse-myths-and-superstitions

12. Charles Amter, "8 Best Solar Eclipse Music Festivals," *Variety*, August 14, 2017, http://variety.com/2017/music/news/solar-eclipse-music-festivals-oregon-eclipse-moonfest-moonstock-1202523862/

13. "Eclipse of the Sun Blamed on Black Squirrel: A Choctaw Legend," First People—Native American Legends, accessed June 7, 2017, http://www.firstpeople.us/FP-Html-Legends/EclipseOfTheSunBlamedOnBlackSquirrel-Choctaw.html

14. "Eclipse of the Sun Blamed on Black Squirrel."

15. Alan Dundes, *Cinderella: A Casebook* (Madison: University of Wisconsin Press, 1988).

16. Fay Beauchamp, "Asian Origins of Cinderella: The Zhuang Storyteller of Guangxi," *Project Muse*, Tradition 25, no. 2, accessed September 20, 2017, https://muse.jhu.edu/article/436222

17. Jacob Grimm and Wilhelm Grimm, "Household Stories by the Brothers Grimm: Aschenputtel," translated by Lucy Crane, Project Gutenberg, accessed September 3, 2017, https://www.gutenberg.org/files/19068/19068-h/19068-h.htm

18. Grimm and Grimm, "Household Stories by the Brothers Grimm: Aschenputtel."

19. Paul Chi, "First Look: The Making of Cinderella's Wedding Gown," *Vanity Fair*, February 11, 2015, https://www.vanityfair.com/hollywood/2015/02/cinderella-wedding-gown-first-look

20. John Lloyd and John Mitchinson, *The Book of General Ignorance* (New York: Harmony Books, 2006).

21. Antariksh Bothale, "What Qualities Would the Glass in Cinderella's Slippers Need to Have in Order for Her to Walk and Dance Comfortably?" *Huffington Post*, December 6, 2017, https://www.huffingtonpost.com/quora/what-qualities-would-the_b_1934501.html

22. Theodore Roszak, *The Making of a Counter Culture* (Berkeley: University of California Press, 1995).

23. Lucy Hammer, *Discovering Your Spirit Animal* (Berkeley, CA: North Atlantic Books, 2009).

24. Sam Silver, "Squirrel," *Nordic Wiccan* (blog), February 17, 2013, http://nordicwiccan.blogspot.com/2013/02/squirrel.html

25. Macy and Hart, *White Shamans and Plastic Medicine Men.*

26. Silver, "Squirrel."

Bibliography

Adler, Bill, Jr. *Outwitting Squirrels: 101 Cunning Stratagems to Reduce Dramatically the Egregious Misappropriation of Seed from Your Birdfeeder by Squirrels.* Chicago: Chicago Review Press, 2014.

Alden, William. "Computer Bugs and Squirrels: A History of Nasdaq's Woes." *New York Times*, August 22, 2013. https://dealbook. nytimes.com/2013/08/22/computer-bugs-and-squirrels-a-history-of-nasdaqs-woes/

Amter, Charles. "8 Best Solar Eclipse Music Festivals." *Variety*, August 14, 2017. http:// variety.com/2017/music/news/solar-eclipse-music-festivals-oregon-eclipse-moonfest-moonstock-1202523862/

"Anima 2016." *unifrance.* Accessed August 20, 2017. https://en.unifrance.org/festivals-and-markets/882/anima

Audubon, John James. *Viviparous-Quadrupeds-North-America.* Memphis: General Books LLC, 2012.

Bakeless, John. *America as Seen by Its First Explorers: The Eyes of Discovery.* Mineola, NY: Dover, 2011.

Bale, Miriam. "These Criminals Are Throwbacks." *New York Times*, January 16, 2014. https://www.nytimes.com/2014/01/17/ movies/in-the-nut-job-a-surly-squirrel-plans-a-heist.html

Baran, Stanley J. *Introduction to Mass Communication.* New York: McGraw-Hill, 2014.

Barkowitz, Ed. "Squirrel Driving Phillies Nuts." *Philadelphia Enquirer*, October 5, 2011. http://www.philly.com/philly/sports/phillies/ Squirrel_driving_Phillies_Cardinals_nuts. html

Barnett, Lindsay. "PETA Wants to Use Michael Jackson's Song 'Ben' to Help Lab Rats." *L.A. Unleashed*, July 7, 2009. http:// latimesblogs.latimes.com/unleashed/2009/ 07/peta-wants-to-use-michael-jacksons-song-ben-to-help-lab-rats.html

Beauchamp, Fay. "Asian Origins of Cinderella: The Zhuang Storyteller of Guangxi." *Project Muse*, Tradition 25, no. 2. Accessed September 20, 2017. https://muse.jhu.edu/article/ 436222

Berardinelli, James. "Over the Hedge (United States, 2006)." *Reelviews Movie Reviews.* www.reelviews.net/reelviews/over-the-hedge

"Black Squirrel Productions | Augustana College." Accessed August 10, 2017. https:// www.augustana.edu/student-life/groups/ black-squirrel-productions

"Black Squirrel Squabbles." *Roadside America*, May 6, 2018. https://www.roadsideamerica. com/story/29130

Blakeslee, Sandra. "Kentucky Doctors Warn Against a Regional Dish: Squirrels' Brains." *New York Times*, August 29, 1997. https:// www.nytimes.com/1997/08/29/us/kentucky-doctors-warn-against-a-regional-dish-squirrels-brains.html

Bothale, Antariksh. "What Qualities Would the Glass in Cinderella's Slippers Need to Have in Order for Her to Walk and Dance Comfortably?" *Huffington Post*, December 6, 2017. https://www.huffingtonpost.com/ quora/what-qualities-would-the_b_1934501. html

"Bridgestone Tires Squirrel Advert." YouTube (video), posted by Will Riker, July 7, 2018. https://www.youtube.com/watch?v=_ mP5D-0fIgk

Broad, William. "Nuclear Pulse: Awakening to the Chaos Factor." *Science*, May 29, 1981. http://science.sciencemag.org/content/212/ 4498/1009

Bruner, Raisa. "Squirrel Almost Collides with Daniela Ulbing at Olympics." *Time*, February 26, 2018. http://time.com/5175480/squirrel-snowboard-olympics/

Burt, Stephen. "Squirrel Girl Is Not the Hero We Deserved. She's the One We Needed." *Slate*, May 21, 2015. http://www.slate.com/blogs/browbeat/2015/05/21/squirrel_girl_why_you_should_be_reading_the_unbeatable_squirrel_girl_marvel.html

Camus, Albert. *The Plague*. New York: Vintage, 1971.

Capooth, Wayne. "Massive Squirrel Migrations Recorded in North America." *Delta Farm Press*, July 21, 2006. http://www.deltafarmpress.com/massive-squirrel-migrations-recorded-north-america

Casamassina, Matt. "Conker's Bad Fur Day—Review." IGN, March 2, 2001. http://www.ign.com/articles/2001/03/03/conkers-bad-fur-day

Case, Steven. "State Mammal of North Carolina: Gray Squirrel." *NCpedia*, 2012. https://www.ncpedia.org/symbols/mammal

Castanga, John. "What Business Can Learn from a Squirrel." *QuickSilver Edge Strategic Communications*, February 6, 2015. http://quicksilveredge.com/views-from-the-edge/

Castillo, Monica. "Review: 'The Nut Job 2' Squirrels Away the Laughs for Itself." *New York Times*, August 11, 2017. https://www.nytimes.com/2017/08/11/movies/the-nut-job-2-nutty-by-nature-review.html

Casto, Stanley D. "The Texas Gray Squirrel Migration of 1857." *East Texas Historical Journal* 41, issue 2 (2003): 48–50.

Cavna, Michael. "RIP, June Foray: The 'Queen of Animation' Voiced 'Rocky and Bullwinkle' Roles." *Washington Post*, July 27, 2017. https://www.washingtonpost.com/news/comic-riffs/wp/2017/07/27/rip-june-foray-first-lady-of-animation-acting-voiced-rocky-and-bullwinkle-and-tweety-roles/?utm_term=.83c622c1ccb3

"Character: Nutsy Squirrel." *Comic Vine*. Accessed August 26, 2017. https://comicvine.gamespot.com/nutsy-squirrel/4005-16839/

Chi, Paul. "First Look: The Making of Cinderella's Wedding Gown." *Vanity Fair*, February 11, 2015. https://www.vanityfair.com/hollywood/2015/02/cinderella-wedding-gown-first-look

Choi, Charles Q. "Ancient Squirrel-Like Creatures Push Back Mammal Evolution." *LiveScience*, September 10, 2014. https://www.livescience.com/47774-ancient-squirrels-push-back-mammal-evolution.html

Christiansen, Tom. "Smite's Newest Norse God Is a ... Squirrel?? Meet Ratatoskr!" *EPIC BREW* (blog), May 16, 2015. https://epicbrew.net/2015/05/16/smites-newest-norse-god-is-a-squirrel-meet-ratatoskr/

"City of Olney Municipal Code." *City of Olney*. Accessed August 26, 2017. www.ci.olney.il.us/docs/Title_6__Animals__5_16_12.pdf

Corrigan, Don. "The Great Truck Nutz Controversy." Popular Culture Association (PCA), paper presentation, Boston, Massachusetts, April 2012.

Coupland, Douglas. *Marshall McLuhan: You Know Nothing of My Work!* New York: Atlas & Company, 2010.

"Crazy Squirrel Is Executed by Police Officer." *The Dispatch* (Moline, Illinois), April 3, 1929. https://www.newspapers.com/image/338598190/

Dargis, Manohla. "Woodland Creature Stumbles into Peril in 'Over the Hedge.'" *New York Times*, May 19, 2006. https://www.nytimes.com/2006/05/19/movies/woodland-creatures-stumble-into-peril-in-over-the-hedge.html

DeGioia, Phyllis. "Squirrels as Pets: A Really Bad Idea." *VetzInsight*, November 7, 2016. https://www.vin.com/vetzinsight/default.aspx?pid=756&id=5454945

Ditko, Steve, and Will Murray. *The Coming of ... Squirrel Girl*. Marvel Super-Heroes vol. 3, #8, Marvel Super-Heroes Winter Special, 1991.

Downie, Leonard. *The New Muckrakers*. New York: Mentor Books, 1976.

Drennan, Heather. "Tony LaRussa: All-Star for Animals." *PETA* (blog), November 2, 2011. https://www.peta.org/blog/tony-larussa-star-animals/

Dundes, Alan. *Cinderella: A Casebook*. Madison: University of Wisconsin Press, 1988.

Dyssean, Theo. "How a Tongue Twister Led to Spies Being Called 'Secret Squirrels.'" *NEWSREP*, November 10, 2016. https://

thenewsrep.com/66922/how-a-tongue-twister-led-to-the-phrase-secret-squirrel/

Ebert, Roger. "Over the Hedge." rogerebertwww, May 18, 2006. https://www.rogerebert.com/reviews/over-the-hedge-2006

Eck, Kevin. "Twiggy the Waterskiing Squirrel Proves Love of Sports, Pees on Reporter." *TVSpy*, January 9, 2015. http://www.adweek.com/tvspy/twiggy-the-waterskingsquirrel-proves-love-of-water-sports-pees-on-reporter/138613

"Eclipse of the Sun Blamed on Black Squirrel, Choctaw Legends." First People—Native American Legends. Accessed June 7, 2017. http://www.firstpeople.us/FP-Html-Legends/EclipseOfTheSunBlamedOnBlackSquirrel-Choctaw.html

Ess, Ramsey. "There's Never Been a Better Time to Revisit 'Rocky and Bullwinkle.'" *SPLITSIDER*, January 23, 2017. http://splitsider.com/2017/01/theres-never-been-a-better-time-to-revisit-rocky-and-bullwinkle/

Fabing, Howard D. "On Going Berserk: A Neurochemical Inquiry." *Scientific Monthly* 83, no. 5 (November 1956): 232–237.

Farber, Manny. *Farber on Film: Mugging Main Street*. Edited by Robert Polito. New York: Library of America, 2009.

Forsyth, Adrian. *Mammals of North America: Temperate and Arctic Regions*. Buffalo, NY: Firefly Books, 1999.

Foster, John S., Jr., Earl Gjelde, William R. Graham, Robert J. Hermann, Henry (Hank) M. Kluepfel, Richard L. Lawson, USAF (Ret.), Gordon K. Soper, Lowell L. Wood, Jr., and Joan B. Woodard. *Report of the Commission to Assess the Threat to the United States from Electromagnetic Pulse (EMP) Attack, Volume 1. Executive Report* (2004). http://www.dtic.mil/dtic/tr/fulltext/u2/a484497.pdf

Fowler, Richard. *A Squirrel's Tale*. Tulsa, OK: EDC Publishing, 1983.

Fox, Ken. "Over the Hedge—Review." *TV Guide*. https://www.tvguide.com/movies/over-the-hedge/review/279933/

Freeman, Don. *Earl the Squirrel*. New York: Puffin Books, 2005.

"Gaming's Most Notorious Anti-Heroes." IGN, March 5, 2012. http://www.ign.com/articles/2012/03/05/gamings-most-notorious-anti-heroes

Gardiner, Josephine. "Squirrel Nutkin: Anarchy for Under Fives." *Channel Light Vessel* (blog), May 11, 2015. http://emeraldlamp.blogspot.com/search?q=squirrel+Nutkin

Geller, P. "Ratatosk." Mythology.net. Accessed September 18, 2017. https://mythology.net/norse/norse-creatures/ratatoskr/

Godfrey, Linda. *Weird Michigan: Your Travel Guide to Michigan's Local Legends and Best Kept Secrets*. New York: Sterling Publishing, 2006.

Goerling, Ericka. "Marshall McLuhan and the Idea of Retribalization." *McLuhan Galaxy* (blog), August 7, 2014. https://mcluhangalaxy.wordpress.com/2014/08/07/marshall-mcluhan-and-the-idea-of-retribalization

Goldstein, Hilary. "Conker: Live and Reloaded." IGN, June 17, 2005. http://www.ign.com/articles/2005/06/17/conker-live-and-reloaded

"Gray Squirrel: Kentucky State Wild Game Animal." State Symbols USA. Accessed September 22, 2017. https://statesymbolsusa.org/symbol-official-item/kentucky/state-mammal/gray-squirrel

Greeley, Paul. "How a Local News Catch-Phrase Was Born." *TVNewsCheck*, January 6, 2014. http://www.tvnewscheck.com/article/73067/how-a-local-news-catch-phrase-was-born

Grimm, Jacob, and Wilhelm Grimm. "Household Stories by the Brothers Grimm: Aschenputtel." Translated by Lucy Crane. Project Gutenberg. Accessed September 3, 2017. https://www.gutenberg.org/files/19068/19068-h/19068-h.htm

Hall, Charlie. "A Brief History of the ESRB Rating System." *Polygon*, March 3, 2018. https://www.polygon.com/2018/3/3/17068788/esrb-ratings-changes-history-loot-boxes

Hammer, Lucy. *Discovering Your Spirit Animal*. Berkeley, CA: North Atlantic Books, 2009.

Hansen, Will. "Pass the Squirrel, Please: Thanksgiving in 1870." *Newberry Graff Collection*, November 24, 2014. https://www.newberry.org/pass-squirrel-please-thanksgiving-1870

Harris, Jessie Eubank. *Legends and Stories of Famous Trees*. Philadelphia: Dorance, 1963.

Harris, Mark. "It Came from Beneath! The 20 Best Giant Animal Horror Movies." *Thoughtco*, March 20, 2018. https://www.thoughtco.com/best-giant-animal-horror-movies-1873298

Harry, Lou. *The Sugar Bush Chronicles: Adventures with the World's Most Photographed Squirrel*. New York: Sterling Publishing, 2015.

Haugney, Christine. "'Anchorman' Spoof of 1970s TV News Is Basis for Newseum Exhibition." *New York Times*, November 13, 2013. https://www.nytimes.com/2013/11/14/business/media/anchorman-spoof-of-1970s-tv-news-is-basis-for-newseum-exhibition.html

Hedges, Chris. "What Every Person Should Know about War." *New York Times*, July 6, 2003. https://www.nytimes.com/2003/07/06/books/chapters/what-every-person-should-know-about-war.html

Hevesi, Dennis. "Alex Anderson, Creator of Rocky and Bullwinkle, Dies at 90." *New York Times*, October 25, 2010. https://www.nytimes.com/2010/10/26/arts/telvision/26anderson.html

Hickman, Leo. "'If You Want Red Squirrels, You Have to Kill Greys.'" *The Guardian*, September 5, 2012. https://www.theguardian.com/environment/2012/sep/05/red-grey-squirrels-cornwall

Inglis-Arkell, Esther. "Why People in the United States Are Still Dying from the Bubonic Plague." *io9 Gizmodo*, January 25, 2013. https://io9.gizmodo.com/5978781/why-people-in-the-united-states-are-still-dying-from-the-bubonic-plague

Janssen, Kim. "Kamikaze Squirrel Gets Revenge on Alderman Brookins." *Chicago Tribune*, November 22, 2016. http://www.chicagotribune.com/news/chicagoinc/ct-brookins-squirrels-1122-chicago-inc-20161121-story.html

Johnson, M.D. "Squirrel Hunting Myths and Facts: And Why Some Yankees Don't Squirrel Hunt." Realtree, July 4, 2017. https://www.realtree.com/small-game-hunting/articles/squirrel-hunting-myths-and-facts

Johnston, Mike. "And Then Advertising Got Weird: What Is Oddvertising?" *Think Growth.org* (blog), October 28, 2016. https://thinkgrowth.org/and-then-advertising-got-weird-what-is-oddvertising-f595a8741f59

Kaplan, David. "Rocky and Bullwinkle Brave the Comeback Trail." *New York Times*, May 7, 1989. https://www.nytimes.com/1989/05/07/movies/television-rocky-and-bullwinkle-brave-the-comeback-trail.html

Kelly, John. "Experiencing World Events Through the Eyes of a Squirrel," *The Washington Post*, April 10, 2013. https://www.washingtonpost.com/local/experiencing-world-events-through-the-eyes-of-a-squirrel/2013/04/10/dee513f8-a1e5–11e2–9c03–6952ff305f35_story.html?utm_term=.654e3bf2f15e

_____. "Tommy Tucker: Eternity's Satin Doll of a Squirrel Is at Last Located." *Washington Post*, April 18, 2012. https://www.washingtonpost.com/local/tommy-tucker-eternitys-satin-doll-of-a-squirrel-is-at-last-located/2012/04/18/gIQAu5jeRT_story.html?utm_term=.bfd9aaeb92c1

_____. "Tommy Tucker: Washington's Most Famous Squirrel." *Washington Post*, April 8, 2012. https://www.washingtonpost.com/local/tommy-tucker-washingtons-most-famous-squirrel/2012/04/08/gIQAddnZ4S_story.html?noredirect=on&utm_term=.56d72e472b18

Keneally, Meghan. "How Ebola Emerged Out of the Jungle." ABC News, July 28, 2014. https://abcnews.go.com/Health/ebola-emerged-jungle-photos/story?id=24740453

Kenneth, Gilpin N. "Stray Squirrel Shuts Down Nasdaq System." *New York Times*, December 10, 1967. https://www.nytimes.com/1987/12/10/business/stray-squirrel-shuts-down-nasdaq-system.html

"Kent State University Celebrates Black Squirrels with Statue." *Akron Beacon Journal*, October 8, 2009. https://www.ohio.com/akron/news/kent-state-university-celebrates-black-squirrels-with-statue

Kepner, Tyler. "A Gritty Bullpen of Fierce Creatures." *New York Times*, October 18, 2011. https://www.nytimes.com/2011/10/18/sports/baseball/for-st-louis-cardinals-nutty-way-to-win-dont-forget-squirrel. html?_r=1&ref=sports

Kimmett, Colleen. "The Great Squirrel Migration of 1968." *Mental Floss*, April 8, 2017. http://mentalfloss.com/article/94069/great-squirrel-migration-1968

Kolbert, Elizabeth. *Field Notes from a Catastrophe: Man, Nature, and Climate Change*. New York: Bloomsbury, 2015.

Kostelanetz, Richard. "Understanding McLuhan (In Part)." *New York Times*, January 29, 1967. http://www.nytimes.com/books/97/11/02/home/mcluhan-magazine.html

Kury, Theodore J. "What Would It Take for the U.S. to Bury Its Power Lines?" *Fortune*, September 20, 2017. http://fortune.com/2017/09/19/hurricane-destruction-bury-power-lines/

Kutzer, Daphne M. *Beatrix Potter: Writing in Code*. New York and London: Routledge Press, 2003.

LaMarche, Maurice, et al. *Steven Spielberg Presents Animaniacs: Volume 1. Special Features: Animaniacs Live!* Warner Home Video, 2006. DVD.

Leach, Katie. "Kellyanne Conway Interrupts CNN Interview to Tell a Squirrel Hi." *Washington Examiner*, October 27, 2017. https://www.washingtonexaminer.com/kellyanne-conway-interrupts-cnn-interview-to-tell-a-squirrel-hi

"Lewis & Clark Expedition: Scientific Encounters." National Park Service. Accessed September 21, 2017. https://www.nps.gov/nr/travel/lewisandclark/encounters.htm

Lloyd, John, and John Mitchinson. *The Book of General Ignorance*. New York: Harmony Books, 2006.

Logan, Robert K. "The 3 Eras of Communication According to McLuhan and Innis." *McLuhan Galaxy* (blog), June 9, 2015. https://mcluhangalaxy.wordpress.com/2015/06/09/the-3-eras-of-communication-according-to-mcluhan-innis/

Long, Kim. *Squirrels: A Wildlife Handbook*. Boulder, CO: Johnson Books, 1995.

Long, William J. *Secrets of the Woods*. Boston: Ginn & Company, 1902.

MacArthur, John D. "First Great Seal Committee—July/August 1776." *Great Seal*. Accessed September 22, 2017. http://greatseal.com/committees/firstcomm/

Maczko, Ash, and Ashley Witter. "Squarriors." Devil's Due Comics. Accessed August 23, 2017. http://www.devilsdue.net/squarriors.html

Macy, Terry, and Daniel Hart. *White Shamans and Plastic Medicine Men* (indigenous documentary film). Native Voices Program, University of Washington, 1996.

"Magician." Misty Lee. Accessed September 12, 2017. http://mistylee.com/about/

Maslon, Laurence, and Michael Kantor. *Superheroes! Capes, Cowls, and the Creation of Comic Book Culture*. New York: Crown Archetype Publishing, 2013.

Matray, Margaret. "Contractor Sues Virginia Couple for $90K over Squirrel Attack." *Style Weekly*, January 3, 2017. https://www.styleweekly.com/richmond/contractor-sues-virginia-couple-for-90k-over-squirrel-attack/content?oid=2386837

McCaw, Derek. "Clearly, It's Secret(ly) Squirrel Day." *Fanboy Planet*, July 11, 2017. http://fanboyplanet.com/clearly-its-secretly-squirrel-day/

McLuhan, Marshall. *The Gutenberg Galaxy*. New York: Routledge & Kegan, 1962.

———. *Understanding Media: The Extensions of Man*. New York: McGraw-Hill, 1966.

McRobbie, Linda Rodriguez. "The Epic Century-Long English Battle to Rid Itself of American Squirrels." *Atlas Obscura*, April 27, 2016. https://www.atlasobscura.com/articles/the-epic-centurylong-english-battle-to-rid-itself-of-american-squirrels

"Meet the Flying Squirrel Mascots." Flying Squirrels Baseball. Accessed August 23, 2017. http://www.milb.com/content/page.jsp?ymd=20131002&content_id=62329802&sid=t3410&vkey=team3

Messenger, Stephen. "Hero Squirrel Pees on TV News Reporter." thedodowww, January 14, 2015. https://www.thedodo.com/squirrel-pees-on-news-reporter-931954004.html

Miller, Gregory. "5 Times SpongeBob Caused a Controversy." *New York Post*, February 6, 2015. https://nypost.com/2015/02/06/5-times-spongebob-caused-a-controversy/

Minkel, J.R. "The 2003 Northeast Blackout—Five Years Later." *Scientific American*, August 13, 2008. https://www.scientificameri can.com/article/2003-blackout-five-years-later/

Mooallem, Jon. "Squirrel Power." *New York Times*, August 31, 2013. https://www.ny times.com/2013/09/01/opinion/sunday/squirrel-power.html

Mussulman, Joseph. "Eastern Gray Squirrel." *Discovering Lewis & Clark*, revised November 2006. http://www.lewis-clark.org/article/2173

Nafpliotis, Nick. "Is It Good? Squarriors #4 Advance Review." *AIPT!* (blog), September 15, 2015. www.adventuresinpoortaste.com/2015/09/15/is-it-good-squarriors-4-advance-review/

"Native American Totem Animals & Their Meanings." *Legends of America*, March 18, 2018. https://www.legendsofamerica.com/na-totems/

Neurith, Robert. *Shadow Cities: A Billion Squatters, a New Urban World*. New York: Routledge, 2004.

Nugent, Ted, and Shemane Nugent. *Kill It & Grill It: A Guide to Preparing and Cooking Wild Game and Fish*. Washington, DC: Regnery, 2012.

"The Nut Job (2014)." *Box Office Mojo*, January 17, 2014. http://www.boxofficemojo.com/movies/?id=nutjob.htm

"Obsessed with My Pet Squirrel, 'Sugar Bush' | My Crazy Obsession." YouTube (video), posted by TLC, April 24, 2013. https://www.youtube.com/watch?v=NyWSEQDX-jM&t=1s

"The Onion Looks Back at 'It's a Wonderful Life.'" YouTube (video), posted by Peter Rosenthal, *The Onion*, December 23, 2016. https://www.youtube.com/watch?v=GGko87FAMPg

Palm, Allison. "A Squirrelly Outcome—College Selects Black Squirrel as Mascot." *Albion Pleiad*, April 1, 2011. https://www.albionpleiad.com/2011/04/a-squirrely-outcome—94college-selects-black-squirrel-as-mascot/

"Plague." Centers for Disease Control and Prevention. Last modified October 23, 2017. https://www.cdc.gov/plague/

Potter, Beatrix. *The Tale of Peter Rabbit*. London: Frederick Wayne & Co., 1902.

_____. *The Tale of Squirrel Nutkin*. London: Frederick Wayne & Co., 1903.

_____. *The Tale of Timmy Tiptoes*. London: Frederick Wayne & Co., 1911.

Price, Robert. "Patriotic Squirrels Recorded Stealing Family's American Flags." FOX-TV (San Antonio), June 3, 2017. http://foxsanantonio.com/news/local/patriotic-squirrels-recorded-stealing-american-flags-from-familys-yard

Pringle-Harris, Ann. "FARE OF THE COUNTRY; Who Invented Brunswick Stew? Hush Up and Eat." *New York Times*, October 24, 1993. https://www.nytimes.com/1993/10/24/travel/fare-of-the-country-who-invented-brunswick-stew-hush-up-and-eat.html

"Protect Your Car from Wire-Gnawing Squirrels." *The Allstate Blog*, March 17, 2014. https://blog.allstate.com/protect-your-car-squirrels-chewing-on-car-wires/

"Rally Squirrel Raising Money for Charity." KMOV-TV, October 10, 2011. https://web.archive.org/web/20111012164810/http://www.kmov.com/news/local/Rally-Squirrel-raising-money-for-charity—131445878.html

"The Rally Squirrel Song." YouTube (video), posted by Randy Mayfield, October 7, 2011. https://www.youtube.com/watch?v=sk0vDEoTTEc

"Ratatoskr and Meeko: Spiteful Squirrels of Norse and Wabanaki Mythology." *EsoterX* (blog), July 6, 2013. http://esoterx.com/2013/07/06/ratatoskr-and-meeko-spiteful-squirrels-of-norse-and-wabanaki-mythology/

Ray, J. Hamilton. *Squirrels on Skis*. New York: Random House, 2013.

"Red or Dead: Grey Squirrel Cull Goes On." *The Scotsman*, February 28, 2012. https://www.scotsman.com/news/environment/red-or-dead-grey-squirrel-cull-goes-on-1-2141924

Rose, Nancy. *The Secret Life of Squirrels*. New York: Little, Brown, 2014.

Roszak, Theodore. *The Making of a Counter Culture*. Berkeley: University of California Press, 1995.

Roth, David E. "III—Squirrel Hunters to the Rescue." *The Civil War, 1861–1865*. New York: Smithmark, 1992. http://www.cincinnati

cwrt.org/data/ohio%20in%20the%20war/ 1862%20Defense%20of%20Cincinnati/iii_ squirrel.pdf

Rubin, Adam. *Those Darn Squirrels!* New York: Houghton Mifflin Harcourt, 2008.

Rupp, Rebecca. "Time to Savor the Squirrel (Again?)." *National Geographic*, June 24, 2016. https://www.nationalgeographic. com/people-and-culture/food/the-plate/ 2016/06/time-to-savor-the-squirrel-/

Sands, Rich. "TV Guide Magazine's 60 Greatest Cartoons of All Time." *TV Guide*, September 24, 2013. http://www.tvguide.com/ news/greatest-cartoons-tv-guide-magazine-1071203/

Satawa, Rebecca. "What They Probably Won't Tell You during Your Campus Tour: The Top 10 Quirks of Albion College." *Golden Opportunities* (blog), February 21, 2012. http://campus.albion.edu/students/2012/ 02/what-they-probably-wont-tell-you-during-your-campus-tour/

Schappert, Jerry. "Keeping Squirrels Out of Your Car Engine." *Pest Cemetery* (blog), July 8, 2009. http://pestcemetery.com/keeping-squirrels-out-of-your-cars-engine/

"7 Things You Might Not Know about Atom Ant." *Me TV*, March 15, 2016. https://www. metv.com/lists/7-things-you-might-not-know-about-atom-ant

"Shaky Rocket: Foamy the Squirrel." Ill Will Press, May 2, 2018. http://illwillpress.com/ EP/SHAKY.html

Shaw, Hank. "Kentucky Burgoo." *Hunter Angler Gardner Cook.* Accessed September 20, 2017. https://honest-food.net/kentucky-burgoo-recipe/

Sheppard, Deirdre. "The Secret Squirrel Show." Common Sense Media. Accessed September 20, 2017. https://www.common sensemedia.org/tv-reviews/the-secret-squirrel-show

"Shorty Award Winners Cassey Ho and Tara Strong on Fox News Live." *Shorty Awards* (blog), April 11, 2013. http://blog.shorty awards.com/post/47720027964/shorty-award-winners-cassey-ho-and-tara-strong-on

Silver, Sam. "Squirrel." *Nordic Wiccan* (blog), February 17, 2013. http://nordicwiccan. blogspot.com/2013/02/squirrel.html

Simpson, Dave. "Back in Black: Goth Has Risen from the Dead—and the 1980s Pioneers Are (Naturally) Not Happy about It." *The Guardian*, September 29, 2006. https:// www.theguardian.com/music/2006/sep/29/ popandrock

Sisson, Paul. "Plague Squirrels Found in Palomar Campground." *San Diego Union Tribune*, September 17, 2013. http://www. sandiegouniontribune.com/news/health/ sdut-plague-squirrel-campground-palomar-2013sep17-story.html

"Smite in the KJV Bible." *King James Bible Online.* Accessed September 15, 2017. https:// www.kingjamesbibleonline.org/smite

Smith, David Bruce. "Why Didn't Benjamin Franklin Want the American Eagle to Be the National Symbol?" Grateful American Foundation. Accessed September 22, 2017. http://gratefulamericanfoundation.com/ facts/why-didnt-benjamin-franklin-want-the-american-eagle-to-be-the-symbol-of-america/

"Solar Eclipse Myths and Superstitions." Toledo Science Center. Accessed August 25, 2017. https://www.imaginationstation toledo.org/visit/events/solar-eclipse-celebration/solar-eclipse-myths-and-superstitions

"Sonic the Hedgehog." *Electronic Gaming Monthly* 6, no. 8 (August 8, 1993). https:// retrocdn.net/images/9/93/EGM_US_049.pdf

Sopan, Deb. "With a Singing SpongeBob, Nickelodeon Aims for a Broadway Splash." *New York Times*, November 27, 2017. https://www.nytimes.com/2017/11/22/ theater/spongebob-squarepants-the-broadway-musical-nickelodeon.html

Spruch, Grace Marmour. *Squirrels at My Window: Life with a Remarkable Gang of Urban Squirrels.* Boulder, CO: Johnson Books, 2000.

"Squirrel Girl Review! Marvel Future Fight." YouTube (video), posted by CynicalAlex, June 28, 2017. https://www.youtube.com/ watch?v=VedY4pkE6oM

Squirrel World. "Skwerl Migration—History of the Crisis." February 8, 2012. http:// www.scarysquirrel.org/history/migration

Srubas, Paul. "Getting to the Bottom of Booyah." *Green Bay Press-Gazette*, November 19, 2015. https://www.greenbaypress gazette.com/story/news/2015/11/19/getting-bottom-booyah/75528814/

"The Story of Moosylvania." *Flying Moose* (blog). Accessed August 17, 2017. http://flyingmoose.org/moose/moose.htm

"Sugar Bush Squirrel—International Superstar." Accessed June 2, 2017. www.sugar-bushsquirrel.com/

Sula, Mike. "Chicken of the Trees." *Chicago Reader*, August 16, 2012. https://www.chicagoreader.com/chicago/why-eating-squirrels-makes-sense/Content?oid=7215952

Szczepaniak, John. *The Untold History of Japanese Game Developers: Volume 3.* SMG Szczepaniak, 2018.

Tarfuri, Nancy. *The Busy Little Squirrel.* New York: Simon & Schuster, 2007.

Tennyson, Alfred Lord. "In Memoriam A.H.H." Literature Network. Accessed September 2, 2017. http://www.online-literature.com/tennyson/718/

Thorington, Richard W., Jr., and Katie Ferrell. *Squirrels: The Animal Answer Guide.* Baltimore: John Hopkins University Press, 2006.

Thursten, Chris. "Smite World Championship 2015: Grand Finals in Review." *PC Gamer*, January 12, 2015. https://www.pcgamer.com/smite-world-championship-2015-grand-finals-in-review/

"Top 100 Largest Overall Prize Pools." *e-Sports Earnings.* Accessed September 20, 2017. https://www.esportsearnings.com/tournaments

Tumey, Paul. "Gene Ahern Covers the (Comic Book) Conventions." *The Comic Journal*, August 11, 2016. http://www.tcj.com/gene-ahern-covers-the-conventions/

Usher, William. "SMITE Offends Hindus, Catholics, Jews, with Porno-Style Depiction of Kali." *CINEMABLEND.* Accessed September 18, 2017. https://www.cinemablend.com/games/SMITE-Offends-Hindus-Catholics-Jews-With-Porno-Style-Depiction-Kali-44645.html

Vena, Jocelyn. "Jennifer Lawrence's 'Screw PETA' Remark Peeves Animal Rights Org." *MTV News*, April 11, 2012. www.mtv.com/news/1682879/jennifer-lawrence-peta-comments/

Veszy-Wagner, Lilla. "Ratatosk: The Role of the Perverted Intellect." *Psyche: Zeitschrift für Psychoanalyse und ihre Anwendungen* 23, no. 3 (1969): 184–195.

Watts, Melanie. *Scaredy Squirrel at Night.* New York: Kids Can Press, 2009.

"White Squirrels of Olney." *City of Olney.* Accessed June 6, 2017. http://www.ci.olney.il.us/visitors/white_squirrels/index.php

"White Squirrel Wars." *Roadside America*, May 6, 2014. www.roadsideamerica.com/story/29067

Wilson, Gilbert Livingston. *Indian Hero Tales.* New York: American Book Company, 1916.

Wilusz, Ryan. "Squirrel Causes Fire That Destroys Home." *The News Herald* (Morganton, NC), March 26, 2018. http://www.morganton.com/news/squirrel-causes-fire-that-destroys-home/article_4827faca-3132-11e8-afed-1f52b4d8382f.html

Workman, Robert. "Squirrel Girl Crashes THQ's 'Super Hero Squad: Comic Combat.'" *Comic Book Resources*, September 15, 2011. https://www.cbr.com/squirrel-girl-crashes-thqs-super-hero-squad-comic-combat/

Wright, Jo. *Cyril the Squirrel.* Grendon Warks, UK: Lemon Press, 2010.

Yang, Belle. *Squirrel Round and Round.* Somerville, MA: Candlewick Press, 2015.

Young, Ed. "Squirrels Masturbate to Avoid Sexually Transmitted Infections." *Discover*, September 28, 2010. http://blogs.discovermagazine.com/notrocketscience/2010/09/28/squirrels-masturbate-to-avoid-sexually-transmitted-infections/#.WwI71EgvyUk

Zahriyeh, Ehab. "'Hunger Games' Star Jennifer Lawrence on Squirrel Scene in 'Winter's Bone': 'Screw PETA.'" *New York Daily News*, April 10, 2012. http://www.nydailynews.com/entertainment/tv-movies/hunger-games-superstar-jennifer-lawrence-attacks-peta-rolling-stone-interview-article-1.1059041

Zeitchik, Steven. "'Winter's Bone' Wins Grand Jury Prize for Drama at Sundance." *Los Angeles Times*, January 31, 2010. http://articles.latimes.com/2010/jan/31/entertainment/la-et-sundancewinners31–2010jan31

Index